W9-CIF-164

Gods and Myths of the Viking Age

H.R. Ellis Davidson

Gods and Myths of the Viking Age

Bell Publishing Company
New York

This edition was formerly titled *Gods and Myths of Northern Europe*.

First published by Penguin Books Ltd. 1964.

Copyright © MCMLXIV by H.R. Ellis Davidson
All rights reserved.

This edition is published by Bell Publishing Company,
distributed by Crown Publishers, Inc.,
by arrangement with Penguin Books Ltd.
b c d e f g h
BELL 1981 EDITION

Manufactured in the United States of America

Library of Congress Cataloging in Publication Data

Davidson, Hilda Roderick Ellis.
    Gods and myths of the Viking age.

    Originally published by Penguin Books, Baltimore,
which was issued as no. A670 of Pelican books under
title: Gods and myths of northern Europe.
    Bibliography: p.
    Includes index.
    1. Mythology, Germanic.   2. Mythology, Norse.
3. Europe, Northern—Religion. I. Title.
BL860.D36   1981   291.2′11′0948   80-29137
ISBN: 0-517-336448   AACR1

Contents

7058069

Introduction

We will take heart for the future,
Remembering the past.
    T. S. ELIOT, *The Rock*

We are at last beginning to know and understand
the value of the myth.
    MIRCEA ELIADE, *Myths, Dreams and Mysteries*

1. *The Myth-Makers*

The mythology of a people is far more than a collection of pretty
or terrifying fables to be retold in carefully bowdlerized form
to our schoolchildren. It is the comment of the men of one particular age or civilization on the mysteries of human existence
and the human mind, their model for social behaviour, and
their attempt to define in stories of gods and demons their per-
ception of the inner realities. We can learn much from the mythologies of earlier peoples if we have the humility to respect
ways of thought widely differing from our own. In certain respects we may be far cleverer than they, but not necessarily wiser.

We cannot return to the mythological thinking of an earlier
age; it is beyond our reach, like the vanished world of childhood.
Even if we feel a nostalgic longing for the past, like that of John
Keats for Ancient Greece or William Morris for medieval England, there is now no way of entry. The Nazis tried to revive
the myths of ancient Germany in their ideology, but such an
attempt could only lead to sterility and moral suicide. We cannot deny the demands of our own age, but this need not prevent
us turning to the faith of another age with sympathetic understanding, and recapturing imaginatively some of its vanished
power. It will even help us to view more clearly the assumptions
and beliefs of our own time.

For centuries our children have been brought up on the myths
of Greece and Rome. These have dominated our schoolrooms
and inspired our poets, and in them there is much beauty and

wisdom. We have largely neglected however the mythology of our own forbears, the Anglo-Saxons and Vikings who settled in the British Isles and worshipped their gods there before Christianity came. I believe this to have been to our considerable loss, since the northern peoples who created their own mythology should surely arouse as much interest and curiosity as those of the Mediterranean lands.

We know something of the qualities of these peoples from the literature which they have left behind, as well as from tales of their achievements recorded by outsiders. They had courage, vigour, and enthusiasm, an intense loyalty to kindred and leaders, and a keen appreciation of fair dealings between men. They had unusual respect for their women-folk, and at best their conception of marriage allowed for real cooperation and companionship between man and wife. They were great individualists – this was both their weakness and their strength – and resented any attempt to curb their freedom of action. Nevertheless they were capable of considerable self-discipline, and could accept adversity cheerfully, without whining or self-pity. A man who was prepared to die for what seemed to him important was held in honour, whether friend or enemy, and won even greater admiration if he could die with a jest on his lips.

We learn from their literature that they had a keen sense of the dignity of man, and of the sanctity of human relationships. The record of early Christian saints and scholars in Anglo-Saxon England – women as well as men – bears witness to their quick intelligence and aptitude for mystical thought as well as tough intellectual achievement. The group of 'novels' which we call the Icelandic Sagas shows appreciation of both tragedy and comedy in the lives of ordinary folk, at a time long before Hardy and Ibsen. In view of this, it seems worth while to discover what kind of myths were created and treasured by these people, these vigorous individualists who changed the history of western Europe by their achievements.

Unfortunately there are difficulties in the way, and to explain the nature of these something must be said of the history of heathenism in north-western Europe. At the time when Rome was supreme, the Germanic tribes were the barbarians on the outskirts of the Empire, sometimes resisting the Roman armies, sometimes working with them as allies. Rome had considerable influence on their way of life, but in language and in beliefs they seem to have remained largely untouched. When the Empire at last collapsed, the Germanic barbarians, most of them still heathen, pushed forward to overrun the rich lands no longer protected by the Roman armies. The time which we call the Migration period, from about the fourth to the sixth century after Christ, was one of continual movement and restlessness in western Europe. At this time the Angles and Saxons moved westward and took possession of England, bringing with them over the North Sea their heathen beliefs and practices. Elsewhere Franks, Vandals, Alamanni, Ostrogoths, Visigoths, and a score of lesser peoples were striving to find lands on which to settle and some degree of security for themselves and their sons in a bewildering world. As time went on, the independent bands of warriors under their princely leaders became fewer in number. They cancelled each other out, and little settled kingdoms became the order of the day. There was rivalry and strife between these kingdoms, and gradually one absorbed another, many small dynasties vanishing or becoming no more than legends. By the time the great nations emerged, and men thought of Anglo-Saxon England or Merovingian France as established powers, most of the Germanic peoples had given up their heathen beliefs and adopted Christianity.

At the end of the sixth century a little group of missionaries crossed the Channel to bring the Christian faith to Kent. Other Christian teachers were already working in the west of Britain, and before long the temples of the heathen gods were replaced by little churches of wood, brick, and stone, and carved crosses rose everywhere in honour of the Christian God. By A.D. 731 a brilliant Christian scholar in the new monastery of Jarrow in northern England, the man we know as the Venerable Bede, set out to write a book surveying the growth of the Faith from one end of England to the other. Though the heathen religion in Britain was not yet dead, its days were numbered. On the Continent most of the Germanic peoples had already rejected the old gods, with a few exceptions like the Saxons, the Frisians, and the Danes.

In Scandinavia the new Church was much longer gaining a

foothold. Not until the tenth and eleventh centuries were the people of Norway converted by those doughty Christian kings, Olaf Tryggvason and Olaf the Holy. These two waged unceasing battle against the heathen gods, smashing their idols, burning their temples, and either driving out their followers or putting them to a painful death in the name of Christ. Some of those driven out settled in Iceland, where there were no kings and no persecution. But even in Iceland the fires of heathenism were dying down, and in the year 1000 the Icelandic Assembly, after a calm appraisal of the situation, decided for Christianity. Denmark too yielded to the persuasion of the missionaries, and when in 1015 Canute the Dane conquered England he was fully prepared to become a pillar of the Church. The Swedes were the most stubborn in their faithfulness to the heathen religion, but by 1164 a Christian bishop ruled in Uppsala, the old stronghold of Odin and Freyr.

Thus we see why we can learn comparatively little about the heathen myths from England and Germany, where Christianity was established early. We have to turn for information to Scandinavia, where a vigorous heathen population flourished for centuries after Augustine sailed for Kent, or to places in the north-west where the Scandinavian settlers left the marks of their influence. In the last days of their heathenism, Viking adventurers from Norway and Sweden were the scourge and terror of the church in Europe. They swooped down on villages, monasteries, and churches in Britain, France, Germany, and Spain. They burned and plundered, they carried off chalices, crucifixes, and jewelled book covers as loot. It must have seemed to the Christians as if these robust sea-robbers would conquer the western world and usher in a new age of darkness. Vikings ruled in the Orkneys and Shetlands, in the Hebrides, Man, and Dublin. They wiped out the community in Columba's monastery at Iona. In 875 they sacked Lindisfarne, a centre of learning and inspiration renowned through Christendom, and all civilized Europe was shocked and saddened by the news. The few monks who survived massacre wandered for years through the fells with the body of their sainted Abbot Cuthbert, who had made Lindisfarne a place of spiritual power, until they found a resting-place for his remains in Durham. Paris and Hamburg had been plundered in 845; Cadiz and Seville suffered the same fate. In Ireland the wife of a Viking chief, a heathen seeress, spoke her prophecies from the holy altar of Clonmacnoise.

The Viking adventurers were indomitable. They reached the eastern shore of America; they pushed down the Dnieper to Byzantium, where the Christian emperor valued their physical prowess sufficiently to enrol them in his special Varangian guard. They refused to be intimidated by ghosts of the past or the proud civilization of the south, but had the effrontery to cut runic inscriptions on ancient tombs like Maeshowe in Orkney, and on classical monuments like the marble lion of the Piraeus. No haven seemed safe from their longships, and no coast town or village from their favourite weapons: the long sword, the axe, and the firebrand. By 870 they were masters of northern and eastern England. Only the resolution of one young prince, in indifferent health and without powerful allies, kept them from engulfing southern England also, and destroying what three centuries of Christian culture had built. It is hardly surprising that alone among English rulers that prince, Alfred, bears the title Great.

These are the people to whom we turn for our northern myths. They were a formidable body of men, all the more so because they cannot be condemned as a collection of rogues and sadists, blind to all but material values. Of course there were worthless rascals among them, and they could be brutal enough, as the monks at Lindisfarne knew; but their leaders were in many cases men of culture, discrimination, and wit, with love of a good story and a neat jest. They loved fine art and craftsmanship, and treasured their good ships and splendid swords for their beauty as well as their utility in war. A quick-witted poet could win his way in their world as well as a brilliant swordsman, and the man who was both at the same time, like Egill Skallagrimsson the Icelander, or Earl Ragnald of Orkney, had the world at his feet. They were shrewd traders too, with a wily instinct for commerce not unworthy of a modern business magnate. Not a few who sowed their wild oats and built up a promising little fortune a-viking in the western seas grew up to be wise rulers, fathers of fine families, and valuable members of the community; some even came to be saints. From such lively, alert minds one would expect a rich and vigorous mythology, and they do not disappoint us.

2. *The Sources of our Knowledge*

Northern heathenism, that is, the pre-Christian beliefs of the Germanic peoples and the Scandinavians, came to an end in the eleventh century. There were two periods when it presented a threat to Europe : the first was at the time of the fall of Rome, when the Germanic tribes were overrunning the west, and the second was in the ninth and tenth centuries, when the Vikings were a great power and a menace to Christian civilization. In each case Christianity triumphed, and the hostile bands of invaders were converted to the faith. Since they themselves had no desire to make converts, they were at a serious disadvantage, and it was only a matter of time before the new religion replaced the old.

Before this finally happened, however, there was a period of a thousand years in which the old gods were worshipped in the north. This is a long time, and the forms and practices of the heathen religion must have changed greatly during the course of it. We know that there was considerable variety among the religions of the different German tribes, who had no universal faith or church. Moreover there were outside influences to affect the heathen peoples: first from the pagan Mediterranean area, secondly from the East, and thirdly from the Christian Church We must avoid the common error of supposing that the myths which we possess grew out of a fixed and permanent heathen faith possessed by the whole Germanic world.

The heathens themselves left few written records. Such restless adventurers were not the kind of people to sit down and inscribe stories and poems on parchment, and indeed they did not know how to do so. A few wise men could carve runic letters on wood or stone or metal, but this process was not suitable for long and detailed records. The art of writing with a pen only reached the north with the Christian priests. Consequently, our written records from heathen times come either from outsiders, writing Greek or Latin, or from monks in Christian monasteries. One most valuable commentator from early times is the Roman historian Tacitus, living at the end of the first century after Christ, since he was deeply interested in the Germanic way of life, and believed Rome should learn from it. Our difficulty, however, is to decide how far he and many far less gifted recorders of heathen beliefs and practices can be relied upon for accurate first-hand reporting. As far as the poems, stories, spells, riddles, and chronicles written down in the monasteries are concerned, they may have been recorded as much as two or three hundred years after the conversion, and this allows the possibility of prejudice, misinterpretation, or deliberate editing when non-Christian beliefs are being dealt with.

Fortunately it seems that many monks rejoiced in the old stories and poems, and wished to preserve them. England has a great treasure in the form of the complete epic poem, *Beowulf*, the tale of the exploits of a Scandinavian hero of heathen times. It was written down about A.D. 1000, long after the Anglo-Saxons were converted, so it is not free from Christian influence, but it contains information about the heroic past and the way of life in northern Europe before Christianity was established there. Fragments of other heroic poems remain, enough to remind us that our losses have been great. The prose sagas from Iceland have already been mentioned. They were written down in monasteries, and are stories of the adventures and relationships of the early settlers there at the time when most of them were heathen. The sagas are not free from Christian and romantic influences, and the modern tendency is to regard them as brilliant historical novels rather than wholly reliable records of the heathen past, but the memory of heathen customs preserved in them is of considerable value. The sagas of the kings of Norway have recorded more information for us about pre-Christian traditions and the struggles of the early Christian kings to overthrow heathenism. Also from Iceland comes a collection of mythological poems about the heathen gods, which were written down about the thirteenth century, but must contain earlier material. They are unequal in quality, but contain some poetry of great imaginative power. Without these poems, our ideas about heathen religion would be very different, and it is a sobering thought that they are nearly all from one small vellum book of forty-five leaves, the *Codex Regius*, rescued by chance from an Icelandic farmhouse in the seventeenth century. One can only speculate how many other priceless books of this kind have vanished without trace.

The fact must be faced at the outset then that our written sources on the subject of northern heathenism are comparatively late, fragmentary, and of uncertain reliability. In Eliade's book, *Patterns in Comparative Religion*,[1] he asks us to imagine a Buddhist scholar setting out to explore Christianity. He does so

with only a few fragments of the Gospels, a Catholic breviary, various ornaments (Byzantine icons, Baroque statues of the saints, the vestments, perhaps, of an Orthodox priest), but able, on the other hand, to study the religious life of some European village.

This is a salutary exercise, because the evidence connected with the religion of the heathen north is something of this kind, except that we are at a severe disadvantage in that the life of the village now only exists in ancient records of varying reliability. In such a case as Eliade imagines, the Buddhist would no doubt be struck by the wide divergence between the customs of the village and the material in the Gospels and breviary. Should he conclude that the naïve superstitions and inarticulate responses of the villagers were nearer to the essentials of the Christian religion than, say, the opening chapters of St John's Gospel, we know that he would be wrong. It is not that either is 'truer' Christianity than the other, but that the Christian faith exists at many different levels in different societies and in the minds of different men. We fall all too often into the same error when we approach one of the religions of the past. We must be prepared for the simple folk-beliefs of the less sophisticated to be found beside complex symbolism. The important thing is not to allow the crudity of the folk-beliefs to blind us to the depth and importance of the symbolism. Crude and childish ideas about the heathen gods will certainly be found in the myths, either because these satisfied ignorant folk, or because the use of symbols has been misunderstood by the recorder. But it does not follow that all who worshipped these gods were crude and childish in their religious outlook. Indeed the contention put forward in this book is that this was very far from the case.

1. M. Eliade, *Patterns in Comparative Religion*, London, 1958, p. 6.

3. *New Light on the Myths*

It should by now be evident that the study of the northern myths is neither simple nor straightforward. There are, however, more cheering factors to be taken into account. It would be fair to say that the student of early mythology today has a better chance of understanding it than at any previous period since interest in the northern gods was first aroused in the eighteenth century. We have new evidence to draw on, and new disciplines in which to work.

One of the most important of these is archaeology, in which development has been rapid during the last thirty years. We are unlikely to discover fresh written records from the heathen period, but the emergence of a new ship-burial or heathen temple is something which can happen at any time. Such discoveries can show us the way in which the people who worshipped the gods lived, the nature of their religious ceremonial, and how they treated their dead. Funeral rites in particular can tell us much about the use of religious symbolism, and what the worship of the gods meant to those who believed in them. A major archaeological discovery, like that of the Anglo-Saxon ship-burial at Sutton Hoo, may cause us to revise many of our former ideas about religious practice and symbolism. Sacred places like Jelling in Denmark and Old Uppsala in Sweden have been excavated not long ago; as recently as 1962 the site of the first little Christian church in Greenland, set up by the wife of Eric the Red, was discovered. Indeed archaeological evidence increases to an almost bewildering extent: from England alone the excavation of new Anglo-Saxon cemeteries of the pagan period and revaluation of records of earlier excavations are bringing to light fresh facts every year.

There is no doubt that all our resources are needed if we are to read archaeological evidence aright. We want knowledge of written records, the history of religions, and the use of symbolism, as well as the use of all available scientific methods for the preservation of finds. The effort is infinitely worth making, for a temple site or a royal grave, wisely excavated and recorded, can be like a voice speaking directly to us from the past.

Introduction

Other sources of knowledge are less dramatic, demanding the slow amassing ot data rather than sudden discovery. Such sources are the study of place-names, particularly of places named after the heathen gods; the study of religious symbolism, images of gods or monsters on memorial stones or signs representing the gods; and again the study of early inscriptions in Latin or in runes. All these kinds of evidence need to be used with much caution, for it is tempting to base wild assumptions on isolated details. But if assessed prudently, such evidence can throw light on the past, and students of religion too pedantic or cowardly to take it into account cannot hope to make real progress. Moreover there must be ready and generous cooperation between experts in different fields of knowledge if we are to make profitable use of the wealth of new information piling up concerning the pagan religion from which the myths emerged.

Above all, it is fair to say that we are now beginning to understand better the true meaning of the myth because of the great strides made in psychology and the study of the human mind. Every age, from that of Tacitus onwards, has shown interest in the legends of the past, and each has been influenced in its approach by its own particular interests and preconceptions. At the close of the nineteenth century it was believed that myths were essentially attempts to explain natural phenomena. Gods, giants, monsters, and demons who appeared in them were interpreted as standing for the sun and moon, wind, frost, or winter darkness, or for some other manifestation of the natural world. The god Freyr was a sun god, pure and simple. The monster Grendel in the poem *Beowulf* symbolized the dangerous climate of the fens, bringing plague to the king's hall. The capture of Arthur's queen Guinevere represented the triumph of winter. The weaknesses of this method as a universal key to mythology were well illustrated by Andrew Lang's brilliant piece of satire, triumphantly proving Gladstone to be a solar myth. When this method of interpretation went out of fashion, there was great faith for a while in the study of folklore as a means of tracing the lost religions of the past. Popular beliefs still found among country folk concerning the old gods, like the idea in Sweden that the last sheaf of the harvest should be left for Odin's horse, were held to throw new light on the nature of the beliefs of heathen times. The limitations of this approach have been clearly revealed by Jan de Vries, in two detailed studies of folk-beliefs about Odin and Loki.[1] He has shown that popular folklore associated with an ancient god is just as liable to become one-sided, distorted, and over-simplified as are the themes of great poems retold in ballad form.

A new step towards the understanding of myth was made when C. G. Jung showed how the symbolism of ancient legends was echoed in the dreams of his patients, in cases where they were quite unfamiliar with the tales. It became clear that certain symbols, such as the dragon emerging from his den, or the climbing of a tree up to heaven, have a widespread significance for mankind. They recur in many parts of the world, in many periods. Our tale of Jack and the Beanstalk, for instance, is paralleled in Polynesia by the story of the hero Maui climbing to the sky; Jacob's ladder is echoed by the rite of the priest-king of Ancient Ur ascending the Ziggurat, and by the magician-shaman in Siberia in our own times climbing a ladder cut in a beech tree. The symbols are found in folk-tales, in nursery rhymes, and in the imagery of poets, as well as in the legends of the gods. Such symbols may be borrowed in the first instance by one religious system from another, but the reason why they are retained and develop such vigorous life in the new context seems to be due to the deep appeal which they possess to the human mind. They express something of the desires, urges, and fears common to men of every age, to which, in Dr Johnson's words, 'every bosom returns an echo'. Thus it is that when we meet them in a legend or in poetic imagery, we experience immediate recognition of their rightness and power.

This method of approach, like the others, is most dangerous if carried to excess. We must not assume that all myths have equal value, as some writers of Jung's school tend to do. Some have come down to us in a childish or distorted form, some have been copied deliberately by artists or writers, and cannot be regarded as genuine myths expressing an inner experience. We must have the necessary knowledge of the sources and the

1. In *Folklore Fellows' Communications*, Helsingki, 94 (1931) and 110 (1933).

background before we can attempt to assess and interpret the legends themselves. In a number of books on religious imagery Mircea Eliade has put forward an eloquent plea for the discipline of the history of religions rather than that of depth psychology in interpreting the significance of myths.

Indeed the study of the history of religions has made very great progress during recent years. We now know much more than we did about the attitude of early peoples towards the supernatural. Thanks to the work of anthropologists in many different parts of the world, we can now contradict some of the dogmatic theories which were based on insufficient evidence. We can no longer accept the idea that a universal totemism preceded the belief in gods and spirits, as Freud too rashly assumed from the work of early anthropologists like Taylor. We now know that totemism is completely lacking in the life of many of the most primitive tribes. The idea of an impersonal sacred force, like the 'mana' of Melanesia, is apparently not the inevitable precursor of the idea of a god, nor is sun-worship the earliest form of recognizable religion everywhere in the world. We have still much to discover, but it now seems safe to say that at the root of religious beliefs there lies the idea of the sacred, of a power outside man and greater than men. This may be embodied in many different forms : in sacred trees or stones, in the person of the divine king, in the mystery of the Christian incarnation. The instinctive sense of this power, recognized in some form wherever men come together, however simple or complex their society may be, appears to be the moving principle of religious belief.

As our knowledge increases, it also becomes evident that certain patterns are present in the mythologies of the world. These can be traced in widely separate regions and at different ages of civilization. The idea of a Sky God, of a distant father in heaven, is gradually emerging as one of the most widespread conceptions in early religion. The Australian aborigines and many African tribes have such a sky god, the Chinese had an ancient sky god, of whom the emperor was the representative on earth, and the Greek Zeus and the Roman Jupiter appear to have developed out of such a conception. In general however the Sky God remained distant and remote from men's lives.

Other manifestations of the divine became of more immediate importance, such as the worship of dead ancestors or of the totem animal of the tribe, or the deities associated with the earth. Besides the Sky God existed the Earth Mother, the earth who gives birth to all, who gives men food and wealth, and who receives them back to herself when life is over. The Earth as bride of the Sky is one of the universal motifs of world mythology, and there are many myths of how these two were once joined together and had to be separated by force when men were created. The Great Goddess of vegetation and harvest was a development of the Earth Mother. She became increasingly important as agriculture developed among men, and flourished in the fertile Mediterranean lands, under such names as Isis, Demeter, and Cybele. Other divine figures have been emphasized in the work of different scholars. Frazer emphasized that of the Dying God, the male deity linked with the Great Mother, who must perish as the world of nature declines in winter to be reborn in the new life of the spring. As Osiris or Tammuz and under many other names he was lamented throughout the ancient world when his time came to perish in the seasonal round, and in spring he became the symbol of new life emerging from the dead. In the theory occurring throughout his books, Dumézil has taught us to see other figures of widespread significance: the Terrible Sovereign, whose powers are due to magic, the Sovereign Law-Giver, and the Warrior God. Thus Jupiter, at first the Sky God, seems to have developed into the Terrible Sovereign, and remains to some extent in opposition to the warrior Mars.

This is so wide a subject that to dwell on it further would be to defer the main purpose of the book. We have to consider the kind of heritage which our forefathers have left us, and we must decide on its nature before we attempt to see it in the light of other mythologies. It is necessary however to realize that such world patterns in religion exist. When we are studying the myths of our own race, there may be parallels in the myths of other peoples which will help us to understand our own more clearly. The realization of this is perhaps the most exciting recent discovery in the history of religions. It helps us to see the myths of the past as man's attempt to embody his intuitive ideas about the human mind and its environment, to express truths dimly perceived which have roots in his innermost being. Thus the myths may lead us to discover more about our spiritual heritage, and perhaps to realize some of the defects in the spiritual development of the modern world. The study of mythology need no longer be looked on as an escape from reality into the fantasies of primitive peoples, but as a search for the deeper understanding of the human mind. In reaching out to explore the distant hills where the gods dwell and the deeps where the monsters are lurking, we are perhaps discovering the way home.

Chapter 1

The World of the Northern Gods

I am the child of the Earth and starry Heaven, but my origin is of Heaven alone.
   Orphic Grave Tablet

1. *The* Prose Edda

Christianity was firmly established in north-western Europe in the twelfth century, but there was still interest in the heathen legends of the gods. By then men were secure enough in their faith not to fear a resurgence of the ancient paganism, and felt new stirrings of affection for the old tales, never forgotten by the northern poets. The complex, sophisticated verses of the skaldic poets were very fashionable at the courts of kings and in the halls of cultured men, and these poets relied on the myths as their main source of imagery. Their poetry was filled with allusions to the old stories, some of them mere clichés, some neat and witty, and some retaining real poetic fire. In seventeenth-century England the poet Milton enriched his picture of a Biblical Eden by reference to such legends as the descent of Proserpine to Hades, and he could expect an instant response from readers trained in classical lore. In the same way a medieval Icelandic poet could refer to poetry as the ship of the dwarfs, to gold as the tears of Freyja or the cushion of the dragon Fafnir, and to a sword as the fire of the Valkyries: his audience would comprehend his meaning from their knowledge of the myths. He could do this whether he were praising a loved woman, describing adventures in battle, or expressing his enthusiasm for the cause of Christ, and be confident that his hearers would seize on the imaginative implications of his images.

By the twelfth century it was growing more difficult to do

this. The old myths were fading from men's minds: the church-men sometimes condemned them as evil, and cultured young men were reared in the new Christian learning instead of the heathen traditions. It therefore occurred to a gifted Icelandic scholar, Snorri Sturluson, that it would be worth while to write a book about these matters before they were utterly lost. Snorri was a man of extraordinary gifts: chieftain, politician, historian, saga-writer, and poet. He planned his work as a handbook for poets and intellectuals, a guide to poetic imagery. Since he was a brilliant stylist, writing in his native Icelandic, it was no dry antiquarian treatise; he told the old tales of the gods with wit, irony, and a lively delight in their imaginative beauty. He called his book the *Edda*, and it is known as the *Prose Edda* to dis-tinguish it from a collection of poems with the same name. It is from this book of Snorri's, written about 1220, that our main impression of northern mythology has been derived.

There is little doubt that on the whole Snorri has given us a faithful picture of heathen mythology as he found it in the poets. Sometimes he quotes from poems which we still possess, and we can see what he is about; sometimes he gives us stanzas from lost poems, or tells stories which seem to be summaries of narrative poems now vanished; sometimes it is obvious that he is quoting statements which he himself does not under-stand. He was a fine scholar and literary artist, and was able on the whole to resist the temptation to alter his sources so as to rationalize them or to point a Christian moral. But he was primarily a literary artist, not an anthropologist or religious historian, and he was writing in the thirteenth century, not the heathen period. Much of his material came from poets who themselves had written in a Christian age. The question has to be raised then how far in his book we are dealing with an arti-ficial world of myth, far removed from the living faith of the heathen period. For the moment however, provided we re-member his limitations, there seems no better introduction to the mythology of the north than that which Snorri gives us.

2. *The Gods and their World*

Snorri began from a Christian standpoint, but a wise and toler-ant one. When men by their sins broke away from God, he explained in his preface, they lost true understanding of him, and had to begin again from the beginning. As they looked at the wonderful living world around them and the heavens above, they felt that these must have been formed by an almighty creator, one who ruled the stars and existed before them. When certain great heroes came into their world, they believed that these must be the gods, and gave them worship. In this way Snorri explained the existence of the old legends, firmly rejecting the idea that the ancient divinities were devils. He knew that there were many gods and goddesses, and suggested that they came first from Troy, and that Thor was perhaps a grandson of King Priam, thus linking the north to the ancient world. Among the sons of Thor he placed Odin the Wise, who shared with his wife Frigg great powers of magic. Odin and Frigg moved northwards to Germany, and then to Denmark, Sweden, and Norway, leaving one of their sons to rule each kingdom. In Sweden in particular Odin set up chiefs and a code of laws 'after the pattern of Troy', and here was the centre of his rule. His descendants were known as the Aesir.

After this admirably objective introduction, Snorri presented the main body of his material, an account of the gods and their world. The first section of his book was called *Gylfaginning*, 'the deluding of Gylfi'. Gylfi was a Swedish king who wel-comed Odin on his arrival, and he later journeyed to the hall of the Aesir disguised as an old wayfaring man, Gangleri, to test for himself their wisdom and power. His questions were an-swered freely by three mysterious beings whom he found sitting one above the other on three high-seats, and who were intro-duced to him as High One, Just-as-High, and Third. These told him the names and characteristics of the chief gods and goddesses, and described the realms making up heaven and the underworld, the creation of the world, the doings of the gods, and their ultimate destruction by the powers of evil. The account ends with the promise of a new world of gods and men which will arise when the old is destroyed, and Gangleri is then told:

> Now if you find more questions to ask, I don't know how you will set about it, for I have never heard anyone tell more of the story of the world than this. Make what you can of it!

In this way Snorri skilfully avoids responsibility for the material which he is presenting. It is not he who speaks, as in the preface, but three doubtful characters who, you may think, were merely having sport with a naïve and inquisitive Swedish king. All men knew that the cunning old Aesir were past masters at spells to deceive the eyes and the mind. But Snorri guessed that most readers would be won by the persuasive tongues of the Great Three to listen for a while to their account of the vanished world of the gods.

The World Tree

This world had for its centre a great tree, a mighty ash called Yggdrasill. So huge was this tree that its branches stretched out over heaven and earth alike. Three roots supported the great trunk, and one passed into the realm of the Aesir, a second into that of the frost-giants, and a third into the realm of the dead. Beneath the root in giant-land was the spring of Mimir, whose waters contained wisdom and understanding. Odin had given one of his eyes for the right to drink a single draught of that precious water. Below the tree in the kingdom of the Aesir was the sacred spring of fate, the Well of Urd. Here every day the gods assembled for their court of law, to settle disputes and discuss common problems. All came on horseback except Thor, who preferred to wade through the rivers that lay in his path, and they were led by Odin on the finest of all steeds, the eight-legged horse Sleipnir. The gods galloped over the bridge Bifrost, a rainbow bridge that glowed with fire. They alone might cross it, and the giants, who longed to do so, were held back. Near the spring of fate dwelt three maidens called the Norns, who ruled the destinies of men, and were called Fate (*Urðr*), Being (*Verðandi*), and Necessity (*Skuld*). They watered the tree each day with pure water and whitened it with clay from the spring, and in this way preserved its life, while the water fell down to earth as dew. The tree was continually threatened, even as it grew and flourished, by the living creatures that preyed upon it. On the topmost bough sat an eagle, with a hawk perched on its forehead: the same eagle, perhaps, of whom it is said that the flapping of its wings caused the winds in the world of men. At the root of the tree lay a great serpent, with many scores of lesser snakes, and these gnawed continually at Yggdrasill. The serpent was at war with the eagle, and a nimble squirrel ran up and down the tree, carrying insults from one to the other. Horned creatures, harts and goats, devoured the branches and tender shoots of the tree, leaping at it from every side.

Creation

The tree formed a link between the different worlds. We are never told of its beginning, but of the creation of the worlds of which it formed a centre there is much to tell. In the beginning there were two regions: Muspell in the south, full of brightness and fire; and a world of snow and ice in the north. Between them stretched the great emptiness of Ginnungagap. As the heat and cold met in the midst of the expanse, a living creature appeared in the melting ice, called Ymir. He was a great giant, and from under his left arm grew the first man and woman, while from his two feet the family of frost-giants was begotten. Ymir fed upon the milk of a cow called *Auðhumla*, who licked the salty ice-blocks and released another new being, a man called Buri. He had a son called Bor, and the sons of Bor were the three gods, Odin, Vili, and Ve. These three slew Ymir the ancient giant, and all the frost-giants save one, Bergelmir, were drowned in his surging blood.

From Ymir's body they then formed the world of men:

... from his blood the sea and the lakes, from his flesh the earth, and from his bones the mountains; from his teeth and jaws and such bones as were broken they formed the rocks and the pebbles.

From Ymir's skull they made the dome of the sky, placing a dwarf to support it at each of the four corners and to hold it high above the earth. This world of men was protected from the giants by a wall, made from the eyebrows of Ymir, and was called Midgard. The gods created inhabitants for it from two trees on the sea-shore, which became a man and a woman. They gave to them spirit and understanding, the power of movement, and the use of the senses. They created also the dwarfs, creatures with strange names, who bred in the earth like maggots, and dwelt in hills and rocks. These were skilled craftsmen, and it was they who wrought the great treasures of the gods. The gods caused time to exist, sending Night and Day to drive round the heavens in chariots drawn by swift horses. Two fair children, a girl called Sun and boy called Moon, were also set by them on paths across the sky. Sun and Moon had to drive fast because they were pursued by wolves, who meant to devour them. On the day when the greatest of the wolves succeeded in swallowing the Sun, the end of all things would be at hand.

Asgard

Once heaven and earth were formed, it was time to set about the building of Asgard, the realm of the gods. Here there were many wonderful halls, in which the gods dwelt. Odin himself lived in *Válaskjálf*, a hall roofed with silver, where he could sit in his special seat and view all the worlds at once. He had another hall called Valhalla, the hall of the slain, where he offered hospitality to all those who fell in battle. Each night they feasted on pork that never gave out, and on mead which flowed instead of milk from the udders of the goat Heidrun, one of the creatures that fed upon Yggdrasill. Odin's guests spent the day in fighting, and all who fell in the combat were raised again in the evening to feast with the rest. Horns of mead were carried to them by the Valkyries, the maids of Odin, who had also to go down to the battlefields of earth and decide the course of war, summoning fallen warriors to Valhalla. Somewhere in Asgard there was a building with a roof of gold, called Gimli, to which it was said that righteous men went after death. There were other realms beyond Asgard, like Alfheim, where the fair elves lived, and as many as three heavens, stretching one beyond the other.

The Gods

As to the gods who dwelt in Asgard, Snorri twice gives their number as twelve, excluding Odin himself. Odin was the father

and head of the Aesir; he was called All-Father, but had many
other names, among them One-eyed, God of the Hanged, God
of Cargoes, and Father of Battle. He journeyed far and wide
over the earth, and had two ravens to bring him tidings from
afar. His eldest son was Thor, whose mother was Earth. Thor
was immensely strong, and drove in a chariot drawn by goats.
He possessed three great treasures: the hammer Mjollnir, which
could slay giants and shatter rocks; a belt of power which
doubled his strength; and iron gloves with which to grasp the
terrible hammer. Another son of Odin was Balder, said to be
the fairest of all and most deserving of praise; he was white of
skin and bright-haired, and was both wise and merciful. The
gods Njord and Freyr were also dwellers in Asgard, but were
not of the race of the Aesir. Njord came of the Vanir, and was
sent to Asgard as a hostage when the two races were at war,
and Freyr was his son. Njord controlled the winds and the sea,
helped in fishing and seafaring, and brought men wealth, while
Freyr gave sunshine and rain and the gifts of peace and plenty.
Freyr possessed the ship *Skíðblaðnir*, large enough to hold all
the gods, but small enough when folded to lie in a pouch, and
also a wonderful boar with golden bristles. Another god was
Tyr, who could give victory in battle, and it was he who bound
the monster Fenrir and was left as a result with only one hand.
There was also Bragi, who was skilled in the use of words and
in the making of poetry. We hear too of Heimdall, who was
called the white god, and was said to be the son of nine maidens.
His dwelling was beside the rainbow bridge, for he acted as
the gods' warden, guarding heaven from the frost-giants. He
could see for an immense distance, while his ears were sharp
enough to catch the sound of grass growing on earth, and wool
on sheep. He owned *Gjallarhorn*, whose ringing blast could
be heard through all the worlds. There was also among the
gods Loki, the son of a giant, who was handsome to look upon
but given to evil ways. He was a cunning schemer, who both
helped and hindered the gods, and he gave birth to the wolf
Fenrir, to the World Serpent, and to Hel, the ruler of the land
of death. These were the chief of the gods, and beside them
were others of whom we know little: Ull, a famous archer and
skier, Forseti, the son of Balder and a good law-giver, Hoder,

a blind god, and Hoenir, who was sometimes the companion of Odin and Loki in their wanderings. The sons of the great gods, like Vali, Vidar, and Magni, had special parts to play, for they were to inherit the world of Asgard when the older generation had perished.

The Goddesses

There were also certain mighty goddesses. Frigg was the wife of Odin, and like him knew the future of gods and men. Freyja was Freyr's twin sister, and the most renowned of all the goddesses; she helped in affairs of love and had some power over the dead. She drove in a chariot drawn by cats. Freyja was said to have had a husband called Od, who left her to weep tears of red gold at his disappearance. Skadi, the wife of Njord, came from the mountains to marry the sea god. The marriage was not a success, because neither was willing to live away from home, and in the end Skadi went back to the hills, where she went on skis and hunted with the bow. Bragi's wife was Idun, who had one important part to play : she guarded the apples of immortality, on which the gods feasted in order to keep their perpetual youth. Other goddesses are little more than names. Thor's wife, Sif, had wonderful golden hair. Balder's wife was Nanna, and Loki's Sigyn, while Gna and Fulla are mentioned as servants of Frigg. There is also Gefion, to whom unmarried girls went after death.

The Wooing of Gerd

Besides these, we have the maiden Gerd, who was wooed by Freyr. She lived in the north, and he caught sight of her one day as he sat on Odin's seat. The radiance from her white arms lit up the sky and the sea, and as he watched, Freyr was overcome by so intense a desire for her that he could neither eat nor sleep. At last he sent his servant Skirnir down to woo her, giving him his own sword and a horse for the journey. Gerd was at length persuaded to yield to Freyr's wooing and to consent to meet him in nine nights' time. It was on this account, we are told, that Freyr was without a sword when the last great battle of the gods came to be fought.

by his snores. Thor buckled on his belt of strength, but at that moment the giant rose to his feet, and so enormous was he that for once Thor was not prepared to swing his hammer. The giant said his name was Skrymir, 'Big Fellow', and he picked up what they had taken to be a building but now saw to be his glove, with the thumb sticking out on the right to make the side-passage in which they had sheltered.

The giant said they could journey together, and suggested that they should put all their provisions into one bag, which he carried. His great strides took him on ahead, and that evening they found him waiting under an oak. He lay down for a nap while they turned to prepare the supper. But when Thor tried to undo the bag, he could not unfasten the strap, strive as he would. At last in a fury he struck Skrymir on the head with his hammer. But the giant only opened his eyes and asked mildly if a leaf had fallen on his head. In the end they lay down without supper, and once more the noise of Skrymir's snores filled their ears. Thor struck with his hammer a second time, but the only response from Skrymir was to ask whether an acorn had fallen on him. At dawn, when the giant still slept, Thor struck a third time, and this was so mighty a blow that the hammer sank in up to the handle. The giant then sat up and remarked that a bird seemed to have dropped something on him from the tree above. Then he took leave of them, warning Thor to be on his best behaviour when he reached the hall of Utgard, where he assured them there were plenty of fellows bigger even than himself. He strode off through the wood, and to their great relief they saw him no more.

They reached Utgard at midday, and found it no smaller than they had been led to believe. It was indeed so huge that they were able to get in by squeezing between the bars of the mighty gate. In the hall was the king, Utgard-Loki. When at last he noticed his puny visitors, he was not very complimentary in his welcome, but he inquired whether they had any special gifts which they could display before the company. Then followed a series of trials of strength at which Thor and his companions did not acquit themselves as well as might have been expected.

First Loki tried a race at eating with a man called Logi. He was utterly outstripped, for though he rapidly devoured all the meat he was given, Logi swallowed the bones and the trough as well. Next Thialfi, who was a swift runner, ran races with a lad called Hugi, but Hugi was able to reach the end of the course and come back to meet him every time. Then Thor made trial of his strength in a drinking contest. Thor was given a huge horn, which he expected to empty easily, but after three attempts to do so he found that the liquid had only dropped a little below the rim. Next the king suggested that he should try the feat of lifting the cat up from the floor. A great grey cat jumped down in front of him, and Thor grasped it round the middle and exerted all his strength, but was only able to raise one of its paws off the ground. Finally Utgard-Loki called in his old foster-mother to wrestle with Thor. She seemed a decrepit old woman, but Thor with all his power could not get her off her feet. When however she grasped hold of him, he was forced down on one knee before the king stopped the conflict.

The discomfited god and his companions were then given splendid hospitality, and stayed there that night. Next morning Utgard-Loki himself escorted them to the gate, and once they were safely outside, he revealed the truth to them. Thor and his comrades had been deceived by cunning magic, altering the appearance of things. The three blows struck at Skrymir – who in fact was Utgard-Loki himself – had fallen on to the earth, and Thor's hammer had left three mighty pits in the hill which the giant had interposed between himself and the angry god. The bag which could not be undone had been fastened by iron bands. As for the contests in the hall, they had not been what they seemed. Loki's opponent was *Logi* (Fire), which consumes all things more swiftly than any man or god. Thialfi had raced against *Hugi* (Thought), swifter than any man in its flight. The horn offered to Thor had its tip in the ocean, and the great draughts he had drunk had lowered the sea-level down to ebb tide. The cat was in truth the ancient monster, the World Serpent, so that all were terrified when Thor's strength proved great enough to raise it a little way from the depths of the sea. His opponent in the wrestling was no other than *Elli* (Old Age), who can overcome the strongest. When he learned how he had been tricked, Thor in his rage swung his hammer, intending to destroy the stronghold, but even as he did so it vanished from sight, and they were alone on the plain.

Thor's Fishing

Perhaps it was to take vengeance for this humiliation – or so at least it was suggested to Gangleri – that Thor set out to visit the giant Hymir, in the guise of a youth. He asked to go fishing with Hymir, and when sent off to get some bait, he took the giant's biggest ox and cut off its head to take along with them. The boat moved so fast once Thor took the oars that Hymir was astounded, and before long they reached the fishing ground. Thor rowed on still further, although Hymir tried to prevent him for fear of disturbing the Midgard Serpent, and when at last he threw the ox-head out into the sea, it was indeed the serpent which took the bait. Thor had to exert all his divine strength, and before long, digging his heels through the boat and pushing hard against the sea bottom, he hauled up the monster, and they stared fiercely into one another's eyes. At this terrible sight, Hymir was panic-stricken, and as Thor raised his hammer, he cut the line. The serpent sank back into the depths of the sea, and Thor in anger knocked the giant overboard and waded back to shore. Whether he struck off the serpent's head before it sank, or it still lies coiled round the earth, Gangleri was unable to discover.

4. The Doom of the Gods

The Death of Balder

Next Gangleri learned of the event which led to the destruction of the earth and of Asgard, the death of Balder the Beautiful. Balder, son of Odin, had ominous dreams, and the gods, fearing that danger threatened him, sent Frigg to extract an oath from all things on earth, whether living creatures, plants, or things of metal, wood, and stone, that they would do no harm to Balder. After this they found it amusing to fling darts and hurl heavy objects at Balder, knowing that they could do him no hurt. But Loki took on the disguise of a woman, and talked with Frigg. He learned that one little plant, the mistletoe, had taken no oath, since Frigg had thought it too young to threaten Balder. Filled with spite, Loki pulled up mistletoe and persuaded Hoder, the blind god, to throw it at Balder in sport, guiding his hand as he threw. The dart pierced Balder through, and he fell dead to the earth.

Bitter indeed was the grief of the Aesir, and Odin's most bitter of all, since he alone knew the extent of the loss they had suffered. Frigg begged that someone would ride to the kingdom of death and bring Balder back to them. Hermod, another of Odin's sons, agreed to make the perilous journey, riding Odin's horse Sleipnir. The gods meanwhile took up Balder's body and laid it on a funeral pyre built on his own ship, *Hringhorni*. A giantess pushed it off the rollers into the sea, and there Balder was burned on the pyre, with his wife Nanna, who had died of grief, and his horse beside him. Odin laid the gold ring Draupnir, one of the great treasures of the gods, upon the pyre as a last gift. All the gods and goddesses came to Balder's funeral.

Hermod's Ride to Hel

Meanwhile Hermod had been riding down the dark road to the land of the dead, and over the bridge that spanned the Resounding River. There was a maid, Modgud, guarding this bridge, and she came out in wonder to see who came riding with such noise and tumult. Balder, she said, had already passed that way, and five troops of the dead, but this newcomer was not like such travellers, and had the aspect of a living man. At last Hermod reached Hel-gate, and Sleipnir leaped over it with ease. The hall of Hel stood open before them, and Balder was sitting in the high seat. Hel was willing to release him on condition that all things in the world, living or dead, would weep for him. But should any creature refuse to weep, she said, then he must stay with her and never go back to the Aesir. So Hermod bade farewell to Balder, who gave him Draupnir to bear back to Odin and many rich gifts besides, and returned with Hel's answer.

At the summons of the gods, all things did indeed weep for Balder, men and beasts, stones and metals, in the way that we see all things weep after frost, when the air grows warm again. But at last the messenger of the gods came to a giantess, alone in a cave. When they asked her to weep for Balder, her reply was a deadly one:

Alive or dead, the old man's son
has been no use to me.
Let Hel hold what she has!

It was believed that this giantess was no other than Loki himself, seeking in his malice to keep Balder in Hel.

The Aesir were so wrathful that Loki knew that this time he had no hope of mercy if they caught him, so he fled from them, built a house with doors looking out in every direction, and then changed himself into a salmon in the river. But Kvasir, the wisest of the Aesir, found some ashes on the hearth where Loki had been burning a net, and from the shape of this he realized that this was the only way to catch the nimble salmon. They made the net to Loki's pattern, and at the third try they caught him by the tail. Loki was then bound across three flat stones, held down by the entrails of one of his own sons. There he was left to writhe beneath the mouth of a snake, which dropped its poison on to his face. His faithful wife Sigyn sat with a bowl to catch the poison drops, but each time she went to empty it the poison fell on Loki again, and his struggles caused the earth to shake.

Ragnarok

There Loki must lie until Ragnarok, the time of the destruction of the gods. This fearful time will be ushered in by many portents. First there will be great wars through the world, and a time of strife and hatred between men. The bonds of kinship will hold them no longer, and they will commit appalling deeds of murder and incest. There will also be a period of bitter cold, when a terrible pursuing wolf catches the sun and devours her; the moon too is to be swallowed up, and the stars will fall from the sky. The mountains will crash into fragments as the whole earth shakes and trembles, and the World Tree quivers in the tumult. Now all fettered monsters break loose. The wolf Fenrir advances, his great gaping jaws filling the gap between earth and sky, while the serpent emerges from the sea, blowing out poison. The sea rises to engulf the land, and on the flood the ship Naglfar is launched, a vessel made from the nails of dead men. It carries a crew of giants, with Loki as their steersman. From the fiery realm of Muspell, Surt and his following ride out with shining swords, and the bridge Bifrost is shattered beneath their weight. His forces join the frost-giants on the plain of Vigrid, and there the last battle will be fought between this mighty host and the gods.

The note of Heimdall's horn arouses the Aesir to their danger, and Odin rides to the spring beneath the World Tree, to take counsel of Mimir's head. Then with his chosen champions from Valhalla he goes out on to the plain, to encounter at last his ancient enemy, the wolf. Thor meets the World Serpent, and Freyr fights against Surt; Tyr must encounter the hound Garm, broken loose from the underworld, while Heimdall does battle with Loki. All the gods must fall, and the monsters be destroyed with them. Thor kills the serpent, and then falls dead, overcome by its venom. Odin is devoured by Fenrir, but his young son Vidar slays the wolf in turn, setting one foot upon its jaw and tearing it asunder. Tyr and Heimdall both conquer their opponents, but they do not survive the struggle. Only Surt remains to the last, to fling fire over the whole world, so that the race of men perishes with the gods, and all are finally engulfed in the overwhelming sea:

> The sun becomes dark. Earth sinks in the sea.
> The shining stars slip out of the sky.
> Vapour and fire rage fiercely together,
> till the leaping flame licks heaven itself.

Yet this is not the end. Earth will arise again from the waves, fertile, green, and fair as never before, cleansed of all its sufferings and evil. The sons of the great gods still remain alive, and Balder will return from the dead to reign with them. They will rule a new universe, cleansed and regenerated, while two living creatures who have sheltered from destruction in the World Tree will come out to repeople the world with men and women. A new sun, outshining her mother in beauty, will journey across the heavens.

Such is the picture of the beginning and end of the world of gods and men, drawn for Gangleri by the Three Powers.

5. *The Giants and the Dwarfs*

In the second section of this book, Gangleri has disappeared and Snorri fills out his outline by adding more stories about the gods which will serve to explain some of the imagery used by poets. Nearly all the stories which he includes in *Skáldskaparmál* (Poetic Diction) have to do with attempts by the giants to get the better of the gods and to steal their treasures.

The Theft of the Apples

First we hear of the theft of the apples of youth. One day when three of the gods, Odin, Loki, and Hoenir, were journeying together, they tried to roast an ox for their dinner, but the meat would not cook. At last a mighty eagle in an oak called out to them from above, and offered to get the meal cooked for them if they would give him a share. It turned out that his idea of a fair share meant the greater part of the ox, and Loki in a rage attacked him with a stick. He was caught up with the stick, and carried through the air, and the eagle refused to let him go until he promised to bring him Idun and her golden apples. When Loki returned to Asgard, it was easy to lure Idun outside on some pretext, and the giant Thiazi, still in his eagle form, bore her off to his home.

Without the apples of youth, the Aesir began to grow grey and wrinkled, and at last Loki's guilt was discovered, and he was threatened with death unless he righted the wrong that he had done. Accordingly he borrowed the falcon shape of Freyja and flew off to Thiazi's abode. The giant was out fishing, so Loki changed Idun into a nut and flew off with it in his claws. Thiazi discovered the loss and started in pursuit, and Loki flew into Asgard only just in time. The gods were waiting with a heap of wood shavings, and they set fire to these as soon as Loki had flown over the wall, so that the fire singed Thiazi's wings and he fell down inside the stronghold of the gods, and was easily slain.

His daughter Skadi came to avenge her father, and the gods offered her marriage with one of them as compensation for the slaying. She was permitted to see no more than their feet when she made her choice, and so it came about that she married Njord, thinking that she was choosing the handsome Balder. Odin also pleased her by throwing Thiazi's eyes up into heaven, where they became stars.

The Winning of the Mead

Next we hear of the truce made between the Aesir and the Vanir, and how this led to the gift of inspiration coming to gods and men. When the two companies of gods met to make peace, they took a vessel and all spat into it, and from the contents they created the wise Kvasir, who was able to answer all questions. Kvasir however was killed by two dwarfs, who let his blood run into three huge vessels, and mixed it with honey to make a rich mead. Whoever drank of this received the gift of inspiration, and could compose poetry and utter words of wisdom. The malicious dwarfs, however, went too far when they killed a giant called Gilling, and his wife as well. The giant's son, Suttung, took vengeance on them by putting them on a rock and leaving them there to drown. To save their lives they were forced to give him the mead, and it is for this reason that poetry is called 'Kvasir's blood' or 'ship of the dwarfs'.

The gods wished to win the precious liquid back from the giants, and Odin set out to do so. First he sharpened the scythes of nine men labouring in the fields to such good effect that in the end they quarrelled over the possession of his wonderful whetstone, and cut one another's throats. Then he took their place, and hired himself out to their master, the giant Baugi, who was Suttung's brother. The only wage he demanded was a drink of the wonderful mead. Baugi agreed to this, but when it came to the point, his brother would not let Odin have his drink. Then Odin persuaded Baugi to help him to bore a hole into the mountain where Suttung lived, and he crept in, taking the form of a serpent. He slept three nights with Suttung's daughter, and persuaded her to give him three drinks of the mead. In three draughts he emptied all three vessels, and flew off in eagle form back to the Aesir, who had more vessels ready for him. He spat out the mead into them, all but a little that had been lost on the way – known as the poetaster's share – and so it came about that poetry is now said to be the gift of Odin and the Aesir to men.

Thor's Duel

Another tale is that of the giant Hrungnir's duel with Thor. Odin and Hrungnir had a wager together, each insisting that he had the finer horse. Odin galloped off on Sleipnir and Hrungnir after him on his horse Goldmane, and Hrungnir inadvertently found himself inside the realm of the gods before he drew rein. The Aesir allowed him to drink from Thor's great beakers, and he grew boastful, declaring that he was going to sink Asgard into the sea and carry off Freyja and Sif. Thor at this point came in, furiously demanding why a giant was sitting drinking among them, but Hrungnir claimed safe-conduct, and challenged Thor to a duel.

For this duel the giants made a clay man, called Mist-Calf, to support Hrungnir. Hrungnir himself had a sharp, three-cornered heart of stone, and a stone head, and he was armed with a stone shield and a whetstone. Thor came out with Thialfi to meet him, and Thialfi told the giant he had better stand on his shield, in case Thor attacked him from below. Then Thor bore down on Hrungnir with thunder and lightning, and hurled his hammer at him, while the giant threw his whetstone. The weapons met in mid air, and the whetstone was shattered, but one piece lodged in Thor's forehead. The hammer went on to strike Hrungnir's skull and break it in pieces. Meanwhile Thialfi had dealt with the clay figure without much difficulty. The only problem was caused by Hrungnir falling on top of Thor, for no one could move his great leg off the god until Thor's little son, Magni, came up and pushed it away. Magni received the horse Goldmane as a reward. A seeress tried to sing spells to get the piece of whetstone out of Thor's head, but he began to tell her how he had once carried her husband Aurvandil in a basket out of giant-land, and when one toe of Aurvandil had frozen, he had flung it up into the sky to become the star called Aurvandil's Toe. She was so interested that the spell was never finished, and so the stone still remains in Thor's head.

The World of the Northern Gods

Thor's visit to Geirrod

Another tale about Thor tells of his expedition to the realm of Geirrod. Loki had again been out flying in Freyja's feather shape, and he was captured in the hall of Geirrod by the giant himself. Geirrod recognized the hawk by its eyes, and knew it to be Loki, so he shut him up and starved him for three months, until he promised to bring Thor to the hall without his hammer or belt of strength. Loki succeeded in this, but on the way Thor was warned of his danger by a friendly giantess, who lent him her magic staff, another belt, and iron gloves. First Thor was nearly drowned in the river Vimir, for Geirrod's daughter stood astride the stream making it swell, until he struck her with a huge rock, and then climbed out with the aid of a rowan tree. Then he entered Geirrod's hall, and sat down on a seat, but at once felt himself being raised to the roof. He forced the seat down with the aid of his magic staff, and so broke the backs of Geirrod's two daughters, who had been pushing up his chair. Then he went up to Geirrod, who flung a ball of hot iron at him. Thor caught it with his iron gloves, and while Geirrod ducked behind a pillar, he hurled it through the pillar and the giant together. So Thor went back unscathed to Asgard.

The Treasures of the Gods

There is also the story of how the gods obtained their wonderful treasures. One day in a fit of mischief Loki cut off Sif's golden hair, and Thor would have killed him if he had not found two cunning dwarfs to make new tresses of real gold for Sif, which would grow like natural hair. They also made Freyr's wonderful ship and Odin's great spear Gungnir. Loki then challenged two other skilful dwarfs to make three more treasures as good as these, wagering his head that they would not succeed. As they laboured in the smithy the dwarf working the bellows was stung persistently by a fly, but in spite of this they succeeded in forging a marvellous boar with bristles of gold, which could run faster than any steed and light up the darkest night. They also forged the great gold ring, Draupnir, from which eight other rings dropped every ninth night.

As they were making the third treasure, the fly stung the

dwarf again, this time on his eyelid, and he had to raise his hand to brush it away. The third treasure was the great hammer Mjollnir, which would hit anything at which it was thrown and return to the thrower's hand. Because of the interference of the fly, however, which was Loki in disguise, it was a little short in the handle. Nevertheless the gods held that the hammer was the best of all their treasures, and a sure weapon against their enemies, and they declared that Loki had lost his wager. He ran away, only to be caught by Thor and handed over to the dwarfs; they wanted to cut off his head, but Loki argued that they had no right to touch his neck. So in the end they contented themselves with sewing up his lips.

The Ransom of Otter

Odin and Loki also play a part in the story of the otter's ransom, which leads on to the famous tale of the hero Sigurd the Volsung. The two gods were wandering through the world with Hoenir one day, when they saw an otter on the edge of a waterfall, drowsily eating a salmon. Loki flung a stone at the otter and bragged of his double catch. But when that night they stopped at the house of a man called Hreidmar, it transpired that the otter was his son in animal form, and he and his other sons, Fafnir and Regin, threatened to slay the gods in revenge. They had to agree to the ransom imposed by Hreidmar, which was to fill the otter skin with gold and then pile gold over it until it was hidden from sight. To do this, Loki had to catch the dwarf Andvari, who was hiding in the shape of a fish, and make him give up the great golden treasure which he was known to possess. The dwarf tried hard to hold on to a little gold ring, which he said would help him to become rich again, but which would bring destruction on all who possessed it. Loki however insisted on taking that too, and it was needed in the end, since when gold covered the skin, one whisker could still be seen and the ring was used to hide it. It is for this reason that poets use such names for gold as 'otter's ransom' or 'forced payment of the Aesir'.

The wonderful golden treasure only brought ruin to the house of Hreidmar in the end, for his sons slew him in their greed, and then Fafnir turned himself into a dragon and lay upon the gold. His brother Regin urged on the young hero Sigurd the Volsung to slay the dragon, but when Sigurd discovered Regin was tricking him, he slew him as well. Sigurd came into possession of Andvari's ring when he took over the treasure, and this ring ultimately caused his own death and much unhappiness.

6. *Myths outside the* Prose Edda

This concludes the series of stories given in the *Prose Edda* about the gods and their doings. We can add to them one more story in the form of a narrative poem, very similar in spirit to those in Snorri's collection. This is the tale of how the giant Thrym stole Thor's hammer, and the unknown poet tells it with the same ironic humour and imaginative delight which distinguishes Snorri's myths. The poem, *Þrymskviða*, is found in the *Elder Edda*.

The Theft of Thor's Hammer

The story goes that one day Thor discovered that his hammer had been stolen, and he called on Loki to find out what had become of it. Loki borrowed Freyja's falcon shape and went out to search, and he found at last that the giant Thrym had hidden the hammer deep down in the earth, and refused to return it to the gods unless he were given Freyja as his wife. This message caused the greatest consternation in Asgard, and sent Freyja into so great a rage that she shattered her famous necklace as she panted with fury. But Heimdall suggested a plan to get back the hammer without risk to Freyja. Thor was to wrap himself in a bridal veil and journey to Jotunheim in Freyja's place, accompanied by Loki disguised as the bride's handmaid. At first Thor thought such a disguise beneath his dignity, but Loki reminded him tartly that without the hammer there was no hope for Asgard.

Thunder and lightning rent the mountains as they drove off in Thor's chariot, and when they entered Jotunheim they received an enthusiastic welcome. At the feast that night all was nearly discovered because of the bride's voracious appetite, but Loki quickly explained that the reason why Freyja was able to eat an ox and eight salmon was because her ardent longings for the wedding had kept her fasting for eight nights. Again when Thrym tried to kiss the bride, he was terrified by a glimpse of the god's terrible burning eyes beneath the veil, but Loki explained that Freyja had had no sleep for eight nights, so intense was her longing for Jotunheim. Thor's ordeal came to an end when the hammer was at last brought in to hallow the bridal couple, and laid in the lap of the bride. Once he had his hands upon it, it was not long before Thrym and all the wedding party were slain, and Thor returned with Loki in triumph to Asgard.

The Truce with the Vanir

Here then is one myth which Snorri for some reason did not include in his stories about Thor. We know that there were others known to him which were not used in the *Prose Edda*, since some are introduced into another of his works, *Ynglinga Saga*. This gives the history of Sweden from very early times, and includes an account of the ending of the war between the Aesir and the Vanir. We are told that when the truce had been made, the Vanir sent as hostages two of their foremost men, Njord and Freyr, and in return the Aesir sent Hoenir, who was tall and handsome, and Mimir, who was very wise. But Hoenir was of little use in counsel because he was so silent, and the Vanir felt that they had not had a fair exchange. They cut off Mimir's head and sent it to the Aesir. Then Odin took the head and sang spells over it, and was able to talk with it and learn hidden matters.

Gefion

In the same saga there is a story about Gefion, whose name Snorri included among the goddesses. She was sent by Odin to look for land, and King Gylfi of Sweden offered her as much land as she could plough. Gefion visited a giant, had four sons by him, and changed these into a team of oxen. With her mighty team she ploughed round Zealand (the island on which Copenhagen stands) and separated it from Sweden. After this she dwelt at Leire with Skiold, son of Odin.

*

Other myths about the gods and their dealings with Danish kings and heroes are found in the work of a Danish scholar and ecclesiastic who lived in the twelfth century, Saxo Grammaticus. His stories are badly told in complex, pompous Latin, and are frequently muddled, repetitive, and spoiled by moralizing. They have none of the charm of Snorri's work, but they contain material of much interest and value. Other myths are implied or referred to in mythological poems about the gods, some of which are in the form of questions and answers exchanged between two supernatural beings, who test one another's knowledge. The dealings of the gods with famous heroes of old time have not been mentioned in this chapter, but there are many stories about them in the heroic poems and the legendary sagas, and these will be referred to from time to time in the course of this book. Other lost myths can be guessed at from the mythological imagery used by the skaldic poets.

Although it must be realized that Snorri's tales do not exhaust our knowledge about the gods, they do, however, form a good starting point for study. He gives us an impressive picture of the universe, with the World Tree at the centre. We see the gods in never-ending competition with the giants and monsters who threaten their peace and menace their world. We see them divided amongst themselves by jealousies and quarrels, yet ready to combine against a common enemy when the danger becomes acute. Snorri traces for us the beginning of the universe from the primeval heat and cold which existed before the worlds; he lets us realize that it cannot last for ever, since the hostile forces must triumph for a while when the present worlds are overthrown at Ragnarok, before a new cycle begins. In preserving the finest of the myths for us, he has also set them in a memorable framework.

Yet he leaves many questions unanswered. This no doubt will already be obvious to the reader. Who for instance were the twelve great gods of whom Snorri speaks? Was there, so to speak, an official list, and are figures like Hoenir, Kvasir, Hoder, and Mimir to be included among the twelve? Were the first man and woman created from the body of Ymir or from trees on the sea-shore? Did Thor kill the World Serpent before Ragnarok? Is Asgard to be thought of as above the earth or beside it, under a root of the World Tree? Was the tree standing before the creation of the worlds? Why is first Thor and then Odin called the Father of the Gods? What happened to the other sons of Bor? Why were the Vanir at war with the Aesir? Some of these questions had probably occurred to Snorri, but as in the instance of the fate of the Midgard Serpent in the fishing adventure, he may have been unable to give an answer.

There is also the deeper question of how far these gods in the myths ever claimed real worship and allegiance from men. Some of the stories are clearly skilful literary efforts, primarily for entertainment. How much real belief existed in the background? Are Thor and Loki serious or comic figures? Can we respect these sometimes naïve and childish characters of the myths as Snorri represents them?

It is with some of these questions, and in particular with these last, that this book is concerned. To find a simple answer to them may be difficult, and in some cases impossible. We can only attempt a reasoned survey of the gods who appear in the myths, based on our present knowledge.

Chapter 2

The Gods of Battle

We are all puppets in the hand of aegis-bearing Zeus.
In a moment Zeus can make a brave man run away and
lose a battle, and the next day the same god will spur
him on to fight.

Iliad, XVII

1. *Odin, Lord of Hosts*

Violence and battle were always close at hand in the lives of
men of the heathen period in north-western Europe. It seems
fitting then to begin our survey of the beliefs of the north by
concentrating on the gods to whom they turned for help in the
hazards and chances of warfare.

In the late heathen period there is no doubt as to the main
figure who represented the God of Battle, for Odin appears continually as the lord of hosts and giver of victory. In Snorri's
account and in many poems he is shown welcoming to his abode
courageous men who fell in battle. His creatures were the raven
and the wolf who feast upon the slain, while his dwelling was
the hall of the slain, Valhalla. In Norwegian court poetry of the
tenth century, he is pictured choosing champions to fall in battle,
so that after death they can be enrolled in his warrior band and
help him to go out to the last battle of the gods with a magnificent following.

This impressive conception has caught the imagination of
later writers, and it is sometimes assumed that all men hoped to
go to Valhalla after death. The literature however gives us no
real reason to assume that Valhalla was ever regarded as a paradise for all; it was peopled by the chosen ones, the aristocratic
warriors who had worshipped the god on earth. Those who
joined Odin in Valhalla were princely warriors, kings, and distinguished leaders and heroes who followed the god in life and
pledged him their loyal service in return for his help. In the

speech of the warrior Biarki, as quoted by Saxo,[1] it is clearly Odin who is referred to when he says:

War springs from the nobly born; famous pedigrees are the makers of War. For the perilous deeds which chiefs attempt are not to be done by the ventures of common men ... No dim and lowly race, no low-born dead, no base souls are Pluto's prey, but he weaves the dooms of the mighty, and fills Phlegethon with noble shapes.

Like any earthly ruler, Odin handed out weapons to his chosen followers, and once they had received them, they were bound to give him loyal service till death and beyond it. Thus Sigmund the Volsung received a splendid sword, which the god himself brought into the hall and thrust into the great tree supporting the roof. The sword was regarded both as a family heirloom and a gift from Odin, and when Sigmund's time came to die, Odin appeared on the battlefield and shattered the blade with his spear. The pieces of the broken sword were reforged for Sigmund's son, Sigurd, who also found favour with Odin, and was given a wonderful horse bred from Odin's own steed, Sleipnir.

Not only treasures but valuable counsel might be given to chosen warriors. Odin taught Sigmund spells of battle, and he instructed Hadding, another of his heroes, how to draw up his forces in wedge formation. When Hadding profited by this advice, and led out his army, Odin himself in the form of an old man stood behind them, and shot so swiftly with his bow that ten arrows sped as one, while he drove away the storm clouds which the enemy had raised by magic. Similarly he gave advice to Harald Wartooth, king of the Danes, to whom he appeared as 'an old man of great height, lacking one eye and clad in a hairy mantle'.[2] He promised Harald immunity from wounds, and in return Harald vowed to give him 'all the souls which his sword cast out of their bodies'.[3] Saxo has also preserved in the eighth book of his history the story of what happened to Harald when the god's favour was withdrawn. First Odin roused up enmity between him and his great friend King Ring, and then he gave to Ring the cherished secret of wedge

1. Saxo Grammaticus, *Gesta Danorum* (translated Elton, 1894), II, 65, p. 78.
2. ibid, VII, 248, p. 298.   3. ibid, VII, 247, p. 296.

formation. As Harald drove out to meet Ring in battle, he suddenly recognized the god in the place of his own charioteer. He begged him for one more victory, swearing to dedicate to Odin all who fell in battle. But the driver was relentless, and even as Harald pleaded he flung him down from the chariot, and slew him with his own sword as he fell.

The bitterness against the god expressed in this story might be attributed to Saxo the Christian scholar if it stood alone, but it can be matched from many other sources. A fine tenth-century poem, *Hákonarmál*, composed at the death of Hakon the Good of Norway, describes him entering the courts of Odin. He is received with much honour, but his response is a cold one:

> Surely we have deserved victory of the gods ... Odin has shown great enmity towards us ... We will keep our war-gear ready to hand.

The implication is clear: Odin cannot be trusted. This is expressed with even greater freedom in later poetry and by the prose writers:

> You have never been able to order the course of war; often have you given victory to cowards who did not deserve it.   *Lokasenna*

> Balder's father has broken faith – it is unsafe to trust him....
> *Ketils Saga Hœngs*

> I suspect indeed that it is Odin who comes against us here, the foul and untrue....   *Hrólfs Saga Kraka*

Phrases such as this suggest widespread indignation against the treachery of the god. Perhaps it is not too fanciful to catch the same note in the protest of a high priest of the gods at the court of King Edwin of Northumbria in the seventh century, recorded by Bede in his *Ecclesiastical History of the English Nation* (II, 13) less than a century later. Coifi the priest declared that the old religion offered no reward for true and faithful service, and another unnamed speaker in the debate added that heathen men were left with nothing in which they could trust once their earthly life was over. It seems likely that Coifi the priest was the servant of the God of Battle, since his method of destroying and repudiating the temple of the gods was to hurl a spear at it and then to commit it to the flames. This is in accordance with what we know of the sacrificial rites associated with Odin himself.

In Old Norse literature the rites said to belong to Odin are dedication by a spear, hanging, and burning. Snorri tells us in *Ynglinga Saga* that marking with a spear at the time of death and burning of the dead were practices followed by the Swedish worshippers of Odin, and that they claimed to be following their god's own example. According to the poem *Hávamál* (Utterance of the High One), Odin himself recounts how he was pierced with a spear and hanged on a tree, a sacrifice for the attainment of wisdom (see pp. 143-4). We have independent evidence for the sacrifice of men and beasts by hanging as late as the eleventh century in Sweden. In his history of the Archbishops of Hamburg-Bremen,[1] Adam of Bremen gives a grim picture of the bodies of men and animals left hanging from trees round the great heathen temple at Uppsala, when a special festival to the gods was held every nine years. He gives as the source of his information a Christian friend of his, an old man of seventy-two, who had told him that he had seen these sacrifices hanging there. Whether this hanging was preceded by the stabbing of the victim with a spear we do not know. Captives in war were also liable to be put to death by hanging, presumably as a sacrifice to the war god. Procopius, writing in the early sixth century, says of the men of Thule, that is, of Norway and Sweden :

... the sacrifice most valued ... is that of the first man which they capture in war. This sacrifice they offer to Ares, since they believe him to be the greatest of the gods. They sacrifice the prisoner not merely by slaughtering him, but by hanging him from a beam, or casting him among thorns, or putting him to death by other horrible methods.   *Gothic War*, II, 15

Again in *Beowulf* it is noticeable that the king of the Swedes threatens to hang his enemies the Geats after the Battle of Ravenswood 'some of them on the gallows-tree, as sport for the birds' (2940-1).[2]

An account of a sacrifice to Odin by hanging is given in one of the late sagas, *Gautreks Saga*. This has so convincing a ring

1. *Gesta Hammaburgensis ecclesiae Pontificum* (IV, 27).

2. 'Birds' is doubtful, as it is the result of an emendation, but there is no doubt about the threat to hang the prisoners.

that in spite of its late date it may be based on memories of the traditional sacrificial cult of the god. According to this story, a Viking leader, King Vikar, prayed to Odin for a favourable wind, and when lots were drawn to decide who should be given to Odin in return for this, it fell upon the king himself. In this embarrassing situation his men decided to stage a mock sacrifice. Vikar was to stand on a tree-stump with a calf's intestines looped round his neck and fastened to the tree above. Starkad, a famous hero and follower of Odin, was to stand beside him with a long rod in his hand. He thrust this rod at the king, uttering the words, 'Now I give thee to Odin'. At this moment a deadly substitution took place, and the ritual became reality:

He let the fir bough go. The rod became a spear, and pierced the king through. The stump fell from under his feet, and the calf's intestines became a strong rope, while the branch shot up and lifted the king among the boughs, and there he died.   *Gautreks Saga*, 7

Here noose and spear are used together in a ritual killing. Among the many titles of Odin, it is noticeable that we find Spear-Brandisher, and God of Hanged Men.

Snorri also emphasized the importance attributed to the burning of the dead among the followers of Odin. All objects burned on the pyre with their owners were deemed to pass with them to Valhalla, he tells us. The double ritual of hanging and stabbing is accompanied by burning in a tenth-century account of a sacrifice held on the Volga, among the Swedish settlers there. It was witnessed by Ibn Fadlan, an Arab traveller, who left a detailed account of what he saw,[1] and he tells how a slave-girl was sacrificed at the funeral of her master. She was strangled and stabbed at the same time by an old woman called the Angel of Death and her helpers, and the girl's body was then burned beside that of her master on a great pyre formed of a blazing ship. The importance of the burning is emphasized by the words of one of the bystanders, who as the flames mounted high declared that his lord had sent a wind to bear the dead man to paradise because of his love for him. This is fully in accord with what Snorri has to say concerning the funeral rites of Odin.

1. An English translation is given by J. Brøndsted in *The Vikings* (Penguin Books, 1964), pp. 301 ff. A more authoritative version, with notes, is in German, by A. Zeki Validi Togan, *Ibn Fadlan's Reisebericht*, Leipzig, 1939.

The words spoken by Starkad at the sacrifice of King Vikar, 'Now I give thee to Odin', are echoed elsewhere. They could be spoken over an enemy host dedicated to the god, as a spear was flung over them. In the Battle of Fyrisvellir, fought in 960 between the Swedish king Eric and Styrbiorn the Strong, Eric is said to have performed this rite and to have won the victory with the help of Odin. Styrbiorn, according to the story told in *Flateyjarbók*, had prayed to Thor for help, but Eric vowed a sacrifice to Odin:

Eric dedicated himself to him for victory, and offered to die at the end of ten years. He had already made many sacrifices, since he seemed likely to get the worst of it. Not long afterwards he saw a tall man with a hood over his face. He gave Eric a thin stick, and told him to shoot it over the host of Styrbiorn and to say, 'Odin has you all'.

Now when he had shot it, it appeared to him like a javelin in the air, and it flew over Styrbiorn's host. Immediately blindness fell upon Styrbiorn's men and then upon Styrbiorn himself. Then a great wonder came to pass, for an avalanche broke loose on the mountain and fell upon Styrbiorn's host, and all his people were slain.

Flateyjarbók, 11, 61

This practice of hurling a spear was remembered by the composer of *Eyrbyggja Saga* (44). He tells how an Icelander did this over a band of his enemies before a fight 'according to ancient custom, to bring them good luck', although Odin is not mentioned. In the poem on the *Battle of the Goths and Huns* (recorded in a late saga, but believed to contain early traditions), there is an allusion to the spear of Odin which will decide the course of battle. The challenge from the Goths to the Huns ends with the invocation:

May every field of battle be piled with your corpses,
And may Odin let the spear fly according to my words.

Here the flinging of a spear, like the marking with a spear at time of death, is attributed to Odin himself. Odin possessed the great spear Gungnir, and this was evidently used to stir up warfare in the world. In *Voluspá*, the cause of the first war among the gods is said to be brought about by Odin flinging his spear into the host. Thus up to the end of the heathen period the

53

picture of the god as fierce provoker of war and giver of victory persisted in the north.

2. *The Germanic War Gods*

We have good reason to believe that Odin as god of war has developed out of earlier conceptions among the Germanic peoples on the Continent of the god who ruled over the battle-field. The god Wodan, or Wotan, had the same type of sacrifice associated with his name. The Heruli, for instance, worshippers of Wodan, practised a double ritual of stabbing and burning. Among them the victims were not necessarily captives taken in war, but those also who were on the point of death from illness or old age. According to Procopius, writing in the sixth century,[1] they were accustomed to lay such men on the funeral pyre and to stab them to death before their bodies were burned.

We come across continual references to terrible sacrifices in honour of 'Mars' among the Germanic peoples. Jordanes, also in the sixth century,[2] wrote of the worship which the Goths gave to the god of war, who, they believed, had been born among them:

They thought that he who is lord of war ought to be appeased by the shedding of human blood. To him they devoted the first share of the spoil, and in his honour arms stripped from the foe were suspended from trees.

Even more terrible rites were practised by the Cimbri, who may have been a Celtic tribe, but were certainly in close contact with the Germans. Strabo[3] reported of them that they hanged their prisoners up over great bronze bowls; their priestesses, who were old women dressed in white, climbed a ladder and cut the throats of the hanging men so that their blood was received in the bowls below. Orosius, writing in the fifth century, gives a vivid account of the actions of these same Cimbri after they had won a great victory in 105 B.C.:

1. *Gothic War*, VI, 14.
2. *History of the Goths*, translated by C. C. Mierow, Princeton University Press, 1915, vol. IV, p. 61.
3. Strabo, *Geography*, VII, 2, 3.

The enemy captured both camps and acquired an enormous quantity of booty. In accordance with a strange and unusual vow, they set about destroying everything which they had taken. Clothing was cut to pieces and cast away, gold and silver was thrown into the river, the breastplates of the men were hacked to pieces, the trappings of the horses were broken up, the horses themselves drowned in whirlpools, and men with nooses round their necks were hanged from trees. Thus there was no booty for the victors and no mercy for the vanquished. *History of the World*, v, 16

This account of wholesale sacrifice both of living creatures and material things to the god of war may be compared with a description given by Tacitus of a battle between two Germanic tribes, the Hermundari and the Chatti, in the first century. They were fighting for possession of the river which flowed between their lands, which was particularly valuable because of the salt to be obtained there, and also because part of its course passed through what was accounted holy ground: 'They cherished a superstition that the locality was specially near to heaven' (*Annals*, XIII, 57). Accordingly both sides vowed to sacrifice the enemy to Mars and Mercury in return for victory. This was a truly fearful vow, implying as it did the sacrifice of the entire beaten side, with their weapons, their horses, and all else that they possessed. Yet the Hermundari, who won the battle, are said to have carried it out, while the Romans cynically applauded the liquidation of troublesome barbarians in the name of religion.

These isolated references to sacrificial practices among the Germanic peoples in heathen times suggest something of the terror associated in men's minds with the god of battle. Discoveries made in the peat bogs of Denmark give us startling confirmation of the power which he once wielded. The peat soil has preserved piles of booty such as must represent the spoils of many battles, lying not at random, but as if arranged deliberately in some kind of order by the victors. At the four main finds, at Thorsbjerg, Vimose, Nydam, and Kragehul, there was an impressive amount of material, including weapons, armour, clothes, ornaments, tools, pottery, and animal bones. The largest collections must have been built up over a number of years, and the objects left in the holy places gradually sank into the marshy soil until they were hidden from view. Sometimes weapons were bent and broken and rendered useless before they were laid down. In 1950 a fifth discovery of this kind was made at Illerup,[1] and careful excavation made it possible to reconstruct what had taken place. Here the equipment of about seventy warriors had been burned on a pyre, and the swords and shields collected from the ashes, deliberately bent and dented, and carried into the middle of the bog by means of planks laid down on the marshy ground. Some of the weapons were flung into a deep pool, and others left lying on the earth near by, in a spot still reputed to be haunted. In this case the spoil was probably that taken in one battle only, fought about A.D. 400.

We know that mailcoats and weapons were rare and costly treasures, and that the many swords sacrificed at Illerup represented much wealth. Yet men felt impelled to make these strange sacrifices in return for victory, and continued to do so in Denmark from the second to the sixth century after Christ. The explanation given in the literature is that they did this in order to placate the god of battle, perhaps like the Hermundari in the fulfilment of a vow once victory had been won. We do not know what happened to the owners of the swords and mailcoats, spears and horse-trappings preserved in the peat, but the implication is that if not already killed in battle they met with an unpleasant death as part of the expensive sacrifice to the war god.

Tacitus tells us that the Hermundari and the Chatti sacrificed to Mars and Mercury in return for victory. There is little doubt that Mercury represented the Germanic god Wodan at the time when Tacitus wrote. In England the same god, Woden, gave his name to the fourth day of the week, Wednesday, the day which in France is called *Mercredi* after the Roman god. Just as Odin was looked on as the divine ancestor of the Swedes, so Woden was believed to be the founder of many royal dynasties. Most of the Anglo-Saxon kings looked back to him as their divine ancestor. The reason for his identification with Mercury will be discussed more fully in a later chapter (p. 140).

At the time of Tacitus however there is reason to believe that the Roman god of war, Mars, was identified not with Wodan, but with another Germanic god, Tîwaz. Odin in fact appears to

1. H. Andersen, 'Der femte store Mosefund', *Kuml*, 1951, pp. 9 ff.

be the successor of both Wodan and Tîwaz, retaining some of the qualities and attributes of both these gods. In Snorri's account Tîwaz appears as Tyr. He is only a shadowy figure, but Snorri mentions that men prayed to him for victory, and also that he was renowned for his wisdom as well as for his valour. Tîwaz in his day must have been a very great power among the heathen Germans. The third day of the week, sacred in Rome to Mars, was called after him throughout the Teutonic world, so that against *Mardi* in France we have Tuesday in England. In Old Norse his name was used as a synonym for 'god', and Odin bore among his titles that of *Sigtýr*, the *Tyr*, or god, of victory. The name Tîwaz is related to the Greek Zeus, and to the Roman Jupiter (who was originally *Dyaus pitar*, father Dyaus). All three are thought to be derived from *dieus*, the Indo-Germanic word for god, which stands also for the shining heaven and the light of day. It is probable that Tîwaz was the supreme sky god of the Germans as well as their god of battle.

Although Odin had in the main taken the place of Tîwaz at the close of the heathen period, memories of the earlier battle god still lingered. In one of the *Edda* poems dealing with spells to use in battle, men are told to carve runes of victory, giving the name of Tyr.[1] We have what may be instances of this name on weapons. A helmet from Negau in Austria bears an inscription in North Italic letters of the second century B.C., which has been thought by some scholars to give *Teiwa*, an archaic form of the god's name.[2] A spear from Kowel bears the rune which is the initial of the god's name. Another symbol resembling this rune, so small that it could hardly have been noticeable even when new, has been detected on a spear found in an Anglo-Saxon cemetery of the sixth century in Holborough, Kent.[3] These may be signs of the ancient Germanic war god, cut by those who wished to claim his help and protection in battle.

Terrible though the rites associated with Tîwaz were, it seems that he was no mere crude deity of slaughter. Among the titles given to him in inscriptions of the Roman period, we find Mars

1. *Sigrdrífumál*, 5.
2. F. Mossé, 'L'Origine de l'écriture runique', *Conférences de l'Institut de linguistique de l'Université de Paris*, x, 1950–1, p. 55.
3. *Archaeologia Cantiana*, LXX, 1956, pp. 97 ff.

Thingsus. This must mean that Tîwaz was associated with the Thing, the Assembly of the people held to settle disputes and to establish the law. Just as the Lord of Hosts who gave victory in battle to Moses was the same god who delivered to him the tablets of the Law, so Tîwaz appears to have been the protector of law and order in the community as well as ruler over the realm of war. Tacitus tells us that no man might be flogged, imprisoned, or put to death among the Germans save by their priests, 'in obedience to the god which they believe to preside over battle'.[1] If the god of battle punished criminals, then he must surely have been regarded as the supporter of order and justice.

This idea never wholly disappeared in the north, and it may be noticed that the place where the official sword-duel, the *hólmganga*, was fought was close beside the site of the Chief Assembly of Iceland, where the important law cases were held. The appeal to the sword as an arbiter between men has a long and impressive history among the Germanic peoples.[2] According to Tacitus, they were accustomed to use the duel as a form of augury. They used before a battle to secure a captive from the enemy and to match him against a champion of their own. In this way they tested the luck of their side, and the result was held to foreshadow that of the battle to come. Records from the early history of the Germans have many references to single combat between two champions, while behind them the opposing armies waited and watched. The spirit of such a combat is well expressed in the eighth century by Paul the Deacon, who wrote in a history of the Lombards:

See how many people there are on both sides! What need is there that so great a multitude perish? Let us join, he and I, in single combat, and may that one of us to whom God may have willed to give the victory have and possess all this people safe and entire.

History of the Langobards, v, 41 (Foulke's translation)

We know that the Germans were accustomed to take a solemn oath on their weapons, and that this was a very ancient custom, well established in heathen times. This is in accordance with the idea of the god of battle as the supreme arbiter, and it is not

1. *Germania*, 7.
2. See H. R. Ellis Davidson, *The Sword in Anglo-Saxon England*, Oxford, 1962, pp. 193 ff.

difficult to comprehend the effectiveness of such an oath. A man's safety and life depended on the reliability of his weapons, and fighting was a tricky business at best; a broken oath which had been made on sword or spear might result in failure at the moment of crisis. That a man's own weapon should turn against him is one of the more frightening of the curses which could be pronounced against an enemy.

It is probably significant that the one myth about Tyr which has survived in the pages of Snorri concerns the binding of the wolf Fenrir, the adversary of the gods (see p. 31). Only Tyr was brave enough to feed him, and willing to sacrifice his hand in order that the monster should be bound. Later on, the wolf is the special adversary of Odin at Ragnarok. It seems likely that in earlier Germanic myths it was Tîwaz who was matched against him. Snorri tells us that Tyr was killed by Garm, a hound of the underworld, who may well be Fenrir under another name.

At the time of Tacitus, the Semnones, a warlike people who were later known as the Alamanni, lived between the Rhine and the Oder. They worshipped a god called God and Ruler of All (Deus Regnator Omnium). In A.D. 92 their king visited Rome, and Tacitus may well have learned about their religious customs from him or from one of his companions. He tells us[1] that the Semnones gathered yearly in a sacred wood, with other tribes related to them, and that in this place 'hallowed by the auguries of their forefathers and by ancient awe', they witnessed a human sacrifice. Whoever entered the wood had to be bound with a cord as a sign of humility before the god, and if he fell he might not get to his feet but had to roll over the ground. This appears to emphasize the power of the god to bind his followers, as Tyr bound the wolf; the idea of binding is found associated with Odin as war god, and more about this will be said later (pp. 63 and 147). We cannot be certain that Tîwaz was in fact the god of the Semnones, but it seems most probable that he was the supreme deity worshipped in the wood.[2]

1. *Germania*, 39.
2. The stabbing of Helgi in *Fjǫturlundr* (Fetter Grove) in a prose insertion in *Helgakuiða Hundingsbana*, 11, has led some to argue that the Deus Regnator was Wodan. The gap in time however is too great for this to be

It is also possible that the god of the Saxons, known as Saxnot, was the same as the war god Tîwaz. He is mentioned along with Wodan and Thunor as a god who had to be renounced when they were baptized, in an early renunciation formula.[1] He must have been an important deity to be placed alongside the other two, and he was evidently the same god whose name (Seaxneat) is given as that of the founder of the dynasty of the Saxon kings in Essex. Saxnot could originally have been *Sahsginot*, 'sword companion', and this is a fitting name for a war god in whose honour swords were wielded and to whom swords were sacrificed. The worship of Tîwaz under this name may thus have been brought into Essex when the Saxons came over to Britain. Tîwaz was also known in England under the name of Tiw or Tig, as is implied by a few early forms of place-names like Tewin in Hertfordshire and Tuesley in Surrey. At Tysoe, on Edge Hill, seven miles from Banbury, a red horse was cut on the hill slope, and was scoured every Palm Sunday until the end of the eighteenth century; it is possible that here there was a place once sacred to the god, and that the horse was associated with him.

In Tîwaz we have an early Germanic war god, an ancestor of Odin. He had great powers, and extensive sacrifices were made to him. He was a one-handed god, and since a one-handed figure wielding a weapon is seen among Bronze Age rock-engravings in Scandinavia it has been suggested that his worship may go back to very early times in the north, and that the myth of the god binding the wolf is of great antiquity. Dumézil[2] believes that another version has been preserved in the story of the Roman hero, Mucius Scævola, who willingly sacrificed his hand to save his people from destruction. Certainly Tîwaz differs in one respect from Wodan, who seems to have taken over his position as god of battle later in the heathen period. Tîwaz was associated with law and justice, whereas Wodan and Odin are reproached on many occasions for fickleness and treachery.

---

taken as proof. For the idea of ritual binding connected with the gods, Eliade has a most valuable section in *Images and Symbols* (London, 1961), pp. 92–124.

1. MS. Cod. pal., 577, Vatican Library.
2. *Les Dieux des Germains*, Paris, 1959, pp. 71ff.

While Odin is renowned for wisdom and cunning, he is not represented as in any way concerned with justice among men. To find a reason for this change in the character of the war god, it will be necessary to return to the Scandinavian Odin and to consider some of his companions and followers in Asgard and on earth.

3. The Valkyries of Odin

In Snorri's description of the after-life for warriors, there are certain beings who form a link between Odin and the slain, and between the worlds of the living and the dead. These are the female spirits called Valkyries, who wait on the warriors in Valhalla, and no description of the gods of battle can be complete without them. In the descriptions of the poets they appear as women who wear armour and ride on horseback, passing swiftly over sea and land. They carry out Odin's commands while the battle rages, giving victory according to his will, and at the close they lead the slaughtered warriors to Valhalla. Sometimes, on the other hand, they are pictured as the wives of living heroes. Human princesses are said to become Valkyries, as though they were the priestesses of some cult.

Valkyrie names occur frequently in the work of ninth- and tenth-century poets. Many, like *Hildr, Hlǫkk, Guðr*, are simply synonyms for 'battle'. Evidently an elaborate literary picture has been built up by generations of poets and storytellers, in which several different conceptions can be discerned. We recognize something akin to the Norns, spirits who decide the destinies of men; to the seeresses, who could protect men in battle by their spells; to the powerful female guardian spirits attached to certain families, bringing luck to a youth under their protection; even to certain women who armed themselves and fought like men, for whom there is some historical evidence from the regions round the Black Sea. There may be a memory also of the priestesses of the god of war, women who officiated at the sacrificial rites when captives were put to death after battle. The name Valkyrie means, literally, 'chooser of the slain', and in the eleventh century an Anglo-Saxon bishop, Wulfstan, included 'choosers of the slain' in a black list of sinners, witches, and evildoers in his famous *Sermo Lupi*. All the other classes whom he mentions are human ones, and it seems unlikely that he has introduced mythological figures as well. In the tenth-century ship-funeral on the Volga (see p. 52), the old woman who organized the killing of the slave-girl was called the Angel of Death, and had two other women, called her daughters, in attendance. She is described as 'an old Hunnish woman, massive and grim to look upon'. It would hardly be surprising if strange legends grew up about such women, who must have been kept apart from their kind for these gruesome duties. Since it was often decided by lot which prisoners should be killed, the idea that the god 'chose' his victims, through the instrument of the priestesses, must have been a familiar one, apart from the obvious assumption that some were chosen to fall in war.

It seems that from early times the heathen Germans believed in fierce female spirits doing the commands of the war god, stirring up disorder, taking part in battle, seizing and perhaps even devouring the slain. Wulfstan used the word *wælcyrge*, and the same word occurs some centuries earlier, in a number of Old English word-lists, some of which go back to the eighth century. *Wælcyrge*, 'chooser of the slain', is given as the Old English equivalent for the names of the furies: Erinys, Tisiphone, and Allecto.

Earlier evidence still comes from the north of England. Two votive stones were found at Housesteads on Hadrian's Wall in 1883, one of which reads:

Dedicated to the God Mars Thincsus and to the two Alaisiagae, Bede and Fimmilene.

The other refers to 'Mars and the two Alaisiagis'. A third fragment was found which may have been associated with either or both these inscriptions, showing a war god with shield and spear, with a bird beside him. In 1920 an altar was discovered at the same fort, and this also bore an inscription dedicated to the Alaisiagae, calling them goddesses, and giving them the names of Baudihillie and Friagabi.[1] These names have been interpreted as 'ruler of battle' and 'giver of freedom', and they would be suitable ones for Valkyries to bear.

1. R. C. Bosanquet, 'On an altar dedicated to the Alaisiagae', *Arch. Aeliana* (3rd series), 19, 1922, pp. 185 ff.

The conception of a company of women associated with battle among the heathen Germans is further implied by two spells which have survived into Christian times. One comes from Merseburg in south Germany, and is a charm for the unloosing of fetters. It describes how certain women called the Idisi (cf. Old Norse *dísir*, 'goddesses') sat together, some fastening bonds, some holding back the host, some tugging at fetters. It concludes with the words, 'Leap forth from the bonds, escape from the enemy'.

With this may be compared an Old English charm against a sudden pain. It seems at first to be a humble and innocuous charm, until the pain is visualized as caused by the spears of certain supernatural women. At this point it suddenly takes on heroic stature:

> Loud were they, lo, loud, riding over the hill.
> They were of one mind, riding over the land;
> Shield thyself now, to escape from this ill.
> Out, little spear, if herein thou be.
> Under shield of light linden I took up my stand,
> When the mighty women made ready their power
> And sent out their screaming spears. . . .

Later in the spell weapons shot by the gods are mentioned, and the impression is that here we have what was originally a battle spell, like the Merseburg one, which has come down in the world until it could be evoked for a prosaic stitch in the side. A second suggestion of supernatural women in another charm is the term *sigewif*, 'victory-women', used of a swarm of bees.

The unbinding and binding of fetters, the hurling of spears, and the power to ride through the air are all activities associated with Odin. In *Hávamál* he utters a spell to provide 'fetters for my adversaries'. These are not likely to be physical bonds, but rather fetters for the mind, of the kind described in *Ynglinga Saga*:

Odin knew how to act so that his foes in battle became blind or deaf or panic-stricken, and their weapons pierced no more than wands.

A vivid example of such a state is found in one of the sagas from Iceland, *Harðar Saga* (36). The hero Hord was escaping from his enemies when he was suddenly overcome by what is described as 'the war-fetter' (*herfjǫturr*). This was due to hostile magic :

The 'war-fetter' came upon Hord, and he cut himself free once and a second time. The 'war-fetter' came upon him a third time. Then the men managed to hem him in, and surrounded him with a ring of enemies, but he fought his way out of the ring, and slew three men in so doing.

This must not be confused with the onset of panic in battle, for Hord was an exceptionally brave man and a splendid fighter. It seems rather to be a kind of paralysis, like that experienced in a nightmare. Three times he succeeded in shaking it off, but when it overcame him for the fourth time he was surrounded again and killed. It is noteworthy that one of the Valkyrie names is *Herfjǫturr*, 'war-fetter', the same word as in the passage above. The suggested interpretation of one of the names of the Alaisiagae, *Friagabi*, as 'giver of freedom', may be relevant in this connexion.

Old Norse literature has left us with a picture of dignified Valkyries riding on horses and armed with spears, but a different, cruder picture of supernatural women connected with blood and slaughter has also survived. Female creatures, sometimes of gigantic size, pour blood over a district where a battle is to take place; they are sometimes described as carrying troughs of blood or riding on wolves, or are seen rowing a boat through a rain of blood falling from the sky. Such figures are usually omens of fighting and death; they sometimes appear to men in dreams, and they are described more than once in skaldic verse of the tenth and eleventh centuries. The most famous example of this kind of dream vision is that said in *Njáls Saga* to have been seen before the Battle of Clontarf, fought at Dublin in 1014. A group of women were seen weaving on a grisly loom formed from men's entrails and weighted with severed heads. They were filling in a background of grey spears with a weft of crimson. They were called by names of Valkyries. A poem is quoted in the *Saga* which is said to have been spoken by them, and in the course of this they declare that it is they who decide who is to die in the coming battle :

We weave, we weave the web of the spear,
as on goes the standard of the brave.
We shall not let him lose his life;
the Valkyries have power to choose the slain. . . .

All is sinister now to see,
a cloud of blood moves over the sky,
the air is red with the blood of men,
as the battle-women chant their song.

This poem, known as the *Darraðarljóð* or 'Spear-Lay', may not necessarily have been composed about the Battle of Clontarf; it has been suggested that some other battle in Ireland originally inspired it.[1] In any case we have here, at a relatively early date, a picture of Valkyries, 'battle-women', which is in accordance with the other descriptions of terrible female creatures working out the fate of warriors in battle, and bringing down blood and carnage upon men.

Other figures showing a close resemblance to Valkyries of this kind are found in stories of the Celtic peoples. Two 'goddesses', Morrigu and Bobd, are mentioned in the Irish sagas. They were wont to appear on the battlefield, or were sometimes visible before a battle. They could take on the form of birds of prey, and they were accustomed to utter prophecies of war and slaughter. The association of these battle-women with the birds of prey who flock to a battlefield is interesting. In the Old English poem *Exodus* the adjective 'choosing the slain', *wælceasig*, is used of the raven, and one of the earliest Old Norse poems, *Hrafnsmál*, is in the form of a dialogue between a raven and a Valkyrie. The raven, together with the wolf, is mentioned in practically all the descriptions of a battle in Old English poetry, and both were regarded as the creatures of the war god, Odin.

Such striking resemblances between the figures of supernatural battle-women in the literature of the Scandinavians and heathen Germans on the one hand, and the Celtic peoples on the other, are significant. Donahue[2] was led to suggest that there

1. N. Kershaw, *Anglo-Saxon and Norse Poems*, Cambridge, 1922, p. 117.
2. C. Donahue, 'The Valkyries and the Irish War-Goddesses', *Publications of the Modern Language Association* (Baltimore), 56, 1941, pp. 1 ff.

was a belief in fierce battle-spirits connected with the god of war at a time when the Celts and Germans were in close contact with one another, during the Roman period. There is little doubt that the figure of the Valkyrie has developed in Norse literature into something more dignified and less blood-thirsty as a result of the work of the poets over a considerable period. The alarming and terrible creatures who have survived in the literature in spite of this seem likely however to be closer in character to the choosers of the slain as they were visualized in heathen times.

4. *The Berserks of Odin*

The power which Odin was believed to possess over the minds of men at war was not limited to the sapping of their energy and will-power, the imposing of 'fetters' on them in the heat of battle. He could give more positive help, as we see from the phenomenon of the berserks. These were warriors so full of the ecstasy of battle as to be impervious to wounds and to danger, and according to Snorri they derived this power from Odin:

... his men went without mailcoats, and were frantic as dogs or wolves; they bit their shields and were as strong as bears or boars; they slew men, but neither fire nor iron could hurt them. This is known as 'running berserk'. *Ynglinga Saga*, 6

In the later saga-literature the berserk has turned into something which resembles a fairy-tale monster, with whom the hero does battle against overwhelming odds and whom he of course defeats. The main characteristics of the berserk nevertheless are worthy of note. First, he fights in a state of wild frenzy; secondly, he is marked out as a member of a special class free from the laws which govern ordinary members of society. These characteristics have been recorded among the Germanic peoples long before Viking times.

For instance, a class of dedicated warriors was known among the Chatti, the German tribe described by Tacitus in the first century. They wore iron rings round their necks, and could only discard these after they had killed an enemy. Some indeed chose to wear them all their life, as long as they could go on fighting, and 'to such old warriors it always rests to begin the battle'. Tacitus continues:

They are always in the van, and present a startling sight; even in peace they decline to soften the savagery of their expression. None of them has home, land, or business of his own. To whatever host they choose to go, they get their keep from him, wasting the goods of others while despising their own, until old age drains their blood and incapacitates them for so exacting a form of heroism.

Germania, 31 (Mattingly's translation)

Another aspect of the berserks is found among the warriors of the Harii, also described by Tacitus. Like the Chatti these were famed for their strength, and they cultivated the art of terrifying their enemies:

They black their shields and dye their bodies black, and choose pitch dark nights for their battles. The terrifying shadow of such a fiendish army inspires a mortal panic, for no enemy can stand so strange and devilish a sight. *Germania*, 43

The Heruli also, a people who practised cremation and suttee, and who were worshippers of the war god, deliberately cultivated the practice of fighting without armour. Procopius tells us that their only protection was a shield and a cloak, and other writers confirm this.

At the time of Harald Fairhair, king of Norway in the ninth century, there were berserks in the king's bodyguard. In the *Hrafnsmál* they are called wolf-coats, and are said to be men of tried valour who never flinched at battle. We are told in *Heimskringla* that they had a place on the king's warship. Dumézil[1] has suggested that the touching with a spear, the mark of consecration to Odin, may have been the initiation ceremony for members of this band, giving assurance of immortality in the service of the war god whom they worshipped and to whom their lives were dedicated. The berserks who roamed through Scandinavia were apparently viewed as sacred to the god. Dumézil sees them as a necessary element in society, representing the wild and fantastic in contrast with law and order.

The berserks in the stories are frequently said to be shapechangers, and sometimes to take on animal form. Bothvar *Biarki*,

1. G. Dumézil, *Mythes et dieux des Germains*, Paris, 1939, pp. 80 ff.

the celebrated champion of King Hrolf of Denmark, was said to fight in the form of a great bear in the ranks of the king's army, while his human form lay at home and seemed asleep. The basis of such tales may lie in the fierce frenzy, like that of a wild beast, which overcame the berserks in battle. Such fits of rage could be inconvenient in private life, and this is illustrated by a story from the life of the famous poet, Egill Skallagrimsson. His father appears to have been a berserk in his youth, and when he had married and settled down in Iceland, he became over-excited one evening in a game of ball with his child. In a mad frenzy he killed the little boy's nurse, and came very near to destroying his son Egill as well. In another saga a man who suffered from such attacks of berserk rage was said to be healed from them when he became a Christian. The idea of taking on animal shape while in such a rage may have been strengthened by the animal skins which according to tradition such companies of warriors wore. A modern parallel to this is offered by the societies of dreaded leopard-men in Africa.

Memories of initiation into warrior societies survive in the prose sagas. In *Hrólfs Saga Kraka*, a youth had to 'kill' the figure of a monster set up in the king's hall, and to drink its blood. In *Vǫlsunga Saga*, Sigmund and his son, who were outlaws, put on wolf-skins and made a solemn pact to keep certain rules when they fought:

Sigmund and his son put on the skins, and were unable to take them off. The same nature went with them as before, and they spoke in wolf-language; each understood this speech. They stayed out in the wood and went each his own way. They made an agreement between them, that each should be prepared to take on as many as seven men, but no more. He who was outnumbered must call out in wolf-language. 'We must not fail in this,' said Sigmund, 'for you are young and rash, and men will judge you to be a fine quarry.'

We know that companies of warriors living under strict discipline did in fact exist late in the Viking age. Literature has preserved memories of the Vikings of Jomsburg, a band of men living a bachelor life in a warrior community, with rigid rules of obedience. Some of these rules have been recorded for us: no man might be taken into their fellowship who was more than fifty years old, or less than eighteen; no man should break the peace by attacking another of the band, even though a man received into the stronghold had slain another's father or brother; no one might remain in Jomsburg who spoke words of fear or despondency; no one might remain who ran away from some-one of equal strength; no man should keep women in the strong-hold. There is no doubt that foundation for such accounts existed in the Viking age. Impressive fortifications at Trelleborg and Aggersborg have been excavated in Denmark, which were in use in the early eleventh century. They contained lines of bar-rack buildings which made them resemble a Roman camp, and groups of trained men must have lived here as disciplined warriors. King Svein of Denmark no doubt made use of such companies of fighting men in his invasion of England, and it is possible that similar encampments existed in Viking England also. In them we may see the final phase in a long tradition of companies of selected warriors, most of them young bachelors not yet ready to marry and settle down who, along with a few tried veterans, formed the ruler's bodyguard at the courts of the Scandinavian kings. The survival of warrior communities so late in the heathen period may help to account for the richness and vigour of the traditions about the war god in the literature of the north. It is noticeable that in the pages of Saxo's *Gesta Danorum*, written at a time when the great warrior encamp-ments must still have been remembered, the old, tough, devoted warriors who followed Odin, men like Starkad and Hadding, occupy an important place.

5. The Worship of the War God

We have seen that the power of the war god was considerable in northern Europe from very early times, from the period when Tîwaz was regarded as the lord of hosts among the heathen Germans, and also the promoter of justice and order among men. When in the first century after Christ the Hermundari and the Chatti are said to have sacrificed to Tîwaz and Wodan, this may be significant. Wodan, lord of the kingdom of death and ancestor of the German kings, may even then have been chal-lenging the supremacy of Tîwaz on the battlefield.

Later in the heathen period Wodan is seen as the bearer of the spear and the god of the wolf and raven, and he was accepted, by certain tribes at least, as the deity of battle. In Sweden he was known as Odin, the leader of the gods, the deity with power to bind and to loose, whose followers were the terrible 'choosers of the slain' who could strike down men in the conflict or render them helpless to avert death. In this Odin follows in the footsteps of Wodan, the best interpretation of whose name seems to be 'one who makes mad'. Adam of Bremen in the eleventh century sums up this power of the god briefly and decisively : 'Wodan, *id est furor*.' We shall see in a later chapter that Odin was also the god of the dead and supreme practitioner in magic, with the ability to inspire his followers and grant them the ecstatic, trance-like state of intoxication. The ecstasy of battle, which inspired the berserks and filled them with such madness that they knew neither fear nor pain, was naturally viewed as a gift of the same god. In his warrior paradise Valhalla, men were said to divide their time between battle and drinking. These were two means by which they could while on earth achieve forgetfulness of self, and it is therefore fitting that they should be the only occupations in Odin's hall.

We must remember that battle for the Germanic peoples and the Vikings was a very individual affair. The picture of it which emerges from the comments of Greek and Latin historians and again from the poetry and sagas of the people themselves is principally one of single combat between sword-warriors, or of a hand-to-hand struggle between two small bands of men. Under such conditions, faith in Wodan or Odin, who could give supreme confidence and the strength and fury of possession, was an enviable gift; it was a psychological asset likely to bring luck and victory along with it.

Nevertheless men knew that the berserk, freed though he might be for a time from fear and pain, was not inevitably a victor. He might be cut down in battle, for all his strength and furious courage, or wake from his frenzy to find himself crippled for life. The vows made at the ale-drinking to accomplish wild and daring deeds could bring bitter regrets when the men who made them were sober again, as we are reminded more than once in the heroic literature of the north. Thus it is hardly surprising that Odin was remembered as the Arch-Deceiver as well as the god of inspiration.

Throughout the heathen period in northern Europe there was clear need of a god of war. The story of the Germanic peoples and the Vikings is one in which local battles, feuds, invasions, and wars on a national scale are the order of the day. The heroic literature is based on an unsettled society, accustomed to violence and shortness of life. Differences between men were settled for the most part by force of arms, and the natural hero was the warrior chief with his little band of faithful followers, ready to take chances, to trust to their luck with spear and sword, and to risk losing all that they had gained if the fight went against them. Lands, homes, and wives had often to be won by the sword, and always to be defended by it. The leader established his sway over his followers by handing out weapons and armour to be used in his defence, and by the winning of riches in battle. Clearly men reared in such a world were bound to turn to the god whom they served to protect them in the hour of battle, and to grant them the elusive gift of victory, which depended on the spirit of a fighting force – a mysterious, impalpable thing – or sometimes on some slender chance outside men's control.

In the earlier days of Germanic heathenism the terrible whole-sale slaughter of captured forces and criminals implies a belief in a god of battles who demanded that blood should flow in his honour. Blood had to be constantly provided for the mighty deity, or else he would be compelled by his nature to seize on the lives of his worshippers. Pictures of priestesses putting men to a brutal death in his name are reflected in later pictures of the terrible Valkyries of the north, revelling in blood and stirring up battle. Not only must the blood be set flowing, but the panoply of war – swords and mailcoats, shields and spears – must be offered to the god of war, cast into the swamps or the lakes, or burned on the pyre in his honour.

As time went on, the emphasis seems to change from that of a supreme ruler holding in his hand victory or defeat, who taught men the value of law and order among themselves, to that of a more capricious power who bestowed madness on his followers, and who meted out victory or defeat with the arrogance of an earthly tyrant. It is possible that we are led to exaggerate this distinction from the fragmentary evidence left to us, and that Tîwaz also had a strong element of the capricious in his nature. Certainly the madness associated with Wodan and Odin, of whom we know much more, was such as was held to bring dazzling gifts along with it, and at the same time to exact fearful penalties. It would not seem as though Odin was a god whom men could love or respect, although they feared him, and gloried at times in his heady power. But the picture of Odin as the god of battle is an incomplete one. It needs to be finished in the chapter on the gods of the dead.

Chapter 3

The Thunder God

... And thou, all-shaking thunder,
Strike flat the thick rotundity of the world!
Crack nature's moulds, all germens spill at once,
That make ingrateful man.

SHAKESPEARE, *King Lear*, III, ii

1. *Thor in the Myths*

In the myths as presented to us by Snorri, Thor is undoubtedly one of the gods who stands out most clearly. The champion of the Aesir and the defender of Asgard appears as a massive, red-bearded figure, armed with his hammer, his iron gloves, and his girdle of strength. The cult of Thor had a long life in western Europe. In the eleventh century he was still worshipped with enthusiasm by the Vikings of Dublin, and at the close of the heathen period it was he who was thought of as the principal adversary of Christ. In Norway he is described as taking part in a tug-of-war with Christ's champion, King Olaf Tryggvason, over a fire, while in Iceland an enthusiastic woman worshipper of the old gods told a Christian missionary that Thor had delivered a challenge to Christ to meet him in single combat.

Of all the gods, it is Thor who seems the characteristic hero of the stormy world of the Vikings. Bearded, outspoken, indomitable, filled with vigour and gusto, he puts his reliance on his strong right arm and simple weapons. He strides through the northern realm of the gods, a fitting symbol for the man of action. Like the Indian god Indra, who resembles him in some respects, Thor was a tremendous trencher-man, impressing even the giants by his capacity for eating and drinking. When he visited the hall of Thrym disguised as the fair Freyja, he devoured an ox, eight salmon, and three cups of mead, and he ate two out of the three oxen provided for a repast by the giant Hymir when he went on his famous fishing expedition. In the hall

of Utgard-Loki he took part in an epic drinking contest, striving
to empty a great horn whose tip went down into the sea, and
though he was bemused by the cunning of the giant, he lowered
the level of the ocean perceptibly by his efforts. His visit to Hymir was ostensibly to obtain a mighty cauldron in which mead
could be prepared for the gods, and there is mention of certain
huge goblets kept in Asgard for Thor's use. According to another story, Thor's own goats were slaughtered and devoured
with relish by the god and his travelling companions before their
bones and skin were called back to life by the power of his
hammer. There is not much doubt that tales like that of the god
disguised as a bride or of Thor's humiliations in the hall of
Utgard-Loki were primarily for entertainment, acceptable at a
time when the worship of Thor was no longer of serious concern
among men. Nevertheless the very characteristics of the god
seized upon to provide mirth must be in themselves significant,
and much may be learned from them.

Thor's delight in eating and drinking was in accordance with
his great vitality and physical strength. His progress through the
realms of gods and giants was marked by the continual overthrowing of adversaries and overcoming of obstacles. His usual
method of killing his enemies was simple and direct: without
recourse to the tortuous wiles of Odin or Loki, he simply struck
at them with his hammer or hurled it through the air to shatter
their skulls. In this way he slew Hrungnir in a duel, disposed of
Thrym and his relatives, and struck at the Midgard Serpent.
The shattering of rocks and stones is mentioned frequently in
legends of Thor. Once he killed his enemy Geirrod by hurling a
red-hot bolt through a pillar, while another time he used a drinking vessel as a missile, to pass through a pillar and shatter itself
against Hymir's head. He slew giantesses with boulders, or
broke their backs by forcing a weight down upon them. The
argument for trust in Thor given in one of the Olaf Tryggvason
sagas is that:

Thor had done many great works, and had split rocks and shattered
cliffs, while Odin gave men victory.

Oláfs Saga Tryggvasonax, Fornmanna Sǫgur, 101

In such stories we are seeing Thor the Thunder God at work,

felling trees and destroying men with his deadly bolts. Thor's realm is very different from that of Odin. His cult was not an aristocratic one, and indeed a taunt made against him in one of the *Edda* poems was that while Odin received kings who fell in battle, Thor got the thralls. But we shall see that his power extended far, and that he was the god supreme not only over the stormy sky, but also over the life of the community in all its aspects. If part of the mantle of the old sky god, Tîwaz, fell upon Odin, a great part of it undoubtedly covered the broad shoulders of Thor.

2. *The Temples of Thor*

The figure of the god with his hammer is said to have stood in many temples at the close of the heathen period. We hear more of the images of Thor than of those of the other gods, and when he shared a temple with other deities, he is usually said to have occupied the place of honour. Rich robes are mentioned, and sacrifices of meat and bread are said to have been made to him in his temples in Norway. His worshippers would look for guidance from the image of Thor when the time came to make some difficult decision. Adam of Bremen corroborates the evidence of the sagas when he tells us in the eleventh century that Thor's image stood in the heathen temple at Uppsala, and that the god held a sceptre (his hammer?) in his hand. In an eleventh-century Irish poem we find a Christian saint demanding of the king of Dublin that he should take 'the golden castle from the hands of the Black Devil'. Marstrander[1] interprets this as a reference to a black image of Thor in his rich shrine in the Viking stronghold in Dublin. It is known that King Maelseachlainn did in fact take the ring of Thor and 'many other treasures' from this shrine in 994.

Accounts in *Heimskringla* and *Flateyjarbók* of the destruction of such statues of Thor by the Christian kings of Norway imply that they were man-size or even larger. A description of an image of Thor at Thrandheim refers to a chariot drawn by goats, in which Thor sat:

1. C. Marstrander, 'Thor en Irlande', *Revue Celtique*, 36, 1915–16, pp. 241 ff.

The Thunder God

Thor sat in the middle. He was the most highly honoured. He was huge, and all adorned with gold and silver. Thor was arranged to sit in a chariot; he was very splendid. There were goats, two of them, harnessed in front of him, very well wrought. Both car and goats ran on wheels. The rope round the horns of the goats was of twisted silver, and the whole was worked with extremely fine craftsmanship.

Flateyjarbók, I, 268

Skeggi, the man who took Olaf Tryggvason to the temple to see Thor, persuaded him to pull the cord round the horns of the goats, and when he did so, 'the goats moved easily along'. Thereupon Skeggi declared that the king had done service to the god, and Olaf not surprisingly became angry, and called on his men to destroy the idols, while he himself knocked Thor from his chariot. The implication here is that the pulling along of a well-greased chariot formed part of a ritual in Thor's honour.

The noise of the chariot of Thor rattling along was said to cause thunder. Snorri derives the god's name, *Qku-Þórr*, from the verb *aka*, to drive, and interprets it as Thor the Driver or Charioteer. This is in accordance with the picture of a chariot driven by the god across the sky, which in many religions forms part of the conception of the sun god. Such a picture of the thunder god may well be an ancient one in the north. Lappish loan-words for thunder: *atsa-raite, raiððe*, and others, appear to have been derived from an earlier form of Old Norse *reið*, which has the double meaning of a wheeled vehicle and thunder. Descriptions of Thor's arrival in ninth-century skaldic verse emphasize the clatter and roar of a storm, and show that this aspect of the god was by no means forgotten in Iceland. We find for example in a ninth-century poem, *Haustlǫng*:

The Son of Earth drove to the iron game, and the way of the moon resounded before him. ... The holy places of the powers burned before the kinsman of Ull. Earth, ground of the deep, was beaten with hail as the goats drew the wagon-god for his meeting with Hrungnir. ... The rocks shook and the boulders were shattered; high heaven burned.

It was not merely Thor's power over the thunder which was symbolized within the temple. We hear also in many passages in the sagas of a great gold or silver ring on which oaths were sworn, and which was kept in temples where Thor was wor-shipped. There is independent evidence that this ring was sacred to Thor, for in Irish sources the 'ring of Thor' is one of the treasures taken from his temple in 994. Earlier than this, in 876, the heathen Danish leaders in England made a truce with King Alfred, and they are said in the *Anglo-Saxon Chronicle* to have sworn oaths to him on their sacred ring.

Descriptions of this ring suggest that it was an arm-ring and not a finger-ring. Indeed in *Eyrbyggja Saga* Snorri the priest is said to have worn it on his arm, where it protected him from a blow from a sword. In *Hauksbók*, in a passage repeated in several of the sagas, it is said to have weighed two ounces in silver, which would make it not much larger than a wedding ring; the statement in *Eyrbyggja Saga*, settling the weight at twenty ounces, seems more likely to be reliable.[1] The oath for-mula given in the sagas mentions Freyr and Njord and 'the Al-mighty God', usually assumed to be Thor, because of his asso-ciation with the oath-ring. It may also be noted that the General Assembly of Iceland opened on Thor's Day, while Adam of Bremen alludes to the breaking up of Thor's image which stood in the place of the Assembly at Uppsala about A.D. 1030. It would seem that Thor had taken over some of the powers of Tîwaz, and in particular that which hallowed oaths taken between men.

One of Thor's most enthusiastic worshippers described in the sagas was Thorolf *Mostrarskegg*, 'bearded man of Most', whose arrival in Iceland is recorded in *Landnámabók*, and told in the early chapters of *Eyrbyggja Saga* at some length. He came from the little island of Most on the west coast of Norway, and when life grew difficult on account of the tyranny of Harald Fairhair, he consulted Thor as to whether he should leave for Iceland. The reply was evidently favourable, for he took down Thor's shrine, packed its high-seat pillars and most of the timber from it on his ship, and also 'the earth from under the pedestal where Thor had sat'. When he reached Iceland, he flung the high-seat pillars overboard and landed at the point where they were washed ashore. There he marked out the plot of land where he would live, and where he meant to rebuild Thor's

1. F. P. Magoun, 'On the old-Germanic Altar or Oath Ring', *Acta Philologica Scandinavica*, 1949, XX, pp. 277 ff.

temple. He went round the borders of the new estate with fire, and then began building his own house and a mighty sanctuary for his divine friend. The temple is described in detail in the fourth chapter of *Eyrbyggja Saga*. It had pillars, with 'god-nails' in them, the holy ring, a sacrificial bowl in which blood was caught when animals were sacrificed to the god, and images of Thor and other deities.

Here, as well as the bowl of blood and the ring, we have emphasis on the importance of the high-seat pillars. In Scandinavian halls these were the carved wooden pillars flanking the seat of honour, and we see from this and other passages that they also stood in Thor's temple. Thor, as became a god with special dominion over the realm of the sky and over storms, had special power over sea journeys. His worshippers prayed for fair weather and favourable winds, but they did more. Many of those whose arrivals in Iceland are chronicled in *Landnámabók* acted like Thorolf. As they neared the shores of the island, they flung the high-seat pillars overboard so that the god himself might guide them to land. It seems likely that a figure of Thor himself was sometimes carved on these pillars, for there is one specific reference in the sagas to a seat, presumably the high-seat, with Thor carved upon it.

Of the connexion between the thunder god and the great trees of the forest, more will be said below. For the moment we may note the reference to god-nails in the pillars of Thor's temple. A possible clue to the significance of such nails is found in seventeenth-century accounts of heathen religion among the Lapps. They are said to have kept an image of the thunder god in the form of a rude block of wood, with a man's head carved at the top, and two sticks for arms, one holding a mallet. Scheffer[1] says :

Into his head they drive a nail of iron or steel, and a small piece of flint to strike fire with, if he hath a mind to it.

If the nails in the pillar were indeed used for the ritual kindling of fire, we might see an explanation of the strange myth about the duel between Thor and Hrungnir the giant, told by Snorri (see p. 41) and also recounted in ninth-century poetry. The

1. *Acta Lapponia* (English translation, 1674), p. 40.

giant was armed with a whetstone and a stone shield. When Thor appeared with thunder and lightning, he hurled his hammer at Hrungnir while the giant hurled the whetstone at him. The whetstone was smashed to pieces, and one small piece remained in Thor's head, and is said to be there still.

Such a fantastic incident must either be based on obscure poetic imagery or on ritual practice. One suggestion made by Dumézil[1] is that the double duel between the giant and Thor and their two supporters, Mist-Calf and Thjalfi, preserves memories of an initiation ritual, a mock demon being set up for the youth to vanquish, while the myth of the god's combat was taught to him as the inner meaning of the ceremony. The strange fact of the whetstone being left in Thor's head might be explained by the Lapp practice of using the head of the thunder god as a source of fire. The whetstone of the giant, encountering the iron hammer of the god, would be equivalent to the kindling of fire with flint and steel, and this in turn represented the flash of the lightning.

Association of fire with Thor's temple is made in a late saga, *Kjalnesinga Saga*. Here the temple is described in the usual way, but it is also stated that the altar was made of iron on top:

This was the place for the fire which was never allowed to go out. This they called the sacred fire.

This has been usually rejected as an invention of the saga-teller, perhaps imitated from a classical source. It is probable, however, that the association between Thor and fire was a genuine one. It was with fire that Thorolf went round his land, claiming it in the name of the god, and there is some reason to believe that the fires of cremation might be connected with Thor as well as with Odin. There is evidence that a perpetual fire burned in the temple of the thunder god of the Old Prussians, within an oak tree sanctuary. Thor's power over the lightning, the fire from heaven, must not be forgotten, and this aspect of the god was, as we will see, further emphasized by the imitation of thunder within the temple itself.

1. *Mythes et dieux des Germains*, Paris, 1939, pp. 98 ff.

3. The Hammer of Thor

The image of Thor in the temple usually carried a hammer, and we hear much in the myths concerning this weapon of the god. Snorri tells us that the Aesir proclaimed that the hammer Mjollnir was the greatest treasure which they possessed, since it enabled them to hold Asgard secure against the giants. Clearly this hammer was something more than a weapon. It was used at weddings to hallow the bride, for this explains the ruse employed against the giants in the poem *Prymskviða* (pages 44–5). Thor was disguised as a bride because he knew that the moment was bound to come when the hammer would be brought out and laid in his lap, and he would thus get it back into his own hands. This use of the hammer symbol may be of very great antiquity in the north. Scandinavian rock-engravings of the Bronze Age show figures brandishing a weapon which resembles an axe or hammer, and in one group a large figure raises one of these over two small figures standing together, which has led to the suggestion that this is some kind of marriage ritual.[1] There is, however, an enormous gap in time between these early rock carvings and the Viking age, and more corroboration is needed before such a claim can be accepted.

We know that the hammer was raised to hallow the new-born child who was to be accepted into the community, and it seems also to have been used at funerals, since at Balder's death it was fetched to hallow the funeral ship before this was set alight. When Thor had feasted on his goats, he made the sign of the hammer over the bones and skin in order to restore them to life (see page 32). In this new life given by the god, we can see a possible significance in the use of the hammer at sacrifices and funerals, concerning which more will be said below.

Like that of the Christian cross, the sign of the hammer was at once a protection and a blessing to those who used it. An early king of Norway, Hakon the Good, who became a Christian, was bullied into attending autumn sacrifices, and he strove to protect himself from the heathen rites by making the sign of the

1. At Hvitlycke, Tanum, Bohuslän, Sweden, shown in O. Almgren, *Nordische Felszeichnungen als religiöse Urkunden*, 1934, p. 118.

cross over the cup passed round in honour of the gods. When the company objected, one of his friends defended Hakon, saying:

The King acts like all those who trust in their strength and might. He made the mark of the hammer over it before he drank.[1]

Men were accustomed in the tenth century to wear the symbol of Thor in the form of a hammer-shaped amulet on a chain or cord round their necks. Some of these have been found in silver hoards in Denmark and Sweden, and there is an obvious resemblance between the little hammers and the square, equal-armed crosses with figures of Christ on them which were worn at about the same time. Possibly the wearing of Thor's symbol came into fashion as a reaction against the Christian one worn by those converted to the new faith. A mould in which both hammers and crosses were cast can be seen in the National Museum at Copenhagen, and indicates that the silversmiths were prepared to satisfy all tastes in religion. The hammer amulet was also used at an earlier period, though in a slightly different form. Small amulets which resemble long-handled hammers and which may be Thor's hammers were found by Fausset in graves of an Anglo-Saxon cemetery at Gilton, Kent.[2]

A very significant use of the hammer is that mentioned by Saxo, who tells us that large models of it were kept in the temple of Thor in Sweden, and that in 1125 these were carried away by Magnus Nilsson:

He took care to bring home certain hammers of unusual weight, which they call Jupiter's, used by the island men in their antique faith. For the men of old, desiring to comprehend the causes of thunder and lightning by means of the similitude of things, took hammers great and massy of bronze, with which they believed the crashing of the sky might be made, thinking that great and violent noise might very well be imitated by the smith's toil, as it were. But Magnus, in his zeal for Christian teaching and dislike to Paganism, determined to spoil the temple of its equipment, and Jupiter of his tokens in the place of his sanctity. And even now the Swedes consider him guilty of sacrilege and a robber of spoil belonging to the god.   *Gesta Danorum*, XIII, 421 (Elton's translation)

1. *Heimskringla, Hákonar Saga Góða*, 17.

2. H. R. Ellis Davidson, 'Thor's Hammer', *Folklore*, 74, 1963. For the wide use of the hammer amulet in Scandinavia, see P. Paulsen, *Axt und Kreuz in Nord- und Osteuropa*, Bonn, 1956, pp. 205–21.

Saxo evidently believed that the hammers, like the chariot, were used in some kind of ritual to imitate the noise of thunder.

The hammer-shaped weapon is similar to the double axe of antiquity, which also represented the thunderbolt, and which was shown in various forms in temples of the ancient world. Among the early Germanic peoples the god Donar, Thor's predecessor, was considered to resemble Hercules, the mighty male figure armed with a club who battled against monsters, and part of the resemblance was evidently due to the weapon which the god carried. This identification was accepted by the Romans, and there are inscriptions to Hercules from the Roman period, raised by the German soldiers in western Europe. Tacitus tells us[1] that the praises of Hercules used to be chanted by the Germans as they went into battle, and that they believed he had visited them.

The hammer could of course be used as a throwing weapon, and one of the characteristics of Mjollnir was that it would always return to the owner's hand. In this way it was a fitting symbol of the thunderbolt hurled by the angry god. Both Snorri and Saxo tell us that the hammer of Thor was short in the handle. Snorri accounts for this by a story of interference by Loki when the hammer was being forged (see pp. 42–3). Saxo tells us that Hotherus[2] hewed off the shaft of the hammer in battle when he put the gods to flight. The idea of a short handle is borne out by the shape of the Danish amulets, and it is noticeable that these all have a metal ring fitted through the handle. If the hammer was thrown through the air, the handle would need to be short, and a ring would make the throw more effective, as in the case of the 'hammer' thrown in the Highland games. A hammer with a loop fitted through the handle is shown on a Swedish rune-stone from Stenqvista, where it is used as a sign of Thor's protection over the grave.

An object very like a hammer or a double axe is also depicted among the magical symbols on the drums of Lappish shamans, used in their religious ceremonies before Christianity was established. The drums themselves were struck with an implement which resembles a hammer, and here we have another connexion with the metal hammers said to be used in Thor's temple to

1. *Germania*, 3.
2. Presumably the same as Hoder (*Hǫðr*) in Snorri.

imitate the noise of thunder. The name of the Lappish thunder god was Horagalles, thought to be derived from *Þórr karl*, 'old man Thor'. Sometimes on the drums a male figure with a hammer-like object in either hand is shown, and sometimes this is a kind of cross with hooked ends, resembling a swastika. The swastika, or hooked cross, is a sign found in many regions of the world and known from remote antiquity. It was very popular among the heathen Germans, and appears to have been associated with the symbol of fire. There may be some connexion between it and the sun-wheel, well known in the Bronze Age, or it may have arisen from the use of the hammer or axe to represent thunder, which was accompanied by fire from heaven. Thor was the sender of lightning and the god who dealt out both sunshine and rain to men, and it seems likely that the swastika as well as the hammer sign was connected with him.

The Anglo-Saxons worshipped the thunder god under the name of Thunor. Memories of him survive here and there, like the title of High Thunderer, used for the Christian God in a tenth-century charter of Edward the Elder. We have many instances of the swastika symbol from Anglo-Saxon graves of the pagan period, and it is particularly prominent on cremation urns from the cemeteries of East Anglia. On some of these, to be seen in the Cambridge Museum of Archaeology and Ethnology, it is depicted with such care and art that it must surely have possessed special significance as a funeral symbol. Both the swastika and the hammer symbol are found on stones bearing early runic inscriptions in Norway and Sweden, and some of these call on Thor to protect the memorial and place of burial.

The swastika is also found on weapons and sword scabbards. It can be seen on sword hilts from the peat bogs of Denmark as early as the third century A.D. It is clearly marked on a hilt and sword belt found at Bifrons, Kent, in a grave of about the sixth century. By the seventh century, the Christian cross also appears on scabbards, and an elaborate one recovered from the River Seine has the cross and the swastika side by side.[1]

It would seem indeed as though the power of the thunder

1. H. R. Ellis Davidson, *The Sword in Anglo-Saxon England*, Oxford, 1962, pp. 67 and 92-3.

god, symbolized by his hammer, extended over all that had to do with the well-being of the community. It covered birth, marriage, and death, burial, and cremation ceremonies, weapons and feasting, travelling, land-taking, and the making of oaths between men. The famous weapon of Thor was not only the symbol of the destructive power of the storm, and of fire from heaven, but also a protection against the forces of evil and violence. Without it Asgard could no longer be guarded against the giants, and men relied on it also to give security and to support the rule of law.

4. *The God of the Sky*

The mother of Thor was said to be Earth herself, and in the earliest skaldic verse he is described in phrases meaning 'son of Earth'. Of his wife, Sif, we know little, except that she had wonderful golden hair; it has been suggested that this was the sign of an ancient fertility goddess, her abundant, shining hair typifying the golden corn. There was an undoubted link between Thor as the thunder god and the fertility of the earth, on which the lightning strikes and the rain falls, causing increase. Adam of Bremen writes of Thor as the most important of the gods, because of this power over the seasons:

> They say he rules the air which controls the thunder and the lightning, the winds and showers, the fair weather and the fruits of the earth. . . . Thor with a sceptre seems to represent Jove.
>
> *History of the Bishops of Hamburg*, iv, 26

It is in keeping with this link between Thor and the earth, that we find many of the first Icelandic settlers taking with them from Norway not only the high-seat pillars from Thor's temple, but also earth from between the pillars. Moreover they were careful to hallow the land which they took for themselves in the name of the god before they built their dwellings upon it and sowed their crops.

In his association with the natural world, Thor was thus both destroyer and protector. He was regarded in Viking times as a sure guide for those who travelled over the sea, because of his power over storms and wind. He was the god to be invoked for journeying, and even Helgi the Lean, one of the early Icelandic settlers who had been converted to Christianity, was said to continue to call on Thor whenever he had a sea voyage to make. Thor could call down storms against his adversaries, as when he raised a tempest against Olaf Tryggvason by blowing out his beard, urged on by his worshipper, Raud:

Raud said: 'Blow out the bristles of your beard against him, and we will resist them stoutly.' Thor said not much would come of that, but nevertheless they went out, and Thor blew hard into his beard and puffed out the bristles. Immediately a gale came up against the king.   *Flateyjarbók*, 1, 248

Thor is said in *Flóamanna Saga* (21) to appear to a Christian convert in a dream 'big and red-bearded', and to threaten him that it should go hard with him on his journey. He led him to a cliff and showed him great waves breaking over the rocks, saying:

Into such rough seas shall you come and never be delivered from them, unless you turn to me.

Poems quoted in *Njáls Saga* declare that Thor stirred up the storms which shattered the ship of the Christian missionary Thangbrand. Thor's power over the sea might of course be used more positively to benefit his worshippers, as when he is said to have stranded a whale on the shores of Vineland in response to the prayers of Thorhall, one of the explorers. Thorhall boasted to his Christian companions:

Redbeard has got the better of your Christ! I have done this by my poetry which I made about Thor, in whom men trust.

                                        Eiríks Saga Rauða

The connexion between the red beard of Thor and the raising of the wind appears to be emphasized. Perhaps the old explanation, that the beard denoted the lightning, is nearer the truth than the popular suggestion that Thor's beard made him the typical unshaven Viking. The colour of the beard may have been based on the red sky which foretells a storm. Incidentally the fact that one of the most famous worshippers of the god, Thorolf of Most, was known as 'bearded man of Most', suggests his beard was something worthy of notice, even among bearded Vikings. We may note that the terrible glare of Thor's burning eyes is also mentioned more than once in the poetry, and his fearsome voice.

The thunder god with his hammer was, as we have seen, equated with the Roman Hercules. But Donar, the thunder god of the heathen Germans, had other associations more distinguished than this. Adam of Bremen suggested that the god with his sceptre represented Jupiter, and Saxo alludes to Jupiter's hammers. Others saw the association with the supreme sky god of the Romans. The day sacred to Jupiter, *dies Iovis*, the fourth day of the week, Thursday, was dedicated to the Thunderer throughout the Germanic world. We have *Þunresdæg* in Anglo-Saxon England, *Donnerstag* in Germany. It was an important day of the week, and as late as the seventh century Eligius, Bishop of Noyon, had to reproach his congregation because so many of them still kept Thursday as a holy day.[1]

It seems that Donar, Thor's predecessor, like the Greek Zeus, was associated with the great oaks of the forest which covered much of western Europe. The Germans, the Celts (whose thunder god was Tanaros), the Baltic tribes, and the Slavs all had holy groves within the forest where the thunder god was worshipped. Grimm suggested that the connexion between the god and the oak was a practical one, because the oak was the tree most often struck by lightning. The emphasis, however, should probably be laid on the fact that when a great oak is struck by lightning, the sight of its destruction is something unforgettable. A vivid description of such a happening given by Tolstoy in *Anna Karenina* is worth quoting to illustrate this:

... Suddenly there was a glare of light, the whole earth seemed on fire, and the vault of heaven cracked overhead. Opening his blinded eyes, to his horror the first thing Levin saw through the thick curtain of rain between him and the woods was the uncannily altered position of the green crest of a familiar oak in the middle of the copse. 'Can it have been struck?' The thought had barely time to cross his mind when, gathering speed, the oak disappeared behind the other trees, and he heard the crash of the great tree falling on the others.

There is little doubt that this is based on observation, and that Tolstoy had seen an oak falling in a storm. His impression that

1. J. Grimm, *Teutonic Mythology*, (translated Stallybras, 1888), iv, p. 1737.

the heavens had opened and that fire from them was descending on to the earth is significant. As a channel through which the power of the sky god might reach down to the world of men, it is understandable that the mighty oak tree, itself a splendid symbol of age, strength, and endurance, came to be considered specially sacred to the Thunderer.

Groves which the Germans held sacred to the gods are mentioned by Tacitus at the end of the first century. Later on, a number of Christian missionaries – Boniface, Jerome, Bishop Otto, Willebrord – counted the felling of a tree sacred to a heathen god among their achievements in the cause of Christ. There is mention of 'Jupiter's Oak' more than once. The Prussians remained heathen long after Germany as a whole had been converted, and in the sixteenth century writers who visited them described sacred woods in which they made sacrifices and sacred springs which Christians were not allowed to approach. The chief of these sanctuaries was at Romove, where there was a holy oak, in whose trunk were placed images of the gods. Before that of the thunder god, Perkuno, was a fire which was never allowed to go out. The fire was surrounded by curtains, forming a shrine which only the high priest might enter to commune with Perkuno. The name of this god is linked with the Latin word for oak, *quercus*, and it is probable that Donar too was worshipped in sanctuaries of this type. In England there are a number of Anglo-Saxon place-names in the form *Þunre leah*, the meaning of which is 'grove, or forest clearing of Thunder'. One example is the early form of Thundersley in Essex. Similarly in Scandinavia Thor's name is linked with *lundr*, 'grove', and place-names in this form are found in Sweden, west Norway, and Denmark. The Forest of Thor on the north bank of the Liffey outside Dublin existed in the year A.D. 1000. In that year King Brian Boru spent a month destroying it, burning down the undergrowth and demolishing young trees, until, as we are told in an Irish poem, 'the great trees and the lordly oaks alone stood upright'.[1]

In Iceland there were no great oaks, and thus the link between the thunder god and the trees has become blurred in

1. C. Marstrander, 'Thor en Irlande', *Revue Celtique*, 36, 1915–16, p. 247.

the Icelandic sources. But the link was there all the same, and we can discern it in the custom of the settlers to take the oak pillars of Thor's temple with them to Iceland. The pillar, as we have seen, was sacred to the god, and there seems good reason to believe that this was because the pillar represented the sacred tree, in which the power of the god dwelt. In one case in *Landnámabók* we read of an early settler who had no high-seat pillars to bring with him, but when he reached Iceland he prayed to Thor, and the prayer was answered. A great tree was washed ashore, big enough to provide pillars for him and for his neighbours also.

The high-seat pillar formed a support of the hall or temple, and a resemblance between this and the 'lucky' tree, which stood beside the house, and on whose well-being the luck of the family depended, seems a reasonable assumption. In the story of King Volsung, this tree formed a living support to his hall, and there are still a few houses remaining in the British Isles where the building has been supported by a great tree in the centre.[1] The 'lucky' family tree was well-known at one time in Norway, Sweden, Denmark, and Germany. A folk custom still known in England is the raising of a branch from the roof or chimney of a house when the builders have finished the roof (with free drinks all round). One reason given for this is that the house will afterwards be safe from lightning if this ceremony is carried out. In the same way we may assume that pillars hallowed to Thor would protect the dwelling which they supported from the terrors of the storm. Also, like the sacred tree in the forest, they marked the most holy place, where the worshipper might approach the thunder god and learn his will.

5. *Thor and his Adversaries*

Evidence leads us to believe that the cult of Thor was a vigorous one in the north, and that it continued to be so until the close of the heathen period. There are two indications of its widespread influence on the lives of men: the large number of children in Scandinavia who were named after the god, and the many places called after him. In Dublin the Irish referred to

1. Examples are given in *Folklore*, 71, 1960, p. 5.

the Viking settlers as 'people of Thor'. We find men giving respectful and at times devoted allegiance to the god of thunder, in particular among the sturdy Norwegian landowners of good stock though not of royal blood, the independent settlers in Iceland and Ireland, and the adventurers who 'trusted in their own strength and might'. It was in fact a cult which attracted those accustomed to make their own decisions and resentful of too much authority from above.

Thor was the sky god, called upon to hallow and protect the various aspects of men's lives in the community. When we turn from this conception to the picture of the hammer god of myths, there seems at first sight a contradiction. Thor in Asgard spends much of his time 'out killing trolls', or arriving home to dispose of some unwelcome giant who has penetrated the realm of the gods. His adventures are tinged with comedy, and he appears as a being of great strength and uncertain temper, who in moments of crisis simply reaches for his hammer. Myths may be simplified, rationalized, or twisted into comedy, particularly when, as in the case of the myths retold by Snorri, they are recorded after the end of the heathen period. Nevertheless much may still be learned of the nature of a god by the adversaries whom he encounters, and this is true of Thor.

Thor's battles are for the most part with the frost-giants and giantesses, such as Hrungnir, Thrym, Hymir, Geirrod, and their broods. Sometimes they try to lure him into their realms unarmed, but for the most part he goes deliberately to seek them, and kills them without much difficulty once it comes to a direct trial of strength. His most terrible adversary however is the World Serpent, who lies coiled round the earth. Thor's attempt to raise him, when he appears in the form of a great grey cat, is well known; and is a vivid incident in a very amusing tale. But the story of the fishing expedition with the giant Hymir, when Thor drew up the serpent from the ocean depths, was a myth which appears to have been taken seriously. It was at all events well known to poets of the ninth century, for we have four poems all earlier than A.D. 1000 which describe the fishing in some detail: *Ragnarsdrápa*, by Bragi (from the ninth century) *Húsdrápa*, by Ulfr Uggarson, and poems by Gamli Gnævaðarskáld and Eysteinn Valdason (from the tenth century).

The Thunder God

These are predecessors of the better known narrative poem in the *Edda* collection, *Hymiskviða*, which treats the incident on semi-comic lines.

The poem *Húsdrápa* purports to describe a series of carvings in an Icelandic hall, one of which shows Thor hauling up the serpent. This is interesting in view of the fact that in Gosforth church in Cumberland we have what appears to be a carving of the scene, on a stone panel, probably originally part of a cross, now built into the wall of the church. The panel shows two figures in a boat, and a large bait, which could well be the ox-head of the story, at the end of the line. The serpent might have been shown on a lower panel, but in any case is present in stylized form in the serpentine figure which is shown above the boat.[1]

None of the poems make it clear whether the battle between the god and the monster was a conclusive one, and whether we are to regard the hammer-blow struck at the serpent as its bane. In Snorri's prose account, based on *Vǫluspá*, Thor does not slay the serpent until the great final battle, when he himself perishes along with his adversary. Possibly an earlier form of the myth placed the battle at an earlier point in Thor's career, and made him survive it gloriously. In his introduction to the *Prose Edda*, Snorri speaks of Thor as the god who overcame all berserks and giants and 'an enormous dragon', so that he may have been aware of this earlier version of the story. Certainly he seems concerned about the contradiction between two different traditions, as after recounting the fishing incident he remarked that it was not known whether the serpent survived the blow or not. *Hymiskviða* also leaves the result open to doubt, but it may be noted that one of the titles there given to Thor is *orms einbani*, 'sole slayer of the serpent'.

The conquest of a World Monster by the God of the Sky is a recognized pattern in world mythologies. The Indian thunder god Indra, in many ways Thor's counterpart, slew a great dragon in single combat. The conception behind the varying forms of this myth appears to be a fundamental one: that the Sky and Thunder God, the being of enormous strength who defends

1. The scene is also shown on a stone from Altuna, Uppland, Sweden. Here the serpent has taken the bait, but the giant is not shown.

mankind, does battle with the terrible monster threatening man's destruction. Concerning this monster, there will be more to say in a later chapter.

The giants slain by Thor have no special characteristics except that they are huge, powerful, and greedy, being specially jealous of the possessions of the gods. They are always waiting for a chance to attack Asgard and to carry its treasures away. It is implied more than once that Thor was engaged in continual conflict with these beings, and that the stories which survive are only a few out of a large number. In a tenth-century poem by Thorbjorn *Dísarskáld* a long list of unknown names of giants overcome by Thor is given, and the refrain of the poem is 'Thor has guarded Asgard with courage'. Nor did he only fight these battles on behalf of the gods; it is clear that he was also regarded as the Defence of Men (*alda bergr*). He was struggling for mankind, and for the precarious civilization which men had wrested from a hard and chaotic world. If we see his doings in the myths in this light, then they harmonize with the picture given in the prose literature of a god who supported law, helped men to build and to cultivate, to marry and bring up children, and protected them on their journeyings. He guarded not only the halls of Asgard, but the humbler homesteads of Norway and Iceland, marked out and hallowed by his sacred fire and his hammer-sign; he safeguarded their oaths with one another, and invested them with the sanctity of his temple and holy place. As the sky god, he drove his chariot over the circuit of the heavens, and could at will grant the traveller desirable weather and favourable winds. In Asgard he kept the goddesses of peace and plenty safe, so that they could grant their benefits to mankind; on earth, in the stony and storm-beaten lands of the north, he battled with the monsters of cold and violence that unceasingly threatened men's security. It is hardly surprising that he attracted the allegiance of men who struggled against the odds which nature and hostile powers raised against them, nor that, even after he had been long supplanted by Christ, he still played a major part in the old myths of the gods which were recounted in the north.

Chapter 4

The Gods of Peace and Plenty

Crawl to your Mother Earth. She will save you
from the void.

Rigveda, XVIII, 10.

1. *The Deity in the Wagon*

Those gods who determined the course of war and sent thunder
from heaven were essentially powers of destruction, although
they might also give protection from chaos and disorder. Other
powers were said to dwell in Asgard with Odin and Thor
whose province was of a different kind, since their sphere of
influence was over the peace and fertility of the inhabited earth.
These were called the Vanir, and Snorri tells us that the chief
figures among them were the twin deities Freyr and Freyja,
the children of Njord. We are not told much about them in
the myths which he includes in the *Prose Edda*, but it is clear
that he regarded them as powerful beings whose worship continued until late in the heathen period. Freyr he calls *Veraldar
góð*, god of the world. He tells us in *Ynglinga Saga* that he
was the god much loved by the Swedes, because

... in his time the people of the land became richer on account of
peace and good seasons than ever before.

The one story which Snorri tells of Freyr is taken from the
poem *Skírnismál*, and is concerned with his love for the fair
maiden Gerd who dwelled in the underworld with the giants,
and how he sent down Skirnir to woo her. She finally consented
to meet him and become his bride (see p. 30). Magnus Olsen,
in an illuminating study of the poem,[1] interpreted this myth as

1. 'Fra gammelnorsk Myte og Kultus', *Maal og Minne*, 1909, pp. 17 ff.
A different emphasis is given by J. Sahlgren, *Eddica et scaldica*, 1927-8,
pp. 225 ff.

one representing the marriage of the god of the sky with the goddess of the fruitful earth, resulting in rich harvest.

Other evidence exists which implies that the idea of a divine marriage formed an essential part of Freyr's cult, just as it formed a part of the worship of the fertility gods of the Near East. A memory of it survives in an ironic little comedy preserved in *Flateyjarbók*, part of the saga of King Olaf Tryggvason. The hero of this tale is Gunnar Helming, a young Norwegian who quarrelled with King Olaf and fled to Sweden. There he found that the god Freyr was held in much honour, and that at his temple there was an attractive young woman who served the god as his priestess, and was called his wife. Gunnar got on well with the priestess, and when the time came for Freyr to make his autumn journey round the land to bless the season, he was invited to join the party, although the priestess felt that Freyr might not approve of this. Gunnar set out with Freyr's wagon, while an attendant led the beast that pulled it, but they were overtaken by a blizzard on a mountain road, and everyone deserted the god and his wife except Gunnar. For a while he led the wagon, and at last sat down to rest. The priestess then rather ungratefully threatened that Freyr would attack him if he did not go on, and at this Freyr is said to have come down from his wagon and fought with Gunnar. The struggle was a fierce one, but just in time Gunnar remembered the god of King Olaf, and called on him for help. Thereupon he was able to get the better of the 'fiend', who made off, leaving Gunnar to destroy his image. Then Gunnar had the idea of putting on the adornments of the god and impersonating him, and this plan succeeded brilliantly. They arrived at the feast to which they had been invited in spite of the bad weather, and now the god was able to eat and drink with men, which pleased them mightily. Moreover he demanded valuables and clothes from them instead of human sacrifice, which pleased them even more. The season proved a good one, and when in a few months time it was found that Freyr's wife was with child, his reputation grew apace. But this happy state of affairs was ended when news of the doings in Sweden reached the ears of King Olaf. He at once sent a message to Gunnar to return, and the young man stole away with his wife and the large fortune which he had obtained from the credulous Swedes, and went back to Norway.

There is no need to take this story too seriously as a reliable account of the acts of one of Olaf's men, based on historical fact. It is in all probability a piece of brilliant fiction, and may have been partially inspired by classical tales of men who impersonated gods for their own ends. But even if this is so, it provides interesting evidence for the kind of practices associated with Freyr in Sweden. The story would lose its comic point were it not assumed that the image of Freyr was taken round to feasts throughout the winter months, that the Swedes believed that the god in some way was present in his image, and that his priestess, known as his wife, interpreted his messages to men. The naïve delight of the Swedes when they discovered that their god would now be able to eat at feasts and beget children is a mocking commentary on the kind of belief which they had in the powers of Freyr. Incidentally the story throws some light on why the fertility cult never flourished in the north to the extent that it did in the Near East and Mediterranean regions. The picture of Freyr's wagon, harbinger of warmth and fertility, stuck in a snowdrift in the mountains of Sweden is a somewhat pathetic one.

This is not the only account of a god carried round in a wagon. Another story in *Flateyjarbók* (1, 467) shows the Swedish king himself consulting such a god, who is here called *Lýtir*. Little is known of such a deity, but his name seems to have inspired a number of Swedish place-names, and it is possible that it was one of the titles of Freyr. King Eric of Sweden is said to have led the god's wagon to a certain place, and waited until it became heavy, the sign that the god was present within. Then the wagon was drawn to the king's hall, and Eric greeted the god, drank a horn in his honour, and put various questions to him. Here then the privileged person consulting the god was the king himself, and some kind of divination ceremony seems to have taken place.

Earlier in the history of northern Europe, we hear of a goddess who was carried round in a wagon to bring fertility to men. Tacitus knew of such a goddess in Denmark, called Nerthus, and in *Germania*, 40, he gives his famous account of her worship by the Danes. She represented *Terra Mater*, 'Mother Earth', he tells us, and had the power to intervene in the affairs of men. She visited her people in a sacred wagon, which none but the priest might touch, and no one save him was permitted to look inside. When the wagon was not in use, it was kept in a grove on an island. At a certain time the priest knew that she was present in her sanctuary (we are not told how, but possibly, as with Lytir, the wagon became heavy), and then he set out with the wagon, drawn by oxen. Everywhere Nerthus was warmly welcomed by the people :

They do not undertake hostilities nor take up arms; every weapon is put away; peace and quiet then only are known and welcomed.

When the goddess returned to her sanctuary, the wagon, the cloth that covered it, and some symbol (*numen*) which it contained were all cleansed in a sacred lake by slaves who were drowned when their task was over.

There is a long gap between the first century A.D. when Tacitus was writing and the story of Gunnar Helming, and yet there are a number of points of resemblance in the account of the progress of the deity through the district. This gap is bridged to some extent by archaeological evidence. Two elaborate and delicately made wagons were found in a peat-bog at Dejbjerg, in west Denmark, and are thought to date back to about A.D. 200. With them was a small stool of alder wood, which might have served as a seat for the occupant. Clay vessels and a loom-piece found with these objects suggested association with women. Little wagons of this sort could have been used in such a ceremonial progress as Tacitus described. In the ninth century A.D. another beautiful little wagon, delicately carved and ornamented, was buried in a ship at Oseberg, together with other fine wooden objects which seem to have had a ceremonial purpose, and which accompanied the body of a lady of high rank. Tapestries found with the ship show a wagon with a man and woman standing beside it, possibly a representation of such a progress as the stories describe. It is possible also that little figures of the 'driving goddess', female figures wearing neck-rings and kneeling as if to drive a chariot, which have been found in Denmark and are thought to be of Bronze Age date, represent a similar conception of the goddess of fertility, driving out to bless the land with her presence.

In south-eastern Europe one goddess borne round the country-side was Cybele, the Syrian goddess of fruitfulness. An unforgettable account of her progress – again by a cynical and unsympathetic writer – is found in Apuleius's *Golden Ass*. He describes the image as being accompanied by giggling, shrill-voiced priests in women's clothes, pretending to fall into a state of ecstasy and indulging in disgusting practices. Cybele's worship reached Gaul, and tales of St Martin in the fourth century A.D. tell of images covered with white curtains carried round the fields, while Gregory of Tours had heard of similar practices at Autun, in the days of Bishop Simplicius. It has been suggested that Tacitus's account of Nerthus was based on what he knew of the worship of Cybele, but the independent evidence suggests that the fertility deity was indeed worshipped in the north in the way in which he describes, and that similar customs, associated with Freyr and the Vanir, continued in Sweden until the close of the heathen period.

2. *Freyr, God of Plenty*

At the outset we are faced with the question why a fertility goddess, worshipped in Denmark in the first century, had been replaced in the Viking age by a fertility god. The written sources represent Freyr as the sovereign deity of increase and prosperity. According to Adam of Bremen, his image in the temple at Uppsala was a phallic one, and he was the god who dispensed peace and plenty to mortals and was invoked at marriages. Saxo also tells us that there was worship of Freyr at Uppsala. He mentions a great sacrifice called *Fröblod* which took place there at regular intervals, which included human victims. He also refers to the worship of Freyr accompanied by 'effeminate gestures' and 'clapping of mimes upon the stage', together with the 'unmanly clatter of bells'.[1] This implies some kind of performance, possibly ritual drama, which to Saxo and the Danish heroes whom he describes appeared unmanly and debased. It

1. Saxo Grammaticus, *Gesta Danorum* (translated Elton, 1894), VI, 185, p. 228.

may be noted that men dressed as women and the use of clapping and bells have survived into our own time in the annual mumming plays and the dances which go with them. Possibly some kind of symbolic drama to ensure the divine blessing on the fruitfulness of the season was once performed at Uppsala in Freyr's honour. If some kind of ritual marriage formed part of it, it might account for the horror which Saxo felt for such rites.

Saxo and others also state that human sacrifice was part of the cult of the Vanir. In the poem *Ynglingatal* there are puzzling references to a number of early kings of the Swedes meeting with strange and violent deaths. The Swedes evidently believed that their kings had the power to bring peace and plenty to the land, the power attributed to Freyr. It has been suggested that they were regarded in heathen times as the husbands of the fertility goddess – perhaps Freyja, Nerthus, or called by some other name – and that they suffered a real or a symbolic death in that capacity when their time of supremacy came to an end. If that were indeed the case, then the figure of Freyr as the male god of plenty could have evolved gradually out of that of the priest-king. Here however we are dealing with theories and hypotheses, for we have no clear statement from reliable outside observers that such sacrifices of the king did in fact take place, and no archaeological evidence up to now for the existence of such sacrificial rites in Sweden.

We know that Freyr was closely associated with the horse cult, and that sacred horses were kept in his sanctuary at Thrandheim in Norway. When Olaf Tryggvason arrived there to destroy it, it is said that he found a stallion about to be killed 'for Freyr to eat'. The king had the horse brought to him, and rode it to the temple.[1] This meant that he defied Freyr, since it was forbidden to ride the horse which had been given to the god. In the sagas too we hear of horses kept near Freyr's temples in Iceland. The best-known story is that of Hrafnkell, who had a stallion dedicated to the god, and a stud of twelve mares. Hrafnkell shared all his possessions with Freyr, but the horse, called Freyfaxi, 'mane of Freyr', was specially sacred, and no one except Hrafnkell might ride him. When a boy did so on one

1. *Flateyjarbók*, I, 322.

occasion, meaning no harm, Hrafnkell felt forced by his vow to slay the offender. The saga shows the dire results of this action, and how it brought about Hrafnkell's ruin, for in the end his enemies slew Freyfaxi by pushing him over a cliff, and in his bitterness Hrafnkell abandoned the god whom he had worshipped with such devotion. Much of this story is fiction, but must nevertheless be based on traditions about the cult of Freyr which had come down to the story-teller, and as such it merits our attention. Another horse called Freyfaxi is mentioned in *Vatnsdœla Saga*, and the sons of Ingimund, represented as worshippers of Freyr, are there said to be in the habit of attending horse-fights. It seems likely that the horse contests described in several of the sagas, which roused great local excitement in certain districts of Iceland, were originally associated with the cult of Freyr.[1]

Another animal linked with both Freyr and his sister Freyja was the boar. Freyr is said by Snorri to have possessed the boar *Gullinbursti*, made by the dwarfs, whose coat shone in the dark, and who could out-run any steed. Freyja also had a boar, called *Hildisvín*. In the poem *Hyndluljóð* we are told that when she wanted to disguise her protégé, Ottar the Simple, she let him take the shape of her boar. The association of the boar with the deities of fertility is likely to be very old indeed. In early Sweden and in Anglo-Saxon England the boar possessed special significance, since his image is found on ceremonial objects, as well as on those used for war and adornment. Helmets of the seventh century are found with images of the boar on them, and some Swedish helmet-plates show warriors who have helmets with a large boar as a crest. A boar-crested helmet has survived from Anglo-Saxon times, taken from a tumulus at Benty Grange, Derbyshire; the crest is small but exquisitely made in the form of a little boar in gilded bronze with ruby eyes. It was remembered by the Anglo-Saxons that such figures were believed to have protective power, for in *Beowulf* it is said that the boar on the helmet was there to keep guard over the life of the warrior who wore it. When we find an Anglo-Saxon sword from East Anglia bearing three tiny figures of boars stamped on its

1. See G. Gjessing, 'Hesten i forhistorisk kunst og kultus', *Viking*, 7, 1945, pp. 29 ff.

blade, we may assume that they have been placed there for a similar purpose.[1]

Tacitus tells us that the Germanic tribe of the Aestii who lived on the Prussian coast in the first century wore figures (*formae*) of boars as the emblem of their religion. Such figures may have been masks or helmets which covered the face, such as Plutarch tells us were worn by the Cimbri. He does not indicate what kind of animals the Cimbri chose, but in his *Life* of Caius Marius describes these helmets as resembling 'the open jaws of terrible beasts of prey and strange animal faces'. The boar-mask may well have preceded the boar-crested helmet in Sweden, since one of the warriors on a helmet-plate from Vendel is shown wearing a kind of boar-mask, with a tusk protruding on one side. It is clear that some kind of boar-helmet had significance in Sweden and was treasured by the early kings. King Athils was said to possess a helmet called *Hildigǫltr*, 'battle pig', and also to have had a heavy neck-ring called *Sviagriss*, 'piglet of the Swedes'. He won another helmet called *Hildisvín*, 'battle swine', from his opponent, King Ali, and here we have the same name as that of the boar owned by Freyja.

When we are told that Freyja's worshipper, Ottar the Simple, disguised himself as her boar, this might be explained by the donning of a boar-mask by the priest of the Vanir, who thus claimed inspiration and protection from the deity. Although the Vanir were not gods of battle, the protection which they offered would no doubt extend into time of war, and it is noticeable that both Tacitus and *Beowulf* stress the protective power of the emblem. This has been remembered in Cynewulf's poem *Elene*, as Rosemary Cramp pointed out,[2] when Constantine is said to sleep *eofor cumble bepæht*, 'over-shadowed' or 'covered by the boar-sign' at the time when he received the vision of the symbol of Christ. He was thus under the protection of the old heathen sign, either on helmet or standard, when he had his revelation of the new power which was to replace the ancient gods.

1. H. R. Ellis Davidson, *The Sword in Anglo-Saxon England*, Oxford, 1962, pp. 49–50. For boar-helmets, see R. Cramp, '*Beowulf* and Archaeology', *Medieval Archaeology*, I, 1957, pp. 60 ff.
2. op. cit., pp. 59–60.

Besides the horse and the boar, a third symbol which belonged to Freyr was that of the ship. He was said to have owned the ship *Skíðblaðnir*, a vessel large enough to hold all the gods, but able to be folded up when not in use and kept in a man's pouch. This ship could travel at will in any direction, since it always got a favourable wind. It is possible that a cult ship was the base of this tradition, the kind of ship used in processions and folded up when not in use. There is abundant evidence for ships carried in processions and kept in churches in Scandinavia from the Middle Ages down to modern times, some of those from Denmark being used for ceremonies of blessing the fields,[1] and it may be that here we have the tradition of Freyr's sacred boat surviving in a Christian setting. The ship is another religious symbol which can be traced back to very early times in the north. Tacitus knew of a goddess of the Suebi whose symbol was a boat, and he identified her with Isis, which suggests that she was a fertility goddess. It is possible that the unknown 'symbol' of the goddess Nerthus was a ship, but of this we have no proof.

From the time of the Bronze Age onwards, the ship was used in many different forms in funeral ceremonies. Freyr himself had close associations with death and burial, as is emphasized by Snorri in *Ynglinga Saga*. Here we are told that Freyr's own death was kept secret from the Swedes for three years, and during that time he lay in a great burial mound, with a door and three holes in the sides, into which gifts of gold, silver, and copper were placed by the priests. If images of the god were kept in some kind of tomb-like shrine, this may be the explanation of the statement in *Heimskringla* that two wooden men were taken from Freyr's howe and one kept in Sweden while the other went to Thrandheim in Norway. In Iceland also some connexion was made between Freyr and burial mounds. In *Gísla Saga* a priest of Freyr died, and it was said that he was so cherished by Freyr that the god 'would have no frost between them', and so no snow nor frost ever lay on his mound.

The wooden man taken to Thrandheim emphasizes the idea of the cult carried westward, from Sweden to Norway. In Norway, farms, rocks, and fields bear Freyr's name, and his worship was taken west again, by a few settlers who went to Iceland.

1. H. Henningsen, *Kirkeskibe og Kirkeskibsfesten*, 1950.

Place-names suggest that his worship did not gain much ground there, for there are only three places known to be called after him. Memory of some of his worshippers however has survived in the Icelandic sagas. The Hrafnkell who was said to keep horses sacred to Freyr settled in the east in the early tenth century, but whether he was in fact a priest of Freyr, as represented in the saga about him, seems doubtful. A better known worshipper of the god was Thord *Freysgoði*, son of Ozurr, mentioned in several sagas, whose family were known as the *Freysgyðlingar*, but we know no stories about him.

The title *Freysgoði* was also borne by Thorgrim, whose death is described in *Gísla Saga*. He must have been named in honour of Thor, and was in fact the grandson of Thorolf of Most, the famous worshipper of the god. Thorgrim however made friends with Gisli's family, married one of the daughters, became a blood-brother of the sons, and must have forsaken Thor for Freyr. His temple was in the north-west of Iceland. A man described as a priest of Freyr, though he does not seem to have borne the title, was Ingimund, the adventures of whose family are told in *Vatnsdæla Saga*. He is said to have been given a token with Freyr's image on it by King Harald Fairhair, and to have come out to Iceland under the god's guidance. He built a temple in Vatnsdale in the north-west. None were permitted to take weapons into it, and Ingimund was able to obtain a coveted sword from a Norwegian visitor who had unwittingly worn it when entering. Ingimund convinced him that he had angered the god, and must forfeit his weapon, and the sword became a valued heirloom in the family.

Another family of Freyr-worshippers is described in *Víga-Glúms Saga*. They lived in the north, and their founder was Helgi the Lean, who claimed to be descended from King Frodi. When he came out to Iceland he is said to have thrown a boar and a sow overboard to guide him to land, which suggests that he worshipped Freyr, although we know he also invoked Thor, and that he was baptized as a Christian. His son Ingjald built Freyr a temple, the guardianship of which was inherited by Ingjald's grandson, Glum, the hero of the saga. Glum and his mother also had the right to share in the crops grown in a certain field called *Vitazgjafi*, which stood near the temple and was apparently associated with the god. The name of this field has been interpreted as 'certain giver',[1] and it must have been an especially fertile one. Things went badly for Glum, and when he was still a young man he forsook Freyr, and went over to the god of his mother's family. It seems likely that this god was Odin, since his Norwegian grandfather gave him a spear and a sword which were said to be 'lucky' gifts and family treasures. Glum used the spear to slay an overbearing relative in the holy field after he had been denied his share of the grain from it, and so the field was defiled with blood, and the saga implies that Glum aroused Freyr's anger by this deed of violence. He offended the god still further by turning one of Freyr's faithful worshippers off his land, by harbouring his own son after he had been declared an outlaw, and finally by taking a misleading oath in the name of the gods, and thus breaking faith with them. In the end he was forced to leave his land, and this was thought to be on account of Freyr's enmity. Indeed Glum was said to have had a dream that the god was sitting on a chair on the sea-shore, surrounded by a vast crowd, and that he refused to listen to the plea which Glum's dead kinsmen were making on his behalf.

Thus it will be seen that the sagas have preserved memories of a fertility cult associated with Freyr which is strongly at variance with the battle cult of Odin. Its main lines agree with those of the cult of Nerthus as described by Tacitus centuries before. The ban against weapons in Freyr's temples, his anger when blood is shed on his sacred land, the taboo against outlaws in his holy place, are all in accordance with his character as a bringer of peace, and we are reminded of the coming of Nerthus, when weapons were put away and peace reigned supreme. Freyr is linked also with the sun and the fruitful earth; a fertile field stands near his temple, and no frost is allowed to come between him and his faithful worshipper, while we are told also that he was connected with marriage and the birth of children. Like Nerthus, who was known as Mother Earth, and intervened in human affairs, Freyr was the deity who brought fertility to men. Freyr, again like Nerthus, inspired joy and devotion. Men rejoiced to share their possessions with him. Finally the

1. A. Holtsmark, 'Vitazgjafi', *Maal og Minne*, 1933, pp. 111 ff.

dream of Freyr sitting on a chair by the sea reminds us of the god who sat in a wagon, and of Nerthus who journeyed round the land to answer men's prayers. This side of Freyr's cult is apparent in the story of Gunnar Helming, and it may be noted that the god's worshippers in Thrandheim were eager to tell Olaf Tryggvason how their god

... talked to us also, and told us future happenings beforehand, and he gave us peace and plenty.   *Flateyarbók*, I, 322

The impression made by the prose sources is that the worshippers of Freyr were in the minority in western Scandinavia, but that nevertheless they were remembered long after the cult had died out for the devotion which they gave their god.

3. *Companions of Freyr*

While Freyr is the main deity who represents peace and plenty, there are other male figures who seem to resemble him, and who are called by different names. The first of these is represented as a human king who reigned in Denmark in the far past. He was called Frodi, and both Snorri and Saxo agree that his reign was a time of universal peace and unparalleled prosperity. Snorri states that he lived in Denmark at the time when Freyr ruled in Sweden, and suggests that they both reigned at the time of the peace of the Augustines. Saxo's picture is less clear because in the early books of his Danish history he has several kings called Frodi, and some live anything but peaceful lives. But he certainly knew stories about an early king of that name whose reign was calm and prosperous, and who after death was carried round by his people in a wagon for some time, and then finally laid in a burial mound. He even quotes four lines of a poem said to be inscribed over his grave:

Frodi, whom the Danes would have wished to live long, they bore long through their lands when he was dead. The great chief's body, with this turf heaped above it, bare earth covers under the lucid sky.[1]

This Danish Frodi has obvious resemblances to Freyr in Sweden, since Freyr too brought peace to the land, was carried round in a wagon, and had his death concealed for some time,

1. VI, 172, p. 212 (Elton's translation).

while he was finally buried in a mound. The Old Norse word *fróðr* means 'wise', but also has the meaning 'fruitful', 'luxurious', and so would be a fitting title for a god of fertility. Snorri indeed tells us that one of Freyr's titles was *inn fróði*, 'the fruitful'. It seems reasonable to assume then that Frodi was the Danish god of fertility, the equivalent of Freyr in Sweden.

Another being who had some connexion with Denmark, and who possessed a wagon, was known to the Anglo-Saxons. They called him Ing, and his name occurs in the Old English Runic poem, written down in a tenth-century manuscript:

> Ing at first among the East Danes
> was seen of men. Then he went eastwards
> across the sea. The wagon sped after.
> Thus the Heardings have named the hero.

It is usually agreed that the Heardings were the same as the Hasdingi, the royal dynasty of the Vandals. They may have worshipped Ing while they were in south Sweden, and carried his cult to Denmark and further east when they migrated from Scandinavia and settled in Continental lands. Ing appears to be the name or title of a god. The Anglian kings of Bernicia in north-eastern England remembered Ingui, Ingibrand, and Inguec in their genealogies as names of the founder of their line. Freyr himself bore the titles Yngvi or Ingunar, and the royal dynasty of Sweden was known as the Ynglings. Some of the men who were said to have worshipped Freyr in Iceland bore names like Ingjald and Ingimund. It is possible then that Ing was another of the names by which the god Freyr was known in northern Europe.

Another royal ancestor of the Danes was said to have brought them peace and prosperity, and to have journeyed over the sea. This was Scyld, whose story is told in the opening section of the Old English poem *Beowulf*. Here it is said that a ship laden with treasure came across the sea to Denmark, and brought a child who afterwards became the king of the land. When he came to the end of a long and prosperous reign, he departed over the sea as he had come, for the Danes loaded a ship with weapons and precious things and laid their king's dead body upon it, letting the sea bear it away. The full name of this king is given as Scyld Scefing, and the name Scyldings throughout the poem is used of the Danes.

Another version of this legend seems to have survived in England as late as the twelfth century, and appears in William of Malmesbury's *Gesta Regum*. He gives the child's name as Sceaf, and says that he came over the sea with a sheaf of corn beside him. On the whole this late tradition is thought to be untrustworthy, but Sceaf's name is found earlier. The tenth-century *Chronicle* of Aethelweard says that Sceaf came with a boat full of weapons to the island of Scani, and was made king by the inhabitants. Earlier still his name occurs in a ninth-century genealogy of King Egbert of Wessex, included in the *Anglo-Saxon Chronicle*, with the added comment that he was born in the Ark, presumably an optimistic attempt to reconcile native tradition with Biblical lore. Thus, although the allusions vary and are widely scattered, the idea of a young child coming in a ship over the sea and becoming a king in Denmark seems to have long survived in Anglo-Saxon England.

When William of Malmesbury states that Sceaf came in a boat with a sheaf of corn, this suggests folk tradition of some kind. In the thirteenth-century *Chronicle of Abingdon*, it is recorded that when the monks wished to prove their right to certain meadows beside the Thames, they set a sheaf of corn with a lighted candle beside it on a round shield and floated it down the river, the course taken by the shield proving their claim. Since H. M. Chadwick[1] first drew attention to this passage there has been much argument, first as to whether such a custom ever existed as described, and secondly whether it could have any significant connexion with the stories of Scyld and Sceaf. It is not possible here to go into all the complications involved, but it seems worth noticing the fact that a series of traditions has gone on into medieval times bringing together a divine child, a sheaf of corn, and a vessel moving by supernatural power.

We have also another being among the gods of Asgard whose symbol was the shield, and who had some connexions with the Vanir. The god Ull was known as 'god of the shield', and seems

1. H. M. Chadwick, *The Origin of the English Nation*, Cambridge, 1924, pp. 260 ff.

to have used the shield as a boat, since in skaldic verse a shield is called 'ship of Ull'. Ull at one time must have been a deity of some importance, although there is little about him in the pages of Snorri. In Norway and Sweden his name occurs in place-names in two forms, *Ullr* and *Ullin*. Places called after him are in many cases near those called after Freyr, Freyja, Njord, and Njord's wife Skadi, so that it seems natural to assume that he was associated in some way with the Vanir. There is little trace of his worship in Denmark, but a third-century scabbard found in a Danish bog bears a name in runes which means 'servant of Ull', and its owner may have been a worshipper of the god. Ull's name is related to the Gothic word meaning 'majesty', or 'glory', and because of this it has been thought that he was an early Germanic sky god. Snorri however associated him with the bow and with snow-shoes, and Saxo tells us that he crossed the seas on a magic bone, which suggests skates. Skates and snow-shoes would be fitting for a god of winter, or a deity of the northern lakes and mountains. Ull remains a mysterious and shadowy figure, and serves as a reminder of the many northern deities and cults which had faded into oblivion by the time that Snorri wrote his account of the gods.

A more substantial deity is the father of Freyr and Freyja, the god Njord. He must have been concerned with fertility, but in the literature is mainly remembered as a god of the sea and ships, and will be discussed as such in a later chapter. It must be noted here however that his name is the Old Norse equivalent of Nerthus, the goddess described by Tacitus. Many attempts have been made to find an explanation of the relationship between these two deities. Possibly there was originally a male and female pair of deities, Njord and Nerthus, and Freyr took the place of the earlier god. There are traces of other divine pairs: Ullr/Ullin, and Fjǫrgyn/Fjǫrgynn, of whom we know little beyond the names. An alternative theory is that Nerthus was transformed into the male god Njord, and that Njord's wife Skadi, who like Ull is said to have had snow-shoes and a bow, was originally the male partner. But no completely convincing explanation as to why such a change of sex took place has been found.

Snorri tells us a strange tale of the marriage of Njord and Skadi (see page 30). They could not decide where to live, as

Skadi dwelt in the mountains and Njord by the sea, and each was restless and unhappy in the other's abode. An explanation for this story which has been put forward is that it was based on memories of a joint festival lasting for nine days, when a winter deity linked with the hills was joined with a god of warmth from the more fertile regions by the sea.[1] However, if this was the case, the 'marriage' has left only unhappy memories behind.

This brief survey of male figures in the literature who seem to have some connexion with fertility shows how misleading it is to attempt to simplify the cult of the Vanir. The position is sadly complicated, because we seem to be dealing with vague memories and echoes of past beliefs and customs which have left some mark on the literature. Whereas Freyr seems to have been supreme in Sweden at the close of the heathen period, there are a series of male figures bearing different names, possibly local variants of Freyr, or the ghosts of earlier fertility gods displaced by the powerful Swedish deity. Elaborate theories have been woven round these half-forgotten gods, but we lack firm proof as to the nature of their cults or their relationship with one another.

There are certain basic ideas which are associated with these male deities. First we have that of the royal ancestor, as in the case of Freyr and Frodi, Scyld and Sceaf, the first of a line of kings, coming to reign over the land and bring it fruitfulness and peace. There is also an obstinate tradition of a divine infant, who comes over the waves to save his country. Freyr himself may have been associated with such a story; we have the statement in one of the *Edda* poems that he received his hall, Alfheim, as a 'tooth-gift', that is, a present given to a young child. The male gods are also associated with the sea, over which they come, and by which they sometimes return when their work is over. Freyr, Njord, Sceaf, Scyld, Ing, and Ull are all connected with it in some way. The gods sometimes marry the daughters of giants, like Gerd and Skadi. Finally they are associated with death and funeral rites. The body of the dead king is either placed in a mound or committed to the ocean, and it may be borne round among the people before the final resting-place is chosen for it.

1. J. Bing, 'Ull', *Maal og Minne*, 1916, pp. 107 ff.

The Gods of Peace and Plenty

This idea of death in connexion with the male deity brings in a new problem. In the Near East and the Mediterranean regions, we know that the dying gods of vegetation, Osiris, Tammuz, Adonis, and the rest, played a most important part in the religion of fertility. The god's death typified the coming of winter to the world, and all lamented him; then he emerged again from the darkness of death to give new life and bring rejoicing in the spring. In *The Golden Bough* Frazer fitted Balder, the dying god of Asgard, into this death and resurrection pattern, so he too must be mentioned here, although he will be discussed in greater detail in a later chapter.

In the north there are some traces of a dismembered god whose body, like that of Osiris, was formed anew. The clearest resemblance to the myths of the Near East is apparent in the Finnish *Kalevala*, in the story of Lemminkainen, who was cut to pieces, thrown into a river, and resurrected when his mother found the remains of his body and pieced them together. On a more popular level, there are the legends of John Barleycorn, whose 'passion', the beating, soaking, and crushing of the barley grains for the making of ale, is celebrated in many folk-songs. In Asgard there is a minor figure called *Byggvir* (Barley) who appears in the *Edda* poem *Lokasenna*. Loki mocks at him because he is always chattering in the ear of Freyr, and he has a companion called *Beyla*, whose name Dumézil[1] ingeniously interprets as 'bee', symbolizing the other favourite drink, mead made from honey. Among the early ancestors of some Anglo-Saxon royal families there is a *Beow* or *Beaw*, whom some have taken to be a figure symbolizing barley. We have no real evidence however that he was ever worshipped as a fertility god, or regarded as a dying deity whose body grew with the year's growth and was cut down with the harvest.

Balder, son of Odin, was remembered by Snorri for his beauty and his tragic death. Already in the Viking age the resemblance to Christ had been noticed, and in *Vǫluspá* the ending of the poem seems to imply that Balder represents Christ, coming to reign over a new heaven and earth. Balder in his death was mourned by all the world of nature, and in the same way in the most moving of Old English Christian poems, the *Dream of the*

1. 'Deux petits dieux scandinaves', *La Nouvelle Clio*, 4, 1952, pp. 1 ff.

Rood, all creation is said to weep at the death of Christ, as he hung upon the cross. But while Balder's death is deeply lamented, there is no indication in either Snorri's or Saxo's accounts that he was brought back to life to save the world from want. Nor are we told that the crops failed and famine overtook men when he went down into the world of the dead. Part of the essential pattern is missing, and Balder is not linked in any obvious way with the Vanir, the deities of fertility; he is associated rather with the heroes of Odin. On this subject more will be said later.

It seems probable, however, that Snorri's impressive description of Balder's death and the grief it caused owes something to the memory of a god slain for men's preservation and for the fruitfulness of the earth. It may well be this which gives his account – significantly different from Saxo's – its peculiar power, so that it is one of the best known and most loved of all the northern myths. It is hard to doubt that the story owes something to the cult of the Vanir, even if Balder himself were not a true member of that family. The male god of fertility is bound to die, and his death must be universally lamented, as was that of Balder. In lamenting it, we mourn for our own fate, for 'the blight that man is born for'.

But the death of the god is only part of the pattern. New life and renewal of promise are brought in with the spring, and fulfilment with the harvest, and therefore the mourning must be followed by rejoicing. In some religions, this rebirth of hope was linked with a belief in immortality for men, but this does not seem to have been the case in northern Europe. We have the dead Freyr in his mound, the dead Frodi in his wagon. We have the early kings of the Swedes sent down to death in strange and violent forms. We have the body of Halfdan the Black, an early king of Norway, divided among his people, so that four different districts were each said to hold one portion of his dismembered body. No idea of a resurrection however has come down to us in the form in which we find it in the Osiris legend. Although in one sense Freyr returned to men with his priestess and his wagon every year and Nerthus similarly to the Danes in earlier times, both welcomed with universal rejoicing, there is no clear indication that this was a return from the land of the dead. In the same way, the idea of a triumphal return is wholly lacking in the story of Balder, although Hel had promised that universal lamentation would bring him back. Instead we find that the favourite pattern is that of the new, virile successor replacing the older god, or a divine child ruling men for a season and then departing to leave his work to a successor. In the memories of the old northern religion of fertility which are discernible in the literature, the emphasis appears to be on a series of divine rulers and upon a kind of rebirth rather than resurrection from the dead. It is possible here that we are misled because we are dealing with fragments, and with a confused mass of evidence from different periods, but on the whole this emphasis appears to be a consistent one.

It is the function of the male god of fertility to die for the land and for his people, while the goddess never dies. Her function is to weep over him, perhaps to help bring about his return, or to give birth to the divine child who is to take his place. The world first weeps with her and then rejoices at the renewed promise. This helps to make clear the part played by Frigg when she calls upon all things to weep for Balder, and again by the new sons of the gods who avenge their fathers and rule over a new Asgard when the first is destroyed. But the story of Balder does not fit wholly into the pattern. It may also be noted that Freyr leaves no son to avenge him; his descendants, like those of Frodi and Scyld, are the later kings of the land who follow him one by one into the land of the dead, some possibly by way of a sacrificial death. It remains to attempt to discover what was the part played by the goddesses of the north in the pattern of fertility.

4. The Mother Goddess

The usual pattern in early religions is that in which the goddess Mother Earth appears as the wife of the supreme sky god, since the earth is embraced and made fruitful by the god of the heavens. The image of the Earth Mother, from whom we spring, by whom we are nourished, and into which we return when we die, has remained a fundamental one. Tacitus tells us[1] that the goddess Nerthus, worshipped in Denmark in his day, was

1. *Germania*, 40.

Tellus Mater, Mother Earth, but whether she was in fact regarded by her worshippers as the consort of Tîwaz, the sky god, remains a matter for conjecture.

Indeed any clear proof of the worship of the Earth Mother in heathen Scandinavia is hard to find. The mother of Thor, Fjǫrgynn, is little more than a name for us, although her name is used by poets as a synonym for earth. It exists also in the masculine form, *Fjǫrgyn*, and it may be that here we have one of the pairs of fertility deities mentioned in the last section. The only maternal figure surviving in Snorri's Asgard however is the goddess Frigg, the wife of Odin and mother of Balder. Loki and Saxo accuse her of unfaithfulness to her husband Odin, but her essential function seems to be that of revered wife and mother, the consort of the high god, and queen of heaven. In her earlier Germanic form *Frija*, she gave her name to Friday, the day of Venus, throughout the Germanic world.

One of the few myths surviving about Frija is told by Paul the Deacon, the historian of the Lombards, writing in the eighth century. He took it from a still earlier work, part of which has survived, the *Origo Gentis Langobardum*. In this story Frija caused Wodan her husband to give a new name to the tribe of the Winniles and to grant them victory. She told the tribe to come to Wodan at sunrise, bringing their women with them with their long hair hanging over their faces. Then she turned round Wodan's bed to face the east, so that when he awoke he was no longer facing the Vandals, whom he favoured, but the Winniles. His first words were: 'Who are these Longbeards?' As he had now bestowed a name upon them, Frija told him, he must grant them the victory. The connexion between the goddess and name-giving is interesting, and we shall meet it again. It may be noted that in the prose introduction to *Grímnismál* Odin and Frigg are again supporting rival claimants, this time two brothers called Geirrod and Agnar. Frigg by a trick causes Geirrod to torture Odin when he comes to his hall, so that in the end Agnar receives the kingdom and Geirrod perishes by his own weapon.

In the *Edda* poem *Oddrúnargrátr* Frigg is named together with Freyja as a goddess to be invoked by women in labour. She appears also in the opening chapter of *Vǫlsunga Saga* as concerned with the birth of children. King Rerir and his wife besought the gods for a child, and it was Frigg who heard their request and asked Odin to grant it. In view of this association with the family it is interesting to note that the day of this goddess, Friday, was long considered in Germany to be a lucky one for marriages.

It seems probable that there was some connexion between Frigg and her influence over the begetting of children and a group of supernatural women who were long remembered in north-western Europe for their power to determine the destiny of the new-born child. In the eleventh century Bishop Burchard of Worms had to rebuke women for their continued belief in three women known as the *Parcae*, who could affect a child's future; he stated that it was a common custom to lay three places at table for them.[1] There are stories of such women in Old Norse literature; sometimes they were called the Norns. Saxo (vi, 181) has a tale of Fridleif, a Danish king, who took his three-year-old son Olaf into the house of the gods to pray to 'three maidens sitting on three seats'. The first two granted the boy the gift of charm and generosity, but the third decreed that in spite of this he should be niggardly in the giving of gifts.

Inscriptions are known from Roman times in Germany, Holland, and Britain in honour of groups of female beings, generally known as 'the mothers'. Sometimes alone, but often in groups of two or three, they are shown standing, or seated on chairs or stools, sometimes with loose flowing hair, holding fruit or horns of plenty. They are occasionally accompanied by figures in cloaks and hoods, the *Genii Cucullati*, or 'hooded ones'. Carved stones in their honour were set up from the first century A.D. Many are in the Rhineland, but some are further afield, and a few were erected in northern England on Hadrian's Wall. The names given in the inscriptions emphasize the power of giving which these beings possessed; names or titles such as *Gabiae*, meaning 'richly giving', and variations like *Alagabiae*, *Dea Garmangabis* are found. Female deities of this kind seem to have been worshipped by both the Celts and the Germans, and they were evidently associated with fertility and with the protection

1. Corrector, 153 (*Bussbücher und das kanonische Bussverfahren*, ed. H. J. Schmitz, Düsseldorf, 1898), p. 443.

of hearth and home. In some form they were known to the Anglo-Saxons, for Bede mentions them in *De Temporum Ratione* (13), where he tells us that the night before Christmas was known in heathen times as *Modraniht*, 'the night of the mothers'. There seems little doubt that they were closely connected with the birth of children.

It will be remembered that the fertility goddess Nerthus was said to have had a sanctuary on an island. A possible centre for the tribes Tacitus mentions as her worshippers would be Zealand, the island on which Copenhagen stands, and on which Leire, the seat of the Danish kings in early times, was built. A twelfth-century place-name, Niartharum (later Naerum), supports this. Sjaelland (Zealand) was associated with a goddess in Viking times, for Snorri tells us the story of how it was formed by Gefion, whose sanctuary stood at Leire, and who ploughed round the island and separated it from Sweden (see page 45). She seems to be a Danish goddess connected with the plough and with agriculture, who married Skiold, or Scyld, one of the traditional god-kings who came across the sea bringing peace and prosperity to Denmark (page 104). She shows resemblances to Freyja, one of whose names was Gefn, and the names Gefion and Gefn bear a significant likeness to the names of the Mothers in the Roman period, linking up with their powers of giving. Gefion, like Freyja, had a necklace said to have been given to her by a fair youth in exchange for her favours, and she was thought to have some links with the dead, since Snorri stated that unmarried girls went to her after death.

The memory of a goddess who was open-handed in her gifts to men, associated with the earth, survived in Anglo-Saxon England, and has left traces in an old English charm to make the land fertile. This poetic charm is long and complicated in the form in which it was written down, and has obviously been subjected to Christian editing. The following passage however remains as part of the invocation:

> I stand facing the East; I pray for favour.
> I pray to the Great Lord; I pray to the Mighty Ruler;
> I pray to the Holy Guardian of Heaven.
> I pray to Earth and High Heaven.

At this point incense, fennel, hallowed soap, and salt were directed to be rubbed on to the wood of the plough, and seed (to be obtained from a beggar-man) also placed upon it. The chant then continues :

> Erce, Erce, Erce, Earth Mother,
> may the Almighty Eternal Lord
> grant you fields to increase and flourish,
> fields fruitful and healthy,
> shining harvest of shafts of millet,
> broad harvests of barley . . .
> Hail to thee, Earth, Mother of Men !
> Bring forth now in God's embrace,
> filled with good for the use of men.

Here the symbol of marriage between heaven and earth is an effective poetic image, and one that seems likely to be based on an earlier, half-remembered religious tradition. Attempts have been made to interpret Erce as the name of a forgotten earth goddess, but the word may be no more than a cry of invocation. Thus while there is no direct evidence for rites like those of Nerthus and Freyr in heathen England, there are hints that they were not wholly forgotten. The name Gefion seems to be linked with Old English *geofon*, used in poetry as a name for the sea.

Although the conception of the mother goddess remains a shadowy one, and Frigg in particular is an obscure figure, it is no longer customary to dismiss her as of little importance, and to explain her away as a purely literary creation. As Odin's wife and queen of Asgard, she plays a consistent part in the poetry, and lack of detail about her in the myths and the failure to find places named after her may be due to the fact that she was remembered under other titles. She has become overshadowed in Snorri's pages by the more evocative figure of Freyja, and we must now consider why this is so.

5. *The Goddess Freyja*

When Snorri first introduced Freyja into his account of Asgard, he declared that she was the most renowned of the goddesses, and that she alone of the gods yet lived. This implies that he knew something of her worship continuing into his own day in

Scandinavia, and it is well known that fertility cults die hard, particularly in remote country districts. The impressive list of places called after Freyja, especially in south Sweden and south-west Norway, shows that Snorri's estimate was no idle one. There is no case for assuming her to be a mere invention of the poets.

Freyja was called the goddess or bride of the Vanir, and one of Loki's scandalous assertions was that she had love-dealings with her brother Freyr. Snorri puts the matter differently : he tells us that brother and sister marriages were customary among the Vanir, and that Freyr and Freyja were the children of Njord and his unnamed sister (possibly Nerthus). Freyja was associated with love affairs between men and women, and it was said to be good to call on her for help in such cases. Loki accused her of taking all the gods and elves for lovers, while the giantess Hyndla taunted her with roaming out at night like a she-goat among the bucks. A similar insulting comparison was made by an early Christian poet in Iceland, who coupled her name with Odin, and called her a bitch. However, no stories of unseemly behaviour by Freyja have survived, with the exception of a late account in *Flateyjarbók* of how she won her necklace by sleeping one night in turn with each of the four dwarfs who forged it. There are several cases of giants who wanted to carry her off, but she does not seem to have given them any encouragement. However, the jokes made in *Þrymskviða* about Freyja's eagerness for the bridal night, which, according to Loki, had given her an amazing appetite and burning eyes, fit in with the general picture, and confirm the idea that ritual marriage formed some part of the rites of her cult.

Freyja is not concerned only with human love. She seems to have had some authority in the world of death. In *Egils Saga* the hero's daughter, a young woman called Thorgerda, threatened to commit suicide after her brother was killed, and declared 'I shall take no food until I sup with Freyja'. In *Grímnismál* it is even stated that Freyja receives some of those who die in battle; she has half the slain who fall each day, while half go to Odin. Like Frigg she is pictured as a weeping goddess, and her tears are said to be of gold, a favourite image of the early poets. Why she weeps is not very clear. Snorri says that she searches for her lost husband Od, but gives no details. One would expect that this is a memory of the goddess seeking for the slain god of fertility, discussed earlier.

According to Snorri, Freyja had many names. *Gefn*, as we saw, expresses her character as a giver, and links her with the Danish Gefion. Another name, *Mardǫll*, suggests a connexion with the sea (*marr*). Syr, 'sow', reminds us that the boar symbol belonged to her as well as to Freyr. *Hǫrn* is another of her names which occurs in place-names in east Sweden, and may be connected with *hǫrr*, 'flax', indicating a special local variant of the cult of the vegetation goddess. Another possible name used in poetry is *Skiálf*, a name of an early queen of Sweden, married to King Agni, who had a boar-helmet and was presumably a worshipper of the Vanir. Skialf is said to have killed him with the aid of a necklace, and this story is one of those which have been thought to imply a tradition of sacrificial death among the early kings of Sweden.

A necklace is the ornament connected with Freyja, if we are right in assuming that her most cherished possession, the Brísingamen, was worn round the neck. It has been suggested that it was a girdle, and again that it was a piece of amber, but the word *men* is in general used of a woman's ornament worn at the neck, and what we hear about it in the later sources fits in with this interpretation. There appears to be some connexion also with a treasure called the *Brosingamene* mentioned in the Old English *Beowulf*, which is assumed to have been a kind of necklace or collar. The meaning of the name has not been explained, and we do not know whether it was based on a family or tribal name, 'the necklace of the Brisings', or whether the reference is to the brightness of the ornament, from a rare form *brísingr*, 'fire'. A necklace is something which is associated with the mother goddess from very early times. Figurines wearing necklaces found in the Mediterranean area date back as far as 3000 B.C., and small female figures wearing them have survived from the Bronze Age in Denmark and are thought to represent a fertility deity.[1]

1. Students of Freud will recognize the significance of a necklace for a fertility goddess (cf. the ring in Rabelais). It illustrates the familiar tendency to represent the sexual parts of the body by others higher up, and by ornaments worn on these.

We are told also that Freyja possessed a 'feather' or 'falcon' shape. This is mentioned several times in the myths, and is once attributed to Frigg also. Although in Snorri and in *Þrymskviða* it is represented as a kind of flying costume which Loki borrows, there can be little doubt that the original conception was a serious one: Freyja was believed to take on the form of a bird and to travel over vast distances, as Odin and Loki were also able to do.

Freyja's name is specifically linked by Snorri with a special kind of witchcraft known as *seiðr*, for he states that she was a priestess of the Vanir who first taught this knowledge to the Aesir. We know a good deal about *seiðr* from prose sources, and it forms an interesting clue to the nature of her cult. The essentials for performing it were the erection of a platform or lofty seat on which the leading practitioner sat, the singing of spells, and the falling into a state of ecstasy by this leader, who is generally a woman, and is called a *vǫlva*. Sometimes the *vǫlva* was supported by a large company, who acted as a choir and provided the music. At the close of the ceremony, the worker of *seiðr* was able to answer questions put to her by those present, and it is implied that she received her information while she was in a state of trance. The accounts show that questions put to her were concerned for the most part with the coming season and the hope of plenty, and with the destinies of young men and women in the audience. Sometimes the term *seiðr* is used to refer to harmful magic, directed against a victim, but in the majority of accounts it appears to be a divination rite. The term *vǫlva* is found in the poetry and sagas to denote someone with special mantic gifts, a seeress or soothsayer.

We are told more than once that seeresses of this kind used to travel about the land to visit the farms and be present at feasts, and that they would give replies to those who inquired of them. The best-known account of the visit of such a woman to a farm is given in *Eiríks Saga Rauða* (4), and is said to have taken place in the Icelandic settlement in Greenland. It has been questioned whether such practices did in fact take place in Greenland at so late a date, but the account of the costume, equipment, and behaviour of the *vǫlva* has in any case aroused great interest, because it offers so detailed and remarkable a parallel to that of *shamans* and *shamankas* of recent times who have been observed and described by travellers and anthropologists in north-eastern Europe and Asia.[1] This resemblance helps us to understand better the nature of these ceremonies, while it also strengthens the case for the reliability of saga evidence for rites and customs.

As practised in northern Europe and Asia, shamanism is the practice of divination by a professional class of highly trained seers, both men and women. The shaman acts as intermediary between the world of men and the gods, and has the power to descend into the realms of the dead. His spirit is believed to journey forth from his body, which remains in a state of trance. Sometimes the long journey which it takes is described by him in a chant. Sometimes he induces the condition of ecstasy by beating his drum or by an elaborate and exciting dance. His actions and his costume symbolize the inner meaning of the ceremonies in which he takes part. The costume is usually made of animal skins, birds' feathers, and metal likenesses of creatures of the animal world, and sometimes is modelled on some particular creature, such as a bear or a bird. While in his trance, the shaman is believed to be helped or hindered by animal spirits, and may imitate the voices of these creatures with great effect. Sometimes his ascent of the heavens is symbolized by the climbing of a ladder or a tree, and sometimes he is said to ride up to the sky on the back of a goose. The purpose of the ceremony is usually to find the answer to some question of importance for the community, such as the reason for a dearth of food, or an epidemic. Alternatively it may be to heal some sick person, in which case it may be necessary for the shaman's spirit to pursue the soul of the sick man down into the underworld and to overcome by his superior powers the hostile spirits trying to prevent it from returning to the body. The shaman may also reply to individual questions put to him by members of the audience.

We are told in the account of *Eiríks Saga* that the *vǫlva* wore a costume of animal skins, including boots of calfskin and gloves of catskin, and also that a sacrificial meal was prepared for her from the hearts of all living creatures obtainable. She sat

1. The fullest recent study of shamanism is Mircea Eliade, *Le Chamanisme et les techniques archaïques de l'extase*, Paris, 1951.

on a kind of platform high above the audience, upon a cushion stuffed with hen's feathers. She asked that someone should be found to sing the spell necessary for the ceremony, and after some search a young Christian woman admitted that she learned it when a child, and was persuaded to sing it. The *vǫlva* told her afterwards that her singing was so successful that many spirits thronged to hear, and thus she learned from them the hidden things which men wished to know. After the main ceremony was over, she replied to the most important question, which was whether the famine afflicting the community would soon end. She also predicted the destiny of the girl who sang the spell, and told her what her fortunes in marriage would be. Finally men and women went up to put individual queries to her, and received wise answers; in fact 'little that she said went unfulfilled'.

In this account, and in a number of less detailed ones scattered through the sagas, there is much in common with accounts of shamanistic ceremonies described by modern anthropologists. The journey of the shaman's spirit may not be a feature mentioned in the saga narratives, but on the other hand it seems to be implied in the poems. Some poems, like *Vǫluspá* (literally, 'Soothsaying of the *Vǫlva*') are presented as the utterances of a seeress, revealing what is hidden from men. There are also a number of descriptions of supernatural journeyings through terrible cold and darkness and barriers of fire into the 'other world', and these are in accordance with the fearful experiences of the shaman's spirit described elsewhere. It seems established that some form of shamanistic practice was so widespread in the heathen north as to have left a considerable impact on the literature.[1]

All this is relevant to a study of the cult of Freyja. As we have seen, she is said to have been an expert on *seiðr*, and to have introduced it. She could take on bird-form, which meant that she could journey far in some shape other than human. As goddess of the Vanir, the prosperity of the community and marriages of young people were within her province, and these were precisely the subjects on which the *vǫlva* used to be consulted. The *vǫlva* too was accustomed to journey round the countryside

1. See for instance Dag Strömbäck, *Sejd*, Lund, 1935.

and be present at feasts just as Freyja's brother, Freyr, was said to do. Like Freyr, such women were asked to foretell the coming season. We are told of one *vǫlva* in *Landnámabók* who is even said to have worked *seiðr* so that a sound should fill with fish, which means that she took an active part in the bringing of plenty to the land. The seeresses also appear to have foretold the destiny of children. In the story of *Norna-Gest*, included in *Flateyjarbók*, there is a reference to this:

> At that time wise women used to go about the land. They were called 'spae-wives' and they foretold people's futures. For this reason folk used to invite them to their houses and give them hospitality, and bestow gifts on them at parting.   *Flatéyjarbók*, 1, 346

The women in this story were seated when they made their prophecies, since when the people crowded round them, one of them was pushed off her seat, and was very angry. Here then we have memories of a custom which offers us a link with the Mothers and the *Parcae* mentioned earlier. The *vǫlva* in Greenland who was described in such detail was said to be the last survivor of a company of nine women, and the sagas elsewhere represent the seeresses as going about in groups. Possibly at an earlier time than that represented in the sagas, isolated seeresses were less common, and women were not left to conduct ceremonies alone until the organization had broken down owing to the weakening of the old traditions. Such is the state of affairs implied in the story of the Greenland ceremony.

The use of animal fur in the costume of the *vǫlva* links up with the statement made by Snorri that Freyja travelled in a carriage drawn by cats. The link between cats and the goddess has not been satisfactorily explained, but the gloves made of cat-skin, white and furry inside, mentioned in the Greenland account, suggests that cats were among the animal spirits which would aid the *vǫlva* on her supernatural journey. We may note further that in a consultation of a *vǫlva* described in *Vatnsdœla Saga*, she prophesies to a young man in the audience in the name of Freyr, and tells Ingimund that it is the god's will that he go to Iceland. Thus at least in the mind of the saga-teller there was some kind of link between such practices and the cult of the Vanir.

When we find hints that at one time *seiðr* was also practised by men, we may remember the traditional ceremonies, said to be of a shameful nature, associated with Freyr. One of Harald Fairhair's sons, called Ragnvald, was said to have worked *seiðr* with a company of eighty followers. His descendant Eyvind also did *seiðr*, but it is clear that there was great hostility against these two men, and both were killed in the end by members of their own family, and are condemned in Snorri's *Heimskringla* for their wickedness. Such practices in early heathen times seem to be associated then with both the male and female deities of the Vanir. The connexion between women and divination however seems to have been established early among the Germans. Tacitus in his *Histories* (IV, 61) refers to a young woman called Veleda among the Bructeri, who was a seeress secluded in a tower, from which she gave answer to inquirers by means of a relative, who interpreted her replies. He has an interesting comment on this. It was the custom, he says, of the Germans to regard women as endowed with the gift of prophecy, and 'even as goddesses'.

What we know of the practice of *seiðr* may throw some light on the divination associated with the deity in the wagon. The seeresses who travelled alone or in companies and went round to farms in Norway and Iceland may have been the final representatives of the fertility goddess in the north, the deity who, according to Snorri, survived last of all the gods. Here too we may see a link with the widespread cult of the Mothers in earlier times, the appeal to female deities whose blessing on new-born children ensured their happiness in life. We have evidence here for rites in which women were able to participate fully, both as celebrants and as audience, rites bound up with the fertility of the land and also with the rearing of a family and the giving of young girls in marriage. Frigg and Freya appear to be concerned in some way with such rites; both at times appear as the beneficent goddess helping women and girls at the times of marriage and child-birth as well as shaping the destiny of children.

There is little doubt that there was a darker side to *seiðr* and all that it represented. It could include harmful magic, dealing out death to its victims, and this aspect of it in the sagas is more than once found in conjunction with the horse-cult, which we know to be connected with the Vanir. One of the early kings of Sweden was said to have been crushed to death by a *seiðkona* who took on the form of a horse. According to *Landnámabók*, a woman skilled in witchcraft was brought to trial in Iceland for 'riding' a man to death in a similar way. The story is expanded in *Eyrbyggja Saga*, where the picture of the witch is an evil and menacing one. Memories of this evil cult lived on for many years. An English chronicle of the twelfth century states that the wife of King Edgar was accused of witchcraft, and that she was accustomed to take on the form of a horse by her magic arts, and was seen by a bishop 'running and leaping hither and thither with horses and showing herself shamelessly to them'.[1] This may be unreliable evidence for the character of a historic queen, but it is significant that an accusation of witchcraft should be expressed in this particular form. It recalls the accusation against Freyja herself, that she strayed out at night like a she-goat among the bucks. Hints such as this build up a vague but unpleasant picture of the malignant powers and repulsive practices of some women connected with the cult of the Vanir, and they may help to explain the strong prejudice against eating horse-flesh which has survived in this country.[2]

The goddess of the Vanir seems to have flourished under different names in various parts of Scandinavia. In the north we have the arresting but confused set of traditions concerning Thorgerda *Hǫlgabrúðr*, who was worshipped with passionate devotion by Jarl Hakon of Halogaland, and was known as his wife. She appears to be linked with the Vanir, and her image stood in some temples. King Olaf in *Flateyjarbók* is said to have dragged her out along with Freyr, and to have insulted her by pulling her along at the tail of his horse. In Saxo she is said to be one of the 'wives of the kinsfolk' of Freyr, and to have been put into a brothel along with her companions. Thorgerda in the later sagas is represented as consorting with trolls and evil creatures of all kinds, and there is no doubt of the hostility with

---

1. *Historia Eliensis*, 11, 56. See C. E. Wright, *The Cultivation of Saga in Anglo-Saxon England*, 1936, pp. 158–9.

2. The story of Vǫlsi in *Flateyjarbók* (11, 331) where a housewife's 'god' is the generative organ of a horse, fits in with this general picture. See F. Ström, *Diser, Nornor, Valkyrjor*, 1954, pp. 22 ff.

which she was regarded, and of the sinister light which played round her cult for the story-tellers of a Christian age.[1]

Frigg, as we saw, has been left almost wholly free from such aspersions, and yet there is little doubt that Frigg and Freyja are closely connected. As the weeping mother, the goddess associated with child-birth and linked with the benevolent Mothers, Frigg appears to have her roots in the Vanir cult. The two main goddesses of Asgard indeed suggest two aspects of the same divinity, and this is paralleled by the two-fold aspect of the fertility goddess in the Near East, appearing as mother and as lover. Sometimes both roles may be combined in the person of one goddess, but it is more usual for the different aspects to be personified under different names. It is even possible to recognize a triad of goddesses, such as Asherah, Astarte, and Anat of Syria, or Hera, Aphrodite, and Artemis of Greece. Here the three main aspects of womanhood appear side by side as wife and mother, lover and mistress, chaste and beautiful virgin. Frigg and Freyja in northern mythology could figure as the first two of such a trio, while the dim figure of Skadi the huntress might once have occupied the vacant place.

Even in the late sources which are all that remain, it is easy to discern two distinct sides of the cult of the goddess of the Vanir. One was connected with marriage, the family, and the birth of children. This appears to have been eminently respectable, and the visits of the seeresses to families and groups of neighbours in Scandinavia would seem to have been its latest manifestation. Side by side with these reputable practices – which the story-tellers do not shrink from recording – there were others which Saxo and other Christian writers refer to with horror and loathing, and condemn in terms which single them out from other heathen rites. These have only been preserved in hints and garbled accounts, and the hostility felt towards them does not seem to be wholly due to Christian prejudices. The ambivalent nature of the fertility goddess is something familiar to us from what we know of Cybele and Isis in the Roman world, as well as the rich pageant of the Near Eastern divinities,

1. N. K. Chadwick, 'Þorgerðr Hǫlgabrúðr and the Trolla Þing', in *Early Cultures of North-Western Europe* (H. M. Chadwick Memorial Studies), 1950, pp. 397 ff.

and it may help us to understand more of the nature of Frigg and Freyja in Asgard.

6. *The Power of the Vanir*

The deities known as the Vanir are not easy to define in the northern myths, because of the many divine or semi-divine figures who emerge at different points, and whose relationships to one another are complex in the extreme. Yet in some ways they form a clear-cut and convincing group, because we can see the main characteristics of fertility gods and goddesses from other civilizations and other regions of the world repeated once again in the figures of Freyr and Freyja and their following. The fertility pattern is a definite one, easy to recognize, and the northern myths which have to do with the Vanir fall into the accustomed forms.

Snorri saw the Aesir and the Vanir as two powerful companies of gods, able to wage war against one another; yet the only names of male deities of the Vanir which are given in his account are Njord and Freyr, who were given as hostages to the Aesir when the war was over. Who were the rest of the company of the fighting Vanir? The most likely answer seems to be the vast assembly of gods of fertility from many different localities, of which a few names like Ing, Scyld, and Frodi have come down to us, while many more are utterly forgotten. Freyr, the fertility god of the Swedes in the eleventh century, and chief deity after Thor in Uppsala when Adam of Bremen was writing, has become the prototype of the male god of fertility in the literature, but behind him there must have been a vast host representing the givers of peace and plenty to many tribes and families throughout the northern world. Freyr's name is really a title, meaning 'lord', while Freyja meant 'lady'. Perhaps in the lord and lady of the May Day festivities we are seeing their final manifestation, a last glimpse of the fertility powers, humbled from their once high estate. Similarly, Frodi's name is an adjective, describing him as 'the fruitful one', and the list of kings called Frodi in Saxo implies that it was a title which many men bore in turn. The male god must not only have appeared in many different localities, but also have been represented by many different men, priests or priest-kings, who impersonated him; although he was also depicted in temples and appeared in the myths in his own right as the great god of the Vanir, the God of the World, giver of peace and plenty.

In some way the deities of the Vanir are the closest of all the heathen deities to mankind. We have the line of kings, taking it in turn to rule the land and acting as the givers of prosperity if the Vanir favoured them and abode with them. We have the seeresses, a link between men and the Vanir, some-times possibly appearing in the very guise of Frigg and Freyja, coming right into men's homes as the Mothers, or the *Parcae* or the Givers, to convey the blessings of the goddesses. The Vanir were amoral, in the sense that their province was not to distin-guish between good and evil, to bring men the ideals of justice, or to teach them loyalty to one another. They were there to give men the power that created new life and brought increase into the fields, among the animals, and in the home. They brought also the power to link men with the unseen world. Beside the fruits of the earth and the baby in the cradle, their gifts to men included the wise counsels granted through divination, when the god spoke through a human mouth. They offered also the collective excitement of the ceremonies when the god revealed his power to men and women gathering to worship him and the goddesses.

The gift of life brought by the Vanir was a mysterious and impalpable one, but it was essential to men. Without it, good fortune and victory and prudent rule were worthless and empty things, for if the crops failed and children died or there was no quickening in the womb, the community was doomed and with-out hope. Every pagan settlement has thus paid some service to the fertility powers, who possessed the ultimate say as to its future, and the people of the north were no exception. If the grudging soil of the northern lands and the bitter winters and long nights prevented the glorification of the Vanir which might have come with a warmer, more fertile setting, the gift of life which they offered was the more precious because of the precar-ious conditions in the world that waited to receive it.

To get into touch with these life-giving deities might neces-sitate strange, even revolting ceremonies. Orgies have always formed part of the fertility cults, and the reason is given by Eliade:[1]

The awakening of an orgy may be compared with the appearance of the green shoots in the field; a new life is beginning, and the orgy has filled men with substance and with energy for that life. And further, by bringing back the mythical chaos that existed before the creation, the orgy makes it possible for creation to be repeated.

Thus the religion of the Vanir was bound to include orgies, ecstasies, and sacrificial rites. In these, and in the turning to the earth and the dead, whose blessing would help to bring the harvest, it can be seen that the Vanir were the rivals of Odin, god of ecstasy and of the dead. It is hardly surprising that the idea of rivalry between the two cults is sometimes implied in the myths, and is symbolized by the tradition of a war between the Aesir and the Vanir. The Vanir also protected men in battle, and they were the gods of royal houses, worshipped for a long period by the Swedish kings who wore the boar image, and who were believed to be informed for a while by the spirit of the Vanir who possessed them. There seem to have been many who worshipped them with fervour and devotion, finding their cult nearer, more rewarding and comforting than that of the sky god or the wilful god of war. The friendship of the Vanir had none of the treacherous, sliding quality of Odin's favours, and it extended, like his, beyond the grave.

The worshippers of the Vanir were very conscious of the earth, and remembered and venerated the dead ancestors who rested within it. The distant kingdom of the sky was not their concern, although behind the legends of the peace kings the idea of a departure to a land beyond the sea is held out as a promise to men. Indeed there was always a close link between the Vanir and the depths of the earth and sea. The chthonic element is present in their worship, and is emphasized in the myths. The Vanir male gods looked for brides among the giantesses, and Freyr himself looked down into the underworld to find the radiant maiden Gerd to whom he gave his love. The spirits of land and sea are ranged behind the Vanir, and it was they who assisted the seeress in her journeys to the 'other world' and helped her to win hidden knowledge. Behind the goddesses of

1. *Patterns in Comparative Religion*, London, 1958, p. 359.

the Vanir is the conception of the Earth Mother, the Great Goddess who gives shelter to us all. Of the significant part played by the Vanir in myths concerning the realm of the sea and the kingdom of the dead, there will be more to say in the two following chapters.

Chapter 5

The Gods of the Sea

Has thou entered into the springs of the sea?
Or hast thou walked in the recesses of the deep?
Have the gates of death been revealed unto thee,
Or hast thou seen the gates of the shadow of death?

Job, XXXVI

The sea was of such great importance for the peoples of north-western Europe, that it was bound to play a major part in their myths. Many of the old stories have the sea as the background against which the deities play their parts, as in the tales of the ploughing of Gefion, Thor's fishing, the funeral of Balder. The gods are as much at home in the realm of ocean as in the forests and mountains. The men of the north called upon the powers they worshipped for help on their frequent and perilous voyages, and, since the sea was the source of food as well as the chief road for trade, the gods who gave plenty held sway there as well as over the fertile earth. It is worth while to consider briefly the part played by the sea in their mythology and conceptions of the gods.

1. *Aegir and Ran*

The god who appears in Snorri and the poems to be the ruler of the sea is Aegir. He seems to be a personification of the ocean and its mighty strength for good or evil towards men. His name is related to the word for water, and he has much in common with the Greek god Poseidon. The Vikings called the River Eider 'Aegir's Door', while in their poetry the 'jaws of Aegir' devoured ships lost at sea. The ocean has inevitably figured as the greedy destroyer in the poetry of sea-going folk. 'The sea has snapped the ties of my kindred', says Egill in his great poem of mourning, the *Sonatorrek*, composed after his young son was lost at sea. 'Could I have avenged my cause with the sword, the Ale-Brewer would be no more.' It was perhaps to a god of this kind, relentlessly demanding victims, that Saxon pirates in the fifth century were accustomed to sacrifice a tenth of the captives they had taken before sailing for home, choosing their victims by lot. This is referred to as common knowledge in a letter of Sidonius, who describes the expert seamanship of the Saxons: they had no fear of shipwreck, he says, and rejoiced in storms because they gave them the chance to take their foes by surprise. He continues:

Moreover when the Saxons are setting sail from the continent and are about to drag their firm-holding anchors from an enemy shore, it is their usage thus homeward bound to abandon every tenth captive to the slow agony of a watery end, casting lots with perfect equity among the doomed crowd in execution of this iniquitous sentence of death. This custom is all the more deplorable in that it is prompted by honest superstition. These men are bound by vows which have to be paid in victims, they conceive it a religious act to perpetrate their horrible slaughter. This polluting sacrilege is in their eyes an absolving sacrifice.   *Letters*, VIII, 6 (Dalton's translation)

An Old English poetic name for the sea, *garsecg*, means literally 'spear-man', and suggests the image of a fierce warrior, recalling Poseidon with his trident. The weapon of the Norse couple, Aegir and Ran, seems to have been a net, with which Ran would entrap seafarers. A folk-belief quoted in one of the Icelandic sagas is that when people were drowned they were thought to have gone to Ran, and if they appeared at their own funeral feasts, it was a sign that she had given them a good welcome. In a late saga, *Friðjófs Saga*, it is said to have been a lucky thing to have gold on one's person if lost at sea. The hero went so far as to distribute small pieces of gold among his men when they were caught in a storm, so that they should not go empty-handed into Ran's hall if they were drowned. The idea of the hospitality of Aegir and Ran, who were so anxious to throng their underwater realm with the hosts of the dead, may be compared with that of the god of battle. It is by no means inconsistent with their power to destroy.

When however Egill refers to Aegir as the Ale-Brewer, and

the poems make reference more than once to the gods gathering for a banquet in the halls of Aegir, we may discern a different aspect of the god of the sea. In Celtic mythology, cauldrons of plenty are sometimes represented as coming from the land-be-neath-the-waves. The banquet at which Loki made his scandal-ous attacks on gods and goddesses in *Lokasenna* was in Aegir's hall, and it was to obtain a suitable cauldron for the mead at another of Aegir's feasts that Thor went down to the sea to visit Hymir. Snorri in *Skáldskarmál* identifies Aegir with Gymir and Hlér who lived on Hlésey. Gymir, it may be noticed, is the name of the monstrous and terrible giant of the underworld, the father of the beautiful Gerd wooed by Freyr. Hymir, who seems to be a sea-giant, has also a link with the gods, for he is said in *Hymis-kviða* to be the father of Tyr.

Aegir's place indeed should perhaps be among the giants rather than the gods. He is said to have had nine daughters, and it is generally assumed that these are the waves of the sea. They are called by names such as *Gjǫlp*, 'howler', and *Greip*, 'gras-per'. These however are typical giantess names as well, and nine giantesses are said to have been the mothers of the god Heimdall, the most puzzling of the dwellers in Asgard. Certain passages in the poems seem to imply that Heimdall was born of the sea, and that these nine daughters of Aesir were his foster-mothers. We seem to have a link here with Celtic traditions. Jean Young has pointed out that there is a story in an Irish saga of nine giant maidens of the sea who mothered a boy between them.[1] In the tale of Ruad, son of Rigdonn, Ruad was crossing the sea to Norway with three ships, when the vessels ceased to move. He dived down to find out the reason, and discovered nine giant women, three hanging on to each ship. They seized him, and carried him down into the sea. There he spent a night with each in turn, and then was allowed to continue his journey. They told him that one of them would bear him a child, and he promised to come back to them after he left Norway. But after a stay of seven years he broke his promise, and went straight back to Ireland. The nine women discovered this, took the child 'that had been born among them', and set off in pursuit, and when they could not over-

1. *Arkiv für Nordisk Filologi*, 49, 1933, pp. 97 ff.

take Ruad they cut off the child's head and flung it after his father.

A giantess of a similar kind is found in medieval German tradition, and is called *Vrou Wachilt*. She is represented as the mother of the giant Wade, and grandmother of Weland the Smith. The story of the birth of Wade is told in a thirteenth-century saga, *Þiðriks Saga*, composed in Norway but containing much German material. A woman stopped King Vilcinus in a forest, and later appeared out of the sea, holding on to his ship in the same way as the giantesses in the Irish story, and she told him she was going to bear him a child. He took her home with him, but after Wade was born she disappeared. She must be the same woman who comes into a medieval German poem, *Rabenschlacht*. This tells how Wade's grandson, Widia (or Wittich) was fleeing for his life when a 'sea-woman', said to be his ancestress Wachilt, came out of the sea, seized him and his horse, and bore him down to the sea-bottom to save him from his pursuers. Schneider[1] accepted this genealogy of Wachilt, Wade, Weland, Widia as early Germanic tradition. Chambers, reviewing scattered references to Wade,[2] came to the conclusion that he was originally a sea-giant from somewhere in the Baltic region, whose exploits were remembered in Britain because the early settlers knew tales about him. In England his name came to be linked with stone ruins and Roman roads, but in Denmark his connexion with the sea was remembered. An attractive story about him in *Þiðriks Saga* is how he carried his little son Weland on his shoulder as he waded over the deep Groenasund.[3]

These sea-women and their progeny remind us that there was a close link between the giant people of the sea deeps and those who dwelt in the depths of the earth and in caves of the mountains. Poseidon, the Greek god of the sea, to whom Aegir has been compared, was also known as the Earth-Shaker, and had power over the earthquake as well as the storm. The cauldrons associated with Aegir's hall and the giantesses related to him

1. H. Schneider, *Germanische Heldensage*, Berlin, 1928, vol. 1, p. 369.

2. R. W. Chambers, *Widsith*, Cambridge, 1912, p. 95.

3. For this giant family, see 'Weland the Smith', *Folklore*, 69, 1958, pp. 145 ff.

offer us points of contact with Celtic myth, and it is indeed in the lore of the sea that connexions between Norse and Celtic tradition are most clearly perceived. This is not surprising when we remember how it was in their voyaging over the western ocean that the two people came into contact with one another.

2. *Njord, God of Ships*

The god Njord, father of Freyr and Freyja, had close associations with the sea. His dwelling is said in an *Edda* poem to be *Noatún*, 'enclosure of ships', and Snorri tells us that he controlled the winds and the sea, and brought wealth to those whom he helped in fishing and seafaring. Place-names called after him suggest that he was worshipped along the west coast of Norway. Other inland places called after him have an obvious connexion with water, for they are usually at the heads of fiords, by lakes or rivers, or on islands in lakes. Some of the names (those ending in *-ey* for instance) indicate cult centres on islands, like that of the goddess Nerthus in Tacitus's account. The island now called *Tysnesøen* in Norway formerly bore the name *Njarðarlǫg*, 'bath of Njord'. This is of special interest, suggesting that this island in a lake was once sacred to Njord together with the water surrounding it.[1] We are told of Nerthus that her wagon was bathed every year in a sacred lake, and then kept on her island till the time came for it to be used again.

The connexion of ships with the Vanir has already been noted (see page 100). Freyr possessed a ship *Skiðblaðnir*, while other male figures who seem to be linked with Freyr came in a ship across the sea to rule over men, and returned again by ship when their period of earthly rule was over. There is no doubt, moreover, that the symbol of the ship was an important one in the north from the earliest times of which we have archaeological record. In the early rock carvings of the Bronze Age in Scandinavia, horse and ship are often found side by side, and sometimes the sun-wheel is placed with them, a suggestion that these symbols were already linked with the powers governing fertility. Model ships were given as offerings, and at one early

---

1. Another interpretation is 'law-district of Njord'. See J. de Vries, *Altgermanische Religionsgeschichte*, II, p. 470, for discussion of this.

site at Nors in Denmark a hundred small boats, each with a symbol depicted on its side, were packed inside one another and deposited in a clay jar. In the Iron Age it was possible for a real ship to be offered in sacrifice to some power. Such a sacrifice was found in a peat bog at Hjortspring in Denmark, with skeletons of horses and dogs under the large vessel which had been abandoned there.

By the early Iron Age, the ship was also in use as a funeral symbol. Graves in Gotland and elsewhere were carefully made in the shape of a boat, the outline marked out in stones around the burned or buried remains of the dead. By about A.D. 600, the dead were buried or burned inside real boats, or parts of boats. Sometimes in peaty soil the wood of the boats has survived, and in other cases rows of clinch-nails mark the lines of the planks, or these are found among the ashes of cremation burials. As far as our knowledge goes, this custom seems to have begun in Sweden, and spread to Norway and Anglo-Saxon England.[1]

In England it was followed by the heathen kings of East Anglia. In the seventh century, when the kingdom had already been converted to Christianity, but was either suffering a relapse or clinging obstinately to old funeral customs, a ship was buried in the royal cemetery at Sutton Hoo. It was a sea-going vessel, eighty feet long, and it was hauled overland for about half a mile, on to the sandy stretch of heathland above the Deben estuary where burial mounds stood. There it was lowered into the trench prepared for it, and within a gabled burial chamber erected on the deck a king's treasures were laid. There was much rich jewellery, a royal sceptre, a standard, a great ceremonial shield and helmet, a gold-adorned sword, harp, and playing pieces, silver bowls, cups, and drinking horns from the banqueting hall. In this tomb no body was laid, perhaps because the king was lost in battle or at sea, or perhaps because he was given Christian burial while his treasures were laid in the earth according to earlier custom.[2]

1. H. R. Ellis, *The Road to Hel*, Cambridge, 1943, pp. 16 ff. See also C. Green, *Sutton Hoo*, London, 1963, p. 99.

2. R. L. S. Bruce-Mitford, 'The Sutton Hoo Ship-Burial', *Proc. Suffolk Inst. of Archaeology* (Ipswich), 25, 1949, pp. 1 ff.; also Green, op. cit.

The Gods of the Sea

Somewhat later, probably in the ninth century, another richly equipped ship was buried in a great mound at Öseburg in Norway. The grave was entered and robbed, but a series of exquisitely carved wooden objects was recovered and restored, sufficient to show that a rich and elaborate funeral had taken place there. The remains found in the ship were those of a woman. Here, and at two other famous Norwegian ship-burials at Gokstad and Tune, a number of horses and dogs had been slain at the graveside.[1] A series of ship-burials was also discovered in Sweden, at two rich cemeteries at Vendel and Valsgärde. They were not common in Denmark, but one, at Ladby, was on an impressive scale, and bones of horses and dogs show that this too was accompanied by animal sacrifice.

These were the great ship-funerals for people of importance in the community, but many humble folk were also laid to rest in small boats in different parts of Scandinavia, and in places where the Vikings settled. In the early days of the twentieth century Shetelig was able to number the known ship-graves in four figures,[2] and many more have been discovered and excavated since then. Only very recently have we discovered that the ship symbolism must have been important for many of the heathen Angles in eastern England. Apart from the rich Sutton Hoo grave of the seventh century, other ship-graves of earlier date were found in the same cemetery, and another large ship in a burial mound at Snape, further down the coast, unfortunately never properly excavated.[3] Recent excavation in an early Anglian cemetery at Caister-on-Sea, Norfolk, revealed the fact that several graves held bodies covered by part of a boat, recognizable from the clinch-nails still in position. Even in a child's grave, two small pieces of a wooden boat had been raised to form an arch over the body.[4] Association of ships with the dead is further borne out by the careful outline of a ship cut on a cremation urn preserved in Norwich Museum.

1. J. Brønsted, *The Vikings*, Penguin Books, 1964, pp. 139 ff.
2. *Viking Club Saga Book*, IV, 1906, pp. 326 ff.
3. R. L. S. Bruce-Mitford, *Proc. Suffolk Inst. of Archaeology*, 26, 1955, pp. 1 ff.
4. I am grateful for information about this excavation received from Mr Charles Green before the publication of his book cited above. For the Caister ship-graves see Green, op. cit., p. 57.

Clearly then the ship meant something significant to the heathen north, and it was something which was connected with the dead. We have no exact clue from the myths as to what exactly it meant to men's minds, but such indications as we do possess point to association of the ship with the worship of the Vanir. Ship-burial was associated with King Frodi by Saxo. Among the laws attributed to him was one to the effect that every chief should be burned in his own ship if killed in battle, and lesser men in groups of ten to one ship. Frodi, as we have seen, seems to be the Danish equivalent of Freyr. There are not many references to ship-burial in the Icelandic sagas, but two of these are specifically connected with so-called priests of Freyr. Ingimund in *Vatnsdœla Saga* was buried in a ship's boat, and the priest of Freyr in *Gísla Saga*, Thorgrim, was laid in his ship inside a mound. Before they closed the mound Gisli, who was responsible for his foster-brother's death, flung a huge stone down on to the ship, and this offers an interesting parallel to the Oseberg ship-burial, where a great stone was found lying on top of the vessel. It has been suggested that the woman buried at Oseberg may have been a priestess of the Vanir, and it has already been noted (p. 95) that an elaborate little wagon was buried with her.

The most impressive account of a ship-funeral in the early literature comes from Old English poetry, and has taken on new significance now that we know that ship-funeral was a traditional form of burial in East Anglia in heathen times. This is the account in *Beowulf* of the funeral voyage of Scyld, the first king of the Danes, whom we have seen to have certain connexions with the gods of fertility. This account is earlier in date than any of the literary references to ship-funeral from Scandinavia, since it was written down about A.D. 1000, and could have been composed some time considerably earlier than this. The poet tells how the old king was equipped for his journey over the sea:

Never have I heard of a ship more splendidly equipped with swords and mailcoats, the weapons of war and the raiment of battle. In her hold lay a wealth of treasures, which were to journey with him into the realm of ocean. Gifts were prepared for him, and a nation's treasures, whose value was every whit as great as those which others had given him when they sent him forth at the beginning, alone over the waves, while he was but a child. High above him they set a golden standard. Then they let the sea bear him away, and committed him to the ocean. Their hearts were full of grief and their thoughts were heavy. Men who bear rule in halls, heroes beneath the heavens, cannot say in truth who was to receive the cargo which that vessel bore. *Beowulf, 38–52*

This passage reads like a myth to account for a funeral rite, implying that the kings of East Anglia were to be laid in a ship after death because Scyld, one of the founder kings of their race, departed thus from his people, the Danes. Memories of great funeral ceremonies like that at Sutton Hoo could have remained in some men's memory or in family tradition at the time when this passage was composed. We can picture for instance the Sutton Hoo ship bearing the king's treasures being rowed out from the harbour nearest his palace at Rendlesham, and taken up the Deben to a point below the cemetery of the East Anglian kings. If this was the way in which the rulers of the kingdom were borne to their last resting place when a ship was involved in the ceremony, then the description given of Scyld's departure may not be far removed from actual practice. A ship may have borne the dead king away from his sorrowing people, although it was not to be committed to the ocean, as in the poem, but to the earth in the cemetery where a mound was waiting to receive it. There must have been some idea in the minds of those who prepared these elaborate and expensive ship-funerals that the treasures buried with the dead were to pass with them in some way into the mysterious realm of the gods, as did the treasures bestowed upon Scyld in the old story.

Whether in heathen times a dead man was ever launched on a ship which formed his funeral pyre as it sailed, slowly burning, out to sea is something which we cannot know. Such a rite was said to have formed part of Balder's funeral, when he was burned on his ship in the presence of the assembled gods, with his wife and his horse beside him. Two early kings, Haki of Norway and Sigurd Ring of Sweden, were said in late accounts to be sent out to sea when they were dying or dead from wounds received in battle.[1] But we have no early reliable evidence for such a custom, and no eye-witness accounts of such a practice.

1. *Ynglinga Saga*, 23, and *Skjǫldunga Saga*, 27.

Possibly here again such stories are to be viewed as myths, explaining the well-established custom of burning a man in his ship after death. Ship-funeral could have been presented as a re-enactment of the departure in the mythical past of the founder of the race over the sea to the Other World.

As we have seen, such a belief is most likely to have been associated with the Vanir. This conclusion is supported by the use of the ship symbol in the ancient world. It is a very ancient funeral symbol, for in ancient Egypt ships were placed in graves beside some of the pyramids in the Old Kingdom, while model ships were buried in the tombs of Tutankhamen and other rulers of the New Kingdom. In Egyptian belief it was natural to link the ship with the journey of the sun across the heavens, and with the departure of the divine Pharaoh to the realm of the gods. Thus the ship came to stand for the gift of warmth and fertility to men, and since fertility depended on the life-giving water of the River Nile, it was an exceptionally good symbol of new life on earth, and a fitting gift for the dead. The connexion with fertility stands out even more clearly in the ship used as the symbol of Isis in southern Europe. In Roman times, a yearly festival was held at Ostia in her honour when the shipping season re-opened, and on the first full moon of March a ship was blessed and launched without a crew, as a sacrifice to the sea in honour of the goddess. Isis was a fertility deity, whose equivalent in the north was Nerthus, and later Freyja.

About the third century A.D., we know that a goddess had a shrine on the island of Walcheren on the Dutch coast. This was afterwards engulfed by the sand, and many inscribed stones have been found there, some showing the goddess and giving her name as Nehalennia.[1] There is no doubt of her kinship with the Mothers, since she is shown holding fruit and a horn of plenty, and a ship is frequently shown beside her. These stones were probably raised in her honour by travellers who hoped for a safe voyage over to Britain, since her shrine stood at one of the points where passengers embarked to cross the North Sea.

Thus when Njord is renowned as the god of ships, we are faced with a pattern familiar from very early times, the linking of a ship with the deities of peace and plenty. We need to remember

1. A. Houdris-Crone, *The Temple of Nehalennia at Domburg*, 1955.

too that there was an obvious link between the Vanir and the sea for the people of the north, for much of their food came from it. A dearth of fish was as terrible a calamity as a failure of the crops, and on the poor farms folk depended on their store of dried fish to get them through the worst of the winter. Men prayed to the gods for a double harvest, from the earth and from the ocean, and it would naturally be to the Vanir to whom they would turn to bless the fishing boats and to draw the fish into the sounds and fiords.

3. *The Depths of the Sea*

There is little doubt however that the connexion of water with fertility, existing in some form in all the great pagan religions, goes deeper than dependence on sea and river as a source of food. Water is seen as the source of inspiration, of wisdom, even of life itself. It is regarded also as a cleansing and renewing element, from which man can rise new-born. Thus, according to the myth of the end of the northern gods, a new world was destined to rise from the old, and would emerge from the ocean after the fires of destruction had been quenched. This world was in fact the old one cleansed and renewed, since the gold playing-pieces of the ancient gods still lay forgotten in the grass. Out of the sea also came the rulers who were to bring peace and prosperity to the land. The image which men liked to form of them was of a little child voyaging alone in a boat, as the cycle began anew and an infant coming from the sea formed the link between the world of men and that of the gods.

The sea at the same time was the element of destruction. At Ragnarok it was to rise and cover the earth, devouring the dwellings of men and gods along with the overwhelming fire. The chief enemy of Thor, who protected mankind and the gods from chaos and anarchy, was the ancient serpent who dwelt in the ocean depths. This serpent, called by the poets the 'girdle of earth', lay coiled round the world, and it was when he lashed himself into giant rage at the end of the world that the sea covered the land and men and gods perished. The implication in the story of Thor's fishing is that had the god been worsted in his struggle with the monster in the sea, it would have meant the world's destruction then and there. Even in the comic tale of Thor's struggle to lift the serpent in the form of a great grey cat, there was a moment of terror for those who watched to see what the end would be. Like Leviathan and the Kraken, the serpent was a monster of the ocean depths, the eternal enemy of the guardian of the sky. The serpent is linked with the giants, and with the snakes that inhabit the world of death and are its symbols. Beside him we must set the fiery dragon of northern mythology, emerging from the depths of the earth, from rocks, caves, or burial mounds of the dead. To him we shall return in the next chapter.

Thus the fertile sea, source of inspiration and life, and yet a force of destruction, must be set beside the earth, which forms both the cradle of life and its engulfing grave. The dark depths of earth and sea are an essential part of all mythologies. They form the foundations on which the northern Asgard was built.

Chapter 6

The Gods of the Dead

Graves are the mountain tops of a distant,
lovely land.

    Attributed to the *Koran*

1. *Odin and Mercury*

We know that in the early days the Germanic peoples made
costly sacrifices both to Tîwaz and to Wodan, dedicating to them
those who fell in battle or who came into their hands as captives.
Gradually Wodan, whom the Romans called Mercury, supplanted his rival. He was regarded as the ancestor of kings, and
he welcomed them to his halls after death; he was the deity to
whom human sacrifices were offered by burning, strangling, and
stabbing with a spear. In the myths known to Snorri he had
grown greatly in stature, and become Odin, father of the gods
and ruler of Asgard. Even the powerful Thunder God was now
viewed as his son, although Snorri had doubts about this, and
in his preface made Thor the first of the gods of the north.
Odin, as we have seen, was the god of battle, whose symbols
were the spear and the raven, but in the poems and sagas known
to Snorri he is shown in other aspects. He was also the ancient
one-eyed god, crafty and skilled in magic lore, a great shape-
changer, and an expert in the consultation of the dead. He was
the rider on the eight-legged steed, the wanderer up and down
the earth, the god knowing the secrets of travel between the
worlds.

Since the Romans equated Wodan with Mercury, we may
assume that similarities between the two deities existed as early
as the days of Tacitus. Even if Wodan, like Odin, resembled
Mercury in wearing a hat, this is not enough to account for
the identification; the Romans were not likely to be misled by

superficial features of this kind. Mercury was the god of trade, the patron of wisdom and learning, the god who was carried by his winged sandals over land and sea, and the guide who directed souls to the Other World. This gives us a starting point to the study of Wodan as god of the dead.

Like Mercury, Wodan was evidently concerned with trade, for German inscriptions to Mercury in the Roman period bear titles such as Mercator and Negotiator. Among Scandinavian names given to Odin, we similarly find *Farmantýr*, 'god of cargoes'. As for learning, Odin was renowned for his discovery or invention of the runic letters, which for the Germanic peoples before their conversion represented both learning and magic lore. Wodan seems to have had the same reputation. In the Old English poem *Solomon and Saturn*, the reply to the question: 'Who first set down letters?' is 'Mercurius the Giant'. Many myths known to Snorri testify to Odin's habit of wandering about the earth and of flying through the air, either in bird form or on his horse Sleipnir, while in the sagas he frequently appears as the one-eyed stranger, arriving when least expected. His favourite method of travel was on his eight-legged steed, and Wodan before him rode on horseback. The Second Merseburg Charm, in which Wodan heals a horse's leg, suggests that this connexion was known in heathen Germany. Most interesting of the characteristics of Mercury is his function as *psychopompos*, the guide of souls down to the underworld. This in particular is the aspect of Odin which must hold our attention when we come to consider him as God of the Dead.

2. *Odin as a Shaman*

Reference has already been made (pp. 118–19) to the practice of shamanism, a form of religion current up to recent times in north-eastern Europe, and many parts of Asia and America, and one which has by no means wholly disappeared. The shaman's main function is to act as a kind of priest or witch-doctor – though neither term is wholly satisfactory – and to offer himself as a link between the human community to which he belongs and the Other World. While in a state of trance, he is believed to journey in spirit to the furthest heaven or to the land of the dead, so that he may visit the gods to obtain knowledge, or rescue some soul which disease or madness has expelled from its body. He acts as a seer, sometimes foretelling the future, finding the reason for calamities and disease, and answering questions concerning the destinies of those who consult him. We have seen that the *vǫlva*, whose links appear to be with the Vanir, possessed certain of the characteristics of the shaman. The figure of Odin in his aspect as god of the dead undoubtedly fits into the same pattern, and this is an important side of his cult to set beside his character as a war god.

First, the eight-legged horse of Odin is the typical steed of the shaman. In his journeys to the heaven or the underworld, the shaman is usually represented as riding on some bird or animal. The character of the creature varies, but the horse is fairly common in the lands where horses are in general use, and Sleipnir's ability to bear the god through the air is typical of the shaman's steed. Eliade in his detailed study of shamanism throughout the world[1] quotes the story of a Bouriat shamanka from central Asia. She was married to a human husband, but she had for her 'second husband' the ancestral spirit of a shaman. One of her husband's mares gave birth to a foal with eight legs, and he cut off four of them. 'Alas,' cried his wife, 'that was my little horse on which I ride as a *shamanka*,' and after that she left him and disappeared from among men, becoming the protective spirit of her tribe.

Attempts have been made to account for the eight legs of Sleipnir by likening him to the hobby-horses and steeds with more than four feet which appear in carnivals and processions. A more fruitful resemblance seems to be to the bier on which a dead man is carried in the funeral procession by four bearers; borne along thus, he may be described as riding on a steed with eight legs. Confirmation of this is found in a funeral dirge recorded by Verrier Elwin among the Gonds in India.[2] It contains references to Bagri Maro, the horse with eight legs, and it is clear from the song that this is the dead man's bier. The song is sung when a distinguished Muria dies. One verse of it runs:

1. M. Eliade, *Le Chamanisme et les techniques archaïques de l'extase,* Paris, 1951, pp. 407–8.
2. *The Muria and their Ghotul*, Oxford, 1947, pp. 149–50.

> What horse is this?
> It is the horse Bagri Maro.
> What should we say of its legs?
> This horse has eight legs.
> What should we say of its heads?
> This horse has four heads. . . .
> Catch the bridle and mount the horse.

The representation of Odin's eight-legged steed could arise naturally out of such an image, and this is in accordance with the picture of Sleipnir as a horse that could bear its rider to the land of the dead.

There is no doubt that the horse of Odin knew this road well. Saxo has the story of Hadding, who was carried by Odin on Sleipnir, covered with a mantle, over land and sea, until they came to the god's dwelling. In the *Edda* poem *Baldrs Draumar*, Odin rode down the long road to the underworld on Sleipnir and braved the dog that guarded the threshold in order to consult a dead seeress. It was Sleipnir also who carried his rider down the dark and terrible road to Hel's kingdom to seek for Balder, whether it was Odin himself who made the journey (as some have thought) or an emissary. Although we do not often find Odin acting as guide to the dead, the Valkyries, working under his command, performed just this function, and escorted dead kings and heroes to Valhalla. Nor was this characteristic of the god wholly forgotten in Norse literature. In *Vǫlsunga Saga* Odin himself appears like Charon, to row the boat on which Sigmund's dead son was laid. In another late saga, *Egils Saga ok Ásmundar*, he appears as the Prince of Darkness who conducted a giantess down to the underworld.

In the poem *Hávamál* Odin himself is described as hanging on the World Tree, the ash Yggdrasill, pierced with a spear. This recalls the grim record of victims stabbed in the name of Wodan or Odin, said to be left hanging from trees round the temple of the gods at Uppsala and elsewhere. The interpretation in *Hávamál* however goes even further than this, for Odin is represented as speaking these words:

> I know I hung
> on the windswept Tree,
> through nine days and nights.

> I was stuck with a spear
> and given to Odin,
> myself given to myself. . . .

This is a voluntary sacrifice, and its purpose is the acquisition of secret, hidden knowledge, since the god is able to peer down from the tree and lift up the runes which represented magic lore. It was thought at one time that this image of the suffering god hanging from the tree must have been derived from the Christian Crucifixion. But despite certain resemblances, it would seem that here we have something whose roots go deep into heathen thought, and which is no late copy, conscious or unconscious, of the central mystery of the Christian faith. By hanging on a tree, Odin is not sharing in the suffering of the world or saving men from death, he is there to win the secret of the runes:

> They helped me neither
> by meat nor drink.
> I peered downward,
> I took up the runes,
> screaming, I took them —
> then I fell back.

Besides the sacrificial practices of hanging upon a tree, known to be associated with Wodan from early times, we have also significant parallels from shamanistic practice. There is much evidence from various parts of the world concerning the training of young men and women who become shamans, and Eliade has collected this in the study already mentioned. In the accounts of initiation ceremonies undergone by the novice, there are resemblances to this picture of the suffering god.

The World Tree is indeed the centre of the shaman's cosmology, as it is in the world of the northern myths. The essential feature of the initiation ceremony, whether among the Eskimos, the American Indians, or the Siberian peoples, is the death and rebirth of the young shaman, and the torments and terrors which he has to undergo if he is to gain possession of the esoteric knowledge necessary to him in his new calling. Before he can attain ability to heal and to pass to the realms of gods and spirits, he has to undergo a ritual death. This may be experienced in dreams or visions, and the experience may be induced by means of meditation, fasting, or the use of drugs; in any case it causes the initiate terrible suffering. He may imagine himself devoured by birds, boiled in a cauldron, cut open so that serpents or sacred stones can be inserted into his body, or torn into small pieces. If however he is a true shaman, he will survive this mental torture, will be restored to life and wholeness, and will then be able to practise his calling in the community. The World Tree plays a considerable part in these dreams and visions of the young shaman, especially in northern Asia. The Yakuts believed that the soul of the shaman was carried off by the 'Mother Bird of Prey' and placed on a branch of a tree in the underworld, while his body was cut to pieces and devoured by the spirits of illness and death. In other regions it was thought that the new shaman made his drum from branches of the World Tree, while the Mongols believed that shamans tethered their horses to the Tree, as Odin is said to have tethered his horse Sleipnir to Yggdrasill.

The hanging of Odin on the World Tree seems indeed to have two main conceptions behind it. First, Odin is made into a sacrifice according to the accepted rites of the god of death, who is Odin himself. We know that victims were hung from trees before the Viking age, and the custom continued at Uppsala until the tenth century. Secondly, Odin is undergoing a ceremony of initiation, gaining his special knowledge of magic by means of a symbolic death.[1] In his *Prose Edda* Snorri has not shown much of this side of Odin's character, for he has concentrated on showing the god as the All-father and ruler of Asgard. In *Ynglinga Saga*, however, Snorri gives us a somewhat different picture, emphasizing Odin's skill in magic lore, and his power of shape-changing. Here he brings out the shamanistic characteristics of Odin, who like the shaman had the power not only to ride upon an animal but to send forth his spirit in animal forms:

Odin could change himself. His body then lay as if sleeping or dead, but he became a bird or a wild beast, a fish or a dragon, and journeyed in the twinkling of an eye to far-off lands, on his own errands or those of other men.

1. Odin is shown hanging from the tree on an early Swedish carved stone along with scenes that seem to belong to the story of the gaining of the mead.

Like the shamans also, Odin seeks knowledge by communication with the dead. In *Baldrs Draumar* his approach to the dead is shown as it were in double symbolism: he rides down the road that leads to the underworld, and then he proceeds to call up a dead seeress from the grave until she replies to his questions. She is shown in the poem as being forced to answer him against her will:

> Who is this man, unknown to me,
> who drives me on down this weary path?
> Snowed on by snow, beaten by rain,
> drenched with the dew, long I lay dead.

As a refrain throughout the poem we have her reiterated words:

> I have spoken unwillingly;
> now must I be silent.

Fresh insistence by Odin, 'Be not silent, *volva*', prefaces each new question which he puts to the seeress. The poems *Voluspá* and the *Shorter Voluspá* are set in the same pattern, and presented as replies made unwillingly to a persistent questioner. They could indeed be viewed as speeches made by a shaman on awakening from a trance, after a ritual 'death', or journey by the soul to the underworld to gain knowledge of secret things. Possibly there was at one time a connexion between the hanged victims and this power to learn what was hidden from men. Odin declares in *Hávamál* that he knows spells which will make a hanged man walk and talk with him. He is represented as gaining knowledge of the future by consultation of the severed head of Mimir, the hostage said to have been killed by the Vanir. Another version of the story of his relations with Mimir is that he sacrificed one of his eyes so that Mimir, the giant guardian of the spring in the underworld, would permit him to drink from it, and so gain wisdom.

It may be noted that while the ravens, the birds of Odin, are closely connected with battle and the devouring of the slain, they have a different aspect in the poem *Grímnismál*. There the wolves of Odin are called Ravener and Greed, but the ravens have names of a different kind:

> *Huginn* and *Muninn*, Thought and Memory,
> fly over the world each day.

> I fear for Thought, lest he come not back,
> but I fear yet more for Memory.

The birds here are symbols of the mind of the seer or shaman, sent out over vast distances. It seems that the connexion between the god and his ravens is older than the Viking age. He is depicted on his horse with two birds flying above him on a seventh-century helmet from Vendel, Sweden. Possibly two birds on the lid of an early Anglo-Saxon cremation urn found at Newark have some connexion with the god of the dead. Evidence of this kind is admittedly slender, and yet sufficient of it exists to imply continuity between the heathen beliefs of the Dark Ages and those of Viking times. For instance, beside the figure of Odin on his horse shown on several memorial stones there is a kind of knot depicted, called the *valknut*, related to the triskele.[1] This is thought to symbolize the power of the god to bind and unbind, mentioned in the poems and elsewhere (page 59). Odin had the power to lay bonds upon the mind, so that men became helpless in battle, and he could also loosen the tensions of fear and strain by his gifts of battle-madness, intoxication, and inspiration. Symbols resembling this knot of Odin are found beside figures of the horse and the wolf on certain cremation urns from early heathen cemeteries in East Anglia. We know Odin's connexion with cremation, and it does not seem unreasonable therefore to associate them with Woden, god of the dead in Anglo-Saxon England.

The picture of the god as the bringer of ecstasy is in keeping with the most acceptable interpretation of the Germanic name Wodan, that which relates it to *wut*, meaning high mental excitement, fury, intoxication, or possession. The Old Norse adjective *óðr*, from which *Oðinn*, the later form of his name in Scandinavia, must be derived, bears a similar meaning: 'raging, furious, intoxicated', and can be used to signify poetic genius and inspiration. Such meanings are most appropriate for the name of a god who not only inspired the battle fury of the berserks, but also obtained the mead of inspiration for the Aesir, and is associated with the ecstatic trance of the seer.

The connexion of the god of death with inspiration and

1. A figure consisting of three legs radiating from a common centre. The *valknut* is formed of three triangles linked together.

possession seems indeed to go back to the days of early Germanic heathenism, and it continued in the north until the end of the heathen period. The fury and ecstasy supposed to be bestowed upon men is the link between Wodan, worshipped on the Rhine in the first century A.D., and the Scandinavian Odin, god of poetry, magic, and the dead. The worship of Wodan is believed to have travelled northwards, perhaps along with the use of runic letters, with the tribe of the Heruli, and to have established itself at last in Denmark and Sweden beside the worship of the gods of fertility which already prevailed there. It must have reached the shores of the North Sea in the Migration period, and been carried over by some of the invading peoples into Britain. Place-names called after the god are of little help, for they are scattered and rare. It is possible that this gap is due to the fear of the name of the dread deity of death.

In later folk-beliefs Odin was associated with the 'wild hunt', the terrifying concourse of lost souls riding through the air led by a demonic leader on his great horse, which could be heard passing in the storm. Later still, the leader became the Christian Devil. There seems no real reason to assume from this that Wodan was ever a wind god, but it was natural that the ancient god of the dead who rode through the air should keep a place in this way in the memory of the people, and it reminds us of the terror which his name must once have inspired.[1] It has been suggested earlier (page 50) that there appears to have been a definite reaction against the cult of Odin at some time in the Viking age, on account of reiterated accusations of treachery and faithlessness made against him. A renewal of support for the gods of fertility might account for the gradual swing-over from cremation of the dead to inhumation, and for the development of the practice of ship-burial on a grand scale in royal cemeteries on both sides of the North Sea.

The shamanistic element in the worship of Odin can hardly be doubted, but it is not easy to decide how far new influences from the East, coming late to the north, have given a new twist to the cult of a god who already inspired his followers with ecstasy. Two important characteristics of the shamans of northern Europe and Asia, the use of the drum and the dance, do not

1. J. S. Ryan, 'Othin in England', *Folklore*, 74, 1963, pp. 472 ff.

seem to be included among the rites of Odin; and the power of healing does not appear to be associated with him in any way. Resemblances between the Odin traditions and the shamans might be due to certain tendencies once shared by the Germanic peoples with those of the steppes and the tundra, which died out in western Europe with the advent of Christianity. We have seen that there are certain marked shamanistic elements in the fertility cults of Scandinavia also. This raises the whole question of Eastern influences on Scandinavia in the Viking age, about which we know all too little.

3. The Realm of Odin

In Snorri's account the warrior paradise of Odin, Valhalla, is given great prominence, but in fact there is little about it in the poetry, apart from *Grímnismál*. The hall is described as being filled with shields and mailcoats, haunted by wolf and eagle, and provided with hundreds of doors through which the warriors could pour out at any threat of attack. Within it they feasted on pork and mead, served by the maids of Odin. In this picture of Valhalla given by Snorri, two separate conceptions can be discerned. One is that of a life after death as the guest of Odin, god of battle, a life presumably limited to heroes of noble birth and members of royal families claiming descent from the god. The second is that of an unending battle, continuing for ever because those who fall each day are restored to life again in time for the feasting in the evening. We must consider these two conceptions in turn.

The idea of entering Odin's hall after death is well supported by literary evidence. Those who died in the god's service, undergoing a violent death either by battle or by sacrifice, had the entry into his realm. This conception is given vigorous expression in the death-song of Ragnar *Loðbrók*, probably composed no earlier than the twelfth century in its present form, but believed to be based on an earlier death-song containing heathen material. The end of the poem expresses a fierce, exultant belief in the approach of the hero to Odin's hall, where he will be welcomed with feasting and hospitality because he died fearlessly:

It gladdens me to know that Balder's father makes ready the benches for a banquet. Soon we shall be drinking ale from the curved horns. The champion who comes into Odin's dwelling does not lament his death. I shall not enter his hall with words of fear upon my lips.

The Aesgir will welcome me. Death comes without lamenting....

Eager am I to depart. The Dísir summon me home, those whom Odin sends for me from the halls of the Lord of Hosts. Gladly shall I drink ale in the high-seat with the Aesir. The days of my life are ended. I laugh as I die.

The traditional account of Ragnar's death was not of a death in battle. He is said to have been taken captive and then to have perished in a snake-pit. Whether this is to be taken literally or not, it suggests that we are to see his death as a sacrificial one, and that he is the assenting victim. The note of fierce joy which comes out in this passage is echoed elsewhere in connexion with death-rites in Odin's honour. It is found for instance in the description of the burning of a chieftain on the Volga (p. 52), and is the more convincing because reported by an outsider, an Arab eye-witness, who watched the cremation and recorded the words of a man standing beside him:

'We burn them with fire in a twinkling, and they enter Paradise that very same hour.' Then he laughed and said: 'Out of love of him his Lord sent the wind to take him away.'

In spite of Snorri's picture of an exclusively masculine Valhalla, there are grounds for believing that women too had the right of entry into Odin's realm if they suffered a sacrificial death. They too could be strangled and stabbed and burned after death in the name of the god. There are a number of references to the death of a man's wife or betrothed, so that she may be burned upon the funeral pyre with her husband. Balder's wife Nanna is said to have died of grief and to have been laid on the pyre beside him. When Sigurd, king of Sweden, was sent out to sea in a burning ship, the body of a dead princess was placed beside him. When Sigurd the Volsung was slain, Brynhild had a huge pyre made ready and was by her own command burned upon it, so that she might join him as his wife in the other world although they had been kept apart in life. The slave-girl on the Volga was stabbed and strangled so that she too could be burned with her master; she consented to this some time before the funeral ceremony, and was treated with great honour – as though, in fact, she were a true wife – until the day of the burning of the body. A surprising passage in *Flateyjarbók* implies that the custom of suttee was practised in Sweden in honour of Odin until the tenth century. Sigrid the Proud, who afterwards became the wife of King Svein of Denmark, the conqueror of England, left her Swedish husband King Eric, and the reason given was that she wished to avoid being put to death with her husband :

Now at this time Sigrid the Proud had left King Eric, and people said that he felt disgraced by her behaviour. For it was in fact the law in Sweden that if a king died the queen should be laid in howe beside him; she knew that the king had vowed himself to Odin for victory when he fought with his kinsman Styrbiorn, and that he had not many years to live.   *Flateyjarbók*, I, 63

There are so many references either to a deliberate act of suicide by a widow or to a sudden death 'of grief' at the funeral in the literary sources, that some vague memory of the custom of sacrifice of the wife at her husband's funeral seems to have survived from heathen times. Of particular interest is Saxo's account of the love of Signy and Hagbard. They were betrothed against the will of the girl's father, and Hagbard was finally captured and condemned to death. He was to be hanged, and when Signy saw the signal which told her that the execution had taken place, she and her women set fire to the house and hanged themselves while it burned. Hagbard however had managed to delay his execution by a few minutes, as he wished to see whether Signy would be true to him. He saw the flames rising as he stood beside the gallows, and knowing that she must have fulfilled her vow to die with him, he uttered a song of triumph, in which there is a reference to the hope of immortality with his beloved :

Now . . . certain hope remains of renewed love, and death shall prove to have its own delights. Both worlds hold joy.
                                        Gesta Danorum, VII, 237

Like Brynhild and the slave-girl on the Volga, Signy claimed in death the place and privilege of a wife which was not granted to her in life. 'Now they shall enjoy in death what they could not have in life', were the very words spoken in *Qrvar-Odds Saga* when the news of the hero Hjalmar's death was brought, and his betrothed fell back in her chair at the news and died. This indeed seems to be the idea behind such stories. It is implied that the entry into the realm of Odin was open to women as well as men, but a violent death was demanded as the price of entry.

Perhaps the picture given in *Ynglinga Saga* indicates a wider acceptance of Odin's cult on easier terms. Snorri tells us here that all those burned after death went to be with Odin, who had himself established this rite, and that their possessions were burned on the pyre with them. He also mentions the marking with a spear as a sign of belonging to Odin. Snorri is hardly likely to have invented this statement, since it contradicts his own statement elsewhere that Valhalla was only for those killed in battle.

The second conception which forms part of the picture of Valhalla is that of the everlasting battle. This is given in the poem *Vafþruðnismál*, and Snorri seems to have taken it from here and added it to his account of life in Valhalla. The warriors fight all day long, and are restored to life in the evening so that they can feast with Odin and next morning fight anew. This somewhat macabre conception of the animated dead who cannot be laid low is found elsewhere in the literature, notably in tales of magic, but not linked specifically with Odin and Valhalla. It comes into the story of Hild, for instance, for which our earliest source is the poem *Ragnarsdrapa*. Hild was so distressed by the tragic conflict between her father and her lover that she raised those who fell in the fight back to life by her magic powers, and thus the battle never ended.

The true place for the conflict of dead warriors is surely neither in heaven nor on earth, but in the underworld. This is where Saxo's hero Hadding watched the everlasting battle when he was conducted to the land of the dead. He saw two armies fighting, and was told:

These are they who, having been slain by the sword, declare the manner of their death by a continual rehearsal, and enact the deeds of their past life in a living spectacle.   *Gesta Danorum*, I, 31

Another story, from *Flateyjarbók* (1, 206) sets such a conflict inside a burial mound. Here two companies, one in black and one in red, fight without ceasing. The hero Thorstein, a Christian, is the only one who can deal blows to them from which they cannot recover, so that they can rest at peace in the grave.

The hall of the slain, over which in *Grímnismál* Odin is said to rule, and from which Snorri took most of his account of Valhalla, seems indeed to be a picture of the grave itself. Similarly in Book VIII of Saxo's history there is a long description of a gloomy, tomb-like dwelling, with a roof of spears (as in Valhalla), in which lie hosts of the dead. It is represented here as the hall of Geirrod the giant, reached by a long and perilous journey:

It was needful to sail over the Ocean that goes round the lands, to leave the sun and stars behind, to journey down into chaos, and at last to pass into a land where no light was and where darkness reigned eternally.

This can be no other than the underworld, the kingdom of the dead. Valhalla, instead of a bright warrior paradise, seems indeed to be a synonym for death and the grave, described imaginatively in the poems and partly rationalized by Snorri. This world Odin ruled as God of the Dead, as presumably did his predecessor Wodan. Since those who fell in battle came to be dedicated to him by his worshippers, the warrior aspect would naturally come to be emphasized. Possibly another picture was known to the poets, that of a fair dwelling of the gods where benches were made ready for dead kings and favoured mortals. This also belonged to Odin by virtue of his position as All-Father, the high god, which he appears to have usurped from Tîwaz. Such a picture at least is implied in skaldic poems of the tenth century like *Eiríksmál* and *Hákonarmál*, where the kings who die in battle are conducted to Odin's hall by a band of noble Valkyries. The conjunction of these two images of Odin's realm would explain the picture Snorri gives of Valhalla.

4. *The Burial Mound*

There are several links between Odin and the Vanir which at first sight seem puzzling, since the two cults were apparently opposed to one another. The goddess Skadi, wife of Njord, is said to have borne children to Odin. Odin and Freyja are often mentioned together, and we have the strange double of Odin, the god Od (*Óðr*), who is said to have been Freyja's husband, for whom she wept after he left her. We may partly account for such links when we remember that Odin and Freyr were worshipped side by side, and both honoured by the Swedish kings in the great temple at Uppsala. It is thus scarcely surprising if one cult influenced the other, especially in the last period of heathenism, when the powers of the old gods were waning, and distinctions between them became blurred. There is however another reason for a link between the two cults, and that is that the Vanir as well as Odin had undoubtedly power over the realm of the dead.

The Vanir are represented as having close connexions with life in the burial mound, with the symbol of the funeral ship, and with the conception of a journey to the land of the dead across the sea. We know that Freyr himself was said to have been laid in a mound, and to have rested there while offerings were made to him. There is mention of a door in the mound, so that men could enter it, and of wooden figures kept inside. The idea that the dead men rested inside his grave mound as in a dwelling is one found repeatedly in the Icelandic sagas. Sometimes it is crudely and childishly expressed, as when a dead Christian hermit appears in a dream to rebuke a herd-girl for wiping her muddy feet on his house, or a man is buried in a high place, so that he may 'look out over the whole district'. Sometimes we find the pleasant idea of friends buried in neighbouring mounds conversing with one another. Again there are terrifying tales of the doings of the *draugr*, the dead man out of the mound, a vampire-like creature who left his grave to attack man and beast and wreak havoc in the neighbourhood. One of the finest imaginative pictures of the dead man resting in his mound is that of Gunnar in *Njáls Saga*. He had died by violence, and at the time of the dream described had not yet been avenged, yet the picture is a serene and beautiful one :

It seemed to them that the howe was open, and that Gunnar had turned himself in the howe, and looked up at the moon. They thought that they saw four lights burning in the howe, but no shadow anywhere. They saw that Gunnar was merry, with a joyful face.

Brennu-Njáls Saga, 78

The relationship of the dead towards the living might be a hostile one, and the terror of the dead and of their destructive power can be sensed in many stories of hauntings in Iceland. A different relationship however is brought out in the story of an early king in Norway, called Olaf *Geirstaðaálfr*, 'elf of Geirstad'. We are told in *Flateyjarbók* that in time of famine men sacrificed to him in his howe for plenty, even as they were said to have done to Freyr. When Olaf the Holy was born, he was named after this earlier Olaf, his ancestor, and was given his sword and ring, said to have been taken out of the burial mound to be presented to the child at his birth. Consequently men believed that the second Olaf was the first reborn, although the Christian king sternly contradicted such rumours:

> Olaf rode with his bodyguard past the howe of Olaf, Elf of Geirstad, ... 'Tell me, lord ... were you buried here?' The king replied: 'My soul has never had two bodies, it cannot have them, either now or on the Resurrection Day. If I spoke otherwise, there would be no common truth or honesty in me.' Then the man said: 'They say that when you came to this place before, you said – "Here we were once, and here we fare now."' 'I have never said that,' said the king, 'and never will I say it.' And the king was much moved, and clapped spurs to his horse immediately, and fled from the place as swiftly as he might.
>
> *Flateyjarbók*, II, 106

Brøgger[1] put forward the suggestion that it was this earlier Olaf, whom men worshipped after death, who was the occupant of the Gokstad ship-grave, one of the great ship-burials of heathen Norway. This would be another argument for linking Olaf with the cult of the Vanir, in addition to the emphasis on fertility in the story of the sacrifices made to him. The element of ancestor worship implied in this story is indeed what we should expect to find in the cult of Freyr. In the fertility religion, the emphasis is not so much on a world of the gods to which man attains after death if he fulfils certain conditions as on the importance of the veneration of dead ancestors, and the need for the living to remember them at various feasts and festivals, to visit their graves, and perhaps to sit on their burial mounds for wisdom and inspiration. Legends of the peace kings coming over the sea and bequeathing their rule after a while to a

1. 'Oseberggraven Haugbrottet', *Viking*, 1945, pp. 1 ff.

successor play a significant part, as we saw earlier, among the traditions associated with the Vanir. Such legends emphasize the importance of rebirth rather than resurrection or life in a realm of the gods away from the earth.

The title of 'elf' borne by Olaf may be significant. An ancestor of his, Halfdan Whiteleg, had the same title, and is called *Brynálfr* in the poem *Ynglingatál*, which recounts the places where a number of early kings were buried. Regular ceremonies connected with the elves continued in Sweden into the late Viking age. Sigvat the poet, a Christian who served under King Olaf the Holy, has described in one of his verses a journey made for the king in Sweden in 1018. He states in it that he could not find lodging in Gautland because in the late autumn all the people of the district were sacrificing to the elves. In one of the sagas of Iceland, *Kormáks Saga*, a sacrifice to the elves is described. A woman said to have the powers of a *vǫlva* told a man who came to her to be healed of wounds to take a bull which had been sacrificed to a mound

... in which dwell elves ... and redden the outside of the mound with bull's blood, and make the elves a feast with the flesh; and you will be healed. *Kormáks Saga*, 12

The sacrifice of an ox said to be made to the god Freyr in *Gísla Saga* and *Víga-Glúms Saga* may be remembered in connexion with this passage. Freyr himself is said to dwell in Alfheim, and both he and the elves are connected with the sun. Cup-marks on rocks and stone tombs in Sweden are found in association with the sun-wheel on very early monuments, and offerings of milk for the elves have been poured into such cups by Swedish country folk up to our own day. The link between the elves and the dead in the mounds is also in accordance with what we know of Freyr and the Vanir.

An Old English charm against a sudden stitch refers to a pain caused by the shot of either gods, witches, or elves. This charm emphasizes the power of the elves to harm, but the purpose of *alfablót* as referred to in the sagas was to gain their help, and there are indications in the literature that the dwellers in the mounds could give healing, and also help with the birth of children. This last point is well illustrated by the story of the birth of Olaf the Holy. The condition of his mother caused great anxiety because the birth was long delayed, but when a belt taken from the burial mound of Olaf of Geirstad was fastened round the mother, and the sword from it presented to the child who was to be born, all went well, and the baby boy who was to be the future Christian king of Norway was successfully delivered.

Men turned also to the dwellers in the mounds for inspiration. There is a story in *Flateyjarbók*[1] of a man who was able to compose poetry after sleeping on the mound of a dead poet. The inhabitant of the mound appeared to him in a dream and taught him a verse, and after that he also possessed the gift of poetry. This gift did not come from Odin, although he was the god of learning and inspiration, but from the powers under the earth, who came under the sway of the Vanir. We may remember incidentally that Odin did not possess the mead of inspiration until he had stolen it from the giants, and that its making had as much to do with the Vanir as with the Aesir (see pp. 40–1). The practice of a king sitting on the mound of some dead ancestor, mentioned more than once in sagas and poems, may be seen as an extension of this idea, for from the mound he could obtain wisdom and counsel from those within the earth.[2]

Perhaps we should regard stories of the living being shut inside the mounds of the dead as something connected with memories of the Vanir rather than as part of the cult of Odin. The most vivid of such accounts is found in the poem *Helgakviða*, where the princess Sigrun joyfully enters the mound of her dead husband, and clasps him again in death. Notes which accompany the poem state that the lovers Helgi and Sigrun were believed to have been reborn, and to have lived more than once in the world. Here we have the idea of a wife dying with her husband which appears to differ from the traditions of suttee which we have associated with the cult of Odin. In these the wife died usually by strangling before her body was burned, and she was not said to be reborn into this world, but to join her husband or lover in the realm of the gods. Such a distinction may explain the strange words spoken of Brynhild in the *Poetic Edda*, when she was determined to be burned along with the dead Sigurd:

1. *Flateyjarbók, Þáttr Þorleifs jarlaskálds*, 1, 174.
2. H. R. Ellis, *The Road to Hel*, Cambridge, 1943, pp. 105 ff.

Delay her not longer from dying,
that born again she may never be.

5. *Thor and the Dead*

So far no mention has been made of the god Thor in connexion
with the dead. Yet we know the extent of his worship in the
north, and the mark of the swastika or hammer on cremation
urns and memorial stones suggests that he afforded his protection to his worshippers in the realm of death as in life. It seems
as if both cremation and inhumation were associated with Thor.
He had special links with fire, on account of his command over
lightning, but in the later Viking age, when his worship still
flourished, most of his worshippers were buried in the earth.
Cremation lingered on for the most part in Sweden as the rite
of the followers of Odin.

Thor does not seem to have been specially associated with the
burial within a mound, as was Freyr. We have no traditions in
the literature of his 'death', and his establishment of certain
funeral rites, as in the case of Freyr and Odin. It is worth noting
that the famous worshipper of Thor long remembered in Iceland, Thorolf of Most, was not thought to have remained in his
mound after death. It was believed by his kindred that he had
entered the mountains near his home, and that they would join
him there. This is confirmed by the tale of a shepherd, recorded
in *Eyrbyggja Saga*, who, after the death of Thorolf's son by
drowning, claimed to have seen the hill Holyfell standing open,
and Thorstein and his crew being welcomed inside by Thorolf
amid general rejoicing. In *Landnámabók* such a belief is mentioned regarding certain other mountains in Iceland. The people
who are said to have believed that they would 'die into the hills'
were all connexions of Thorolf by ties of kinship or marriage, so
that it seems as if here we have a family belief, perhaps brought
over from Norway by the pioneer Thorolf himself.[1]

As well as building the temple to Thor when he arrived in Iceland, Thorolf also established the sanctity of the hill Holyfell
standing behind Thor's Ness. No man, he said, should look
upon it unwashed, and no living thing should be killed on it.

1. H. R. Ellis, op. cit., pp. 87 ff.

Evidently those who dwelled on the Ness and who were under Thor's protection were to pass into this holy hill after death. Such a conception is closely linked with the importance of the family. Like the idea of the dwelling within the burial mound or the departure over the sea, it emphasizes the significance of man's link with his ancestors, of the continuance of the family rather than the individual, and the importance of one particular sacred locality. The worship of Thor and Freyr is suited to life in a settled community, and in this differs from the cult of Odin, whose cremation pyres might be raised on battlefields far from home.

6. *The Dragon and the Dead*

No study of the conception of the dead in Germanic mythology would be complete without some mention of the powerful image of the fiery dragon. He was regarded as the guardian of the burial mound, and is so described in the Old English poem *Beowulf*:

> Ancient in years, he mounts guard over the heathen gold; yet he is not one whit the better for it.   2276–7

In this poem we have an incomparable picture of the monster, brooding over his treasure in a megalithic stone chamber inside a burial mound. When one cup is removed from his hoard by an intruder, his rage is terrible, and he sallies forth on a punitive expedition, in the form of an incendiary raid against the inhabitants of the land:

> Then did the visitant spit forth embers, and burn up the bright dwellings; the flaming ray wrought mischief to men, for the enemy flying through the air would leave nothing alive . . . He encompassed the people of the land with burning, with fire and flame.

> 2312–22

It was in a battle with this monster, to save his people, that the hero-king Beowulf lost his own life, although he killed the dragon before he himself died from the effects of its fiery breath and sharp teeth.

The vivid description of the dragon in the Anglo-Saxon poem is to some extent corroborated by the dragon set on the king's great shield found in the Sutton Hoo ship-grave. The long teeth, folded wings, and pointed tail can be clearly made out in the stylized and yet powerful figure of the monster. According to the *Anglo-Saxon Chronicle* for the year 793, lights in the sky were described as fiery dragons, and taken for a portent of calamity. This was presumably a display of the aurora borealis, but identification with the northern lights does not explain why the dragon in particular was associated with fire, and also with the graves of the dead. It would however be a natural image for devouring death, and in particular for the greedy fire, swallowing up the dead man and his treasures. The evidence of the Asthall Barrow in Oxfordshire,[1] where, according to archaeological findings, an elaborate cremation burial was held as late as the seventh century, reminds us that the Anglo-Saxons as well as the Scandinavians had the opportunity to watch cremation rites and to hear descriptions of them well into the Christian period. *Beowulf* gives us the most vivid account in the early literature of the north of a great funeral pyre blazing after a battle:

The mightiest of bale-fires rolled up to the clouds, and roared before the mound. Heads melted; closed wounds, terrible gashes of the body, burst open when the blood spurted forth. Fire, greediest of spirits, devoured all those whom war had carried off from both peoples; their flower had perished. 1119-24

Even after cremation of the dead was given up, there is reason to believe that there was ritual burning of the dead within the grave. We have for instance evidence from Stapenhill in Staffordshire, a cemetery of early Anglo-Saxon date, where there were five normal cremation burials, and also a number of inhumation graves with clear signs of burning, encircled by charcoal and blackened earth.[2] Another Anglo-Saxon cemetery, at Kettering, had normal cremation burials together with inhumation burials enclosed between large stones, bearing marks of fire.[3] Similar evidence has been discovered in cemeteries of the Germanic peoples on the Continent. Salin excavated Alamannic

1. *Antiquaries' Journal*, 4, 1924, pp. 113 ff.
2. *Burton-on-Trent Natural History and Archaeological Society Trans.*, 1, pp. 156 ff.
3. F. W. Bull, *Recent Discoveries of Anglo-Saxon Remains, Kettering*, 1904.

cemeteries in France, and found clear signs of burning and of ceremonial fires at Villey-Saint-Étienne and elsewhere.[1] Later this practice was continued and hallowed by the Church, for charcoal was placed in graves, sometimes mixed with incense, as a sign of purification. Whether the earlier use of fire in the grave was connected with the worship of Thunor or of Woden in Anglo-Saxon England our present knowledge is insufficient to decide, but there is no doubt that fire as a funeral symbol continued to be important even when cremation was no longer the accepted burial rite.

The fiery dragon plays no great part in Scandinavian mythology. When the dragon appears in Old Norse poetry and saga he is usually depicted as a serpent. We hear only occasionally of his wings and his power to breathe out fire. The image of the dragon who is the source of fire in Old English literature may be an instance of a mythical figure who has emerged as a result of ritual at the grave. In any case, he has been developed by poets and artists into a creature of such vigour that when we read his description in *Beowulf* it is as if we were given an eyewitness account of his appearance among men. Both in England and Scandinavia the dragon came to be regarded as the guardian of the grave mound, watching over its treasures. Sometimes it is implied that he is to be identified with the dead man buried in the mound, and in some of the late legendary sagas it is said that a man after death became a dragon and guarded the treasure which he had taken into the howe with him. The essential image however appears to be one of devouring death. At the Alamannic cemetery of Oberflacht, the tree coffins preserved by unusual soil conditions were carved with a serpent-dragon extended over the lid, triumphant over the dead within. In the poem *Vǫluspá*, there is mention of a flying dragon *Niðhǫggr*, 'corpse-tearer', who bore away the dead on his pinions, and there seems little doubt from his grim name that he was visualized as the devourer of corpses.

The conception of the flying dragon undoubtedly came from the East, and to some extent we can even trace the road by which he travelled, in the company of the Roman armies who carried the flying dragon as their banner and brought it into Roman

1. E. Salin, *Le Haut Moyen Age en Lorraine*, 1939, pp. 87 ff.

The Gods of the Dead

Britain.[1] But the dragon would not have been welcomed and endowed with such vigorous life had he not fitted in with existing ritual concerning the dead. The serpent-dragon, of which the creature Fafnir, slain by Sigurd the Volsung, may be taken as a typical example, has left his mark in the serpentine ornament and the constantly reiterated snake-motif upon memorial stones raised over the dead. The snake as a symbol of the world of the dead is as recurrent in the art of the north as in its literature.

The dark underworld ruled by Hel as pictured by Snorri in the *Prose Edda* is very much a literary abstraction. But behind this there is a series of glimpses of the grave as the dark dwelling of corpses and serpents, a place of horror and bitter cold and stench and rotting treasures, preserved for us in the *Edda* poems and in Saxo. Sometimes these pictures are linked with the idea of punishment for sin, but they are sufficiently powerful in their own right to be accepted as something more than a reflection of Christian teaching about hell. The northern heathen was by no means immune from the fear of the devouring fire and the engulfing grave. The solutions offered by the great gods – temporary forgetfulness from Odin, belief in rebirth and continuation of the family from Freyr, protective strength and a sense of order provided by Thor – were not in themselves sufficient to silence the threat of the dragon and the monsters. This is made abundantly clear by the unforgettable picture of the gods themselves falling under the power of death, as in the tradition of Ragnarok and the death of Balder. When Balder died, the horse of Odin carried its rider down to the underworld to bring him back to the world of the gods. Balder was found in the hall of Hel, yet the plan for his resurrection failed utterly. He was never restored to life again, and evidence from the earlier poetry indicates that this omission is not due to Snorri. Balder was the son of Odin, and by a surprising twist, typically Icelandic in its irony, the god of the dead was himself defeated by the relentless law of mortality.

1. H. R. Ellis Davidson, 'The Hill of the Dragon', *Folklore*, 61, 1950, pp. 180 ff.

Chapter 7

The Enigmatic Gods

... godlike Shapes, and Forms
Excelling human; princely Dignities,
And Powers that erst in Heaven sat on thrones,
Though of their names in Heavenly records now
Be no memorial.
    Paradise Lost, 1

Looking back over the ground already traversed, we are aware
of three great figures towering over the rest and dominating the
northern heaven, those of the gods Odin, Thor, and Freyr. The
mighty goddess Freyja stands beside her brother, with Frigg,
Odin's consort, as her shadowy and elusive companion. Fading
further into the background can be discerned Njord, father of
Freyr, and Tyr, once a god of war and ruler of the heavens.
What we know of the heathen Germans leads us to believe that
they worshipped a similar group of deities: Wodan, Donar,
Nerthus, and Tîwaz.

But when we have mentioned the great gods, we realize that
these do not by any means exhaust the inhabitants of Asgard, as
Snorri presented them. Many so-called gods play a prominent
part in the myths, and others are mentioned briefly by name, but
we search in vain for any established cult connected with them
in heathen times, while if we try to resolve the difficulty by de-
fining them as literary creations they remain puzzling and con-
tradictory. A number, as we have seen, appear to be associated
with the cult of the Vanir, such as Ing and Scyld, Ull and Byggvir, and the goddesses Gefion and Skadi. Some may originally
have been heroes who in course of time were promoted by antiquaries into heaven. Some may have begun as abstractions used
by the poets, and have gradually developed a literary personality
of their own. Some may have been imported into the north from
foreign sources, and ultimately gained a place in Asgard through
the poets and storytellers.

It is not proposed in this chapter to examine all the opposing theories which have grown up around the enigmatic figures of the lesser gods, nor even to attempt to discuss all the names on Snorri's list. Some of the more interesting claimants to a place in Asgard will be dealt with briefly here and there will be fuller treatment of three outstanding figures who cannot be lightly passed over, Heimdall, Loki, and Balder.

1. *Bragi and Idun*

Bragi deserves mention, as Snorri calls him the god of poetry. In *Lokasenna* he is accused by Loki of avoiding battle and of skulking among the benches. This may be based on the part played by Bragi in tenth-century court poetry, where he is depicted helping to prepare Valhalla for fresh arrivals and welcoming the kings who have been slain in battle to the hall of Odin. On the other hand Loki also refers to Bragi slaying his wife's brother, which means that he played a part in some story unknown to us.

There is record of a poet called Bragi Boddason who lived in the ninth century. It is hardly likely that he was turned into a mythological figure soon after his death, nor indeed that he was called after a god. It is possible that Bragi was a nickname; the word is used to mean poetry in general, and *bragarmál* is poetic diction, while Snorri declares that this meaning comes from the god's name. The word however has another meaning, that of 'leader' or 'foremost one'. When a dead king's funeral feast was held, the cup from which men drank the funeral ale in his honour, and over which solemn oaths might be sworn, was called the *bragarfull*, or 'cup of Bragi'. This means 'the leader's cup', and it could have taken its name either from the chief who was dead or from Odin, foremost of the gods, who would be honoured at funerals in his capacity of god of the dead. Bragi himself is sometimes called the Long-bearded One, and this is one of the titles of Odin. It seems possible indeed that he is no more than a reflection of Odin, the god of poetry and inspiration, and that one of Odin's many names has turned through a misunderstanding of the poets into a separate deity. The term *bragarfull* applied to the funeral drink could account for Bragi's association with banquets in Valhalla, where he gradually developed into a prototype of the human poet in the king's hall on earth.

Bragi's wife was said to be the goddess Idun. It was she who guarded the apples of immortality which kept the gods for ever young. Snorri recounts how Loki was forced to steal Idun and her apples for the giant Thiazi, and then to recover them to save the gods from old age and death. Idun is a somewhat colourless figure (though, as her brother is mentioned in *Loka-senna*, presumably at least one more story about her was known) and she does not seem to be fully at home in the northern myths. It has been suggested that she is a literary borrowing, either from the Celtic west or classical sources, and that her golden apples are an imitation of those in the Garden of the Hesperides. Apples and nuts from the land of promise, renewing youth and freeing those who ate them from the tyranny of time, are a familiar feature in Irish sagas, and one that goes back to an early date. It may be noted that on one occasion Loki turned Idun and her apples into a nut, and escaped with it in his claws as he flew in the form of a bird (see p. 39). Here then we have the association between eternal youth and nuts and apples which is found in the Irish stories.

Conceivably however the association of fruit, and particularly the apple, with the gods was already present in Germanic heathenism. Fruit and nuts have been found in early graves, both in southern England and on the Continent, and may have had some symbolic meaning. Nuts are still a recognized symbol of fertility in south-western England. We know too that apples were connected with the Vanir, since it was golden apples which Skirnir offered to Gerd when he went to woo her for Freyr.[1] Again in the Volsung cycle, Frigg gave an apple to the king who sat upon a mound, when he prayed for a son. In an eleventh-century poem by Thorbiorn Brúnarson we may note the strange expression 'apples of Hel'. The poet says that his wife desires his death; she wants him to live under the earth and provides apples of death for him, and the implication here is that the apple was thought of by the poet as the food of the dead.

1. Gerd also refers to her brother's slayer in *Skírnismál*, 16, and it has been suggested that she and Idun are connected in some way.

Moreover, in the Roman period, the goddess Nehalennia, whose shrine stood on the Island of Walcheren, was depicted as a woman sitting in a chair with a bowl of what appear to be apples beside her. She, as we have seen, is linked with the Mothers, and with the goddesses of plenty, the Vanir.[1] Thus while the apple is found as a symbol of perpetual youth in both Old Norse and Irish tradition, we cannot necessarily assume it to be a case of late imitation of Celtic ideas by Scandinavian storytellers.

There is moreover one significant difference in the Norse story of the stealing of the apples and the incident of the fruit stolen from the tree in the Irish story of the Sons of Tuireann, from which it has been suggested that the Idun story has been derived. We are never told that Idun's golden fruit grows upon a tree of the gods, but she seems to have them in a box or bowl, so that she and her treasures could be carried off together. The symbol of the apple of the gods is in any case an ancient one, which must have originated in the Near East, the area from which the cultivated apple-tree came. Its cultivation in northern Europe goes back at least to the time of the Romans, but in the north the native variety of the fruit is small and bitter. In the figure of Idun – given as wife to the god of inspiration and poetry – we must have a dim reflection of an old symbol: that of the guardian goddess of the life-giving fruit of the other world.

2. *Mimir and Hoenir*

Mimir is called the wisest of the Aesir. Snorri describes him as the guardian of the spring beneath the World Tree in the territory of the frost-giants. Elsewhere he is said to have been given as a hostage to the Vanir and killed by them, after which Odin preserved his head and consulted it in all times of perplexity and danger. His name survives in three different forms: Mímir, Mímr, and Mimi. These seem to be no more than variants of one being associated with wisdom and inspiration, who dwelt beside the spring under the tree. An attractive derivation of his name is that linking it with the Latin *memor*, although attempts have

1. Several buckets of apples were found on the Oseberg ship, in a burial which appears to have associations with the Vanir (see pp. 95, 137).

also been made to establish a connexion with Old English *meotud*, 'fate'.

The story of how the Aesir sent Mimir as a hostage to the Vanir, and how he was killed by them because they were dissatisfied with his silent companion Hoenir does not make very good sense as it stands. The tradition of a war between two companies of the gods however is familiar in many mythologies. One explanation is that it was inspired by memories of rivalry between an old and a new cult, or between two contemporary cults in opposition to one another. Dumézil[1] explained it on the basis of a deep-rooted hostility between the gods of fertility on the one hand and the gods of magic on the other. He gives the Celtic myth of a war between the Túatha Dé Donann and the Fomoiri as another example of the same pattern.

Snorri has given us two independent accounts of the war of the gods (see pp. 40 and 45), but in each case the end is the same, and is the gaining of the source of inspiration by Odin and the Aesir. This would imply the triumph of the gods of magic over their opponents, if Dumézil is correct. In one case the source of inspiration was the head of Mimir, and in the other it was the mead created out of the body of Kvasir. There is additional confusion because Kvasir, like Mimir, is sometimes described as the wisest of the Aesir, but his origin seems to be quite different. His name comes from *kvas*, the word for strong beer used by the eastern neighbours of the Germans, and still used in Jutland for crushed fruit. Kvasir was created out of the saliva of the Aesir and the Vanir, as a symbol of the truce between them. Unpleasant as the idea seems to a modern mind, use of saliva may have been a primitive method of fermentation, and in the figure of Kvasir we seem to see something akin to John Barleycorn, symbol of the sacrifice of the fruits of the earth to give the drink of good fellowship and inspiration.

Mimir, however, has been remembered primarily as the guardian of the spring, from which Odin could drink. One stanza of *Vǫluspá* implies that he won this privilege only after sacrificing one of his eyes to Mimir, as the price to be paid for the acquisition of mantic knowledge. If Mimir was the power who possessed

1. G. Dumézil, *Jupiter, Mars, Quirinus*, Paris, 1941, pp. 159 ff.

inspiration before the Aesir, it is among the giants rather than the gods that we should expect to find him. Certainly in the poems a powerful and terrible giant is mentioned more than once in association with the World Tree (sometimes called the Tree of Mimi), and sometimes a magic weapon is connected with this giant figure. Saxo knew a story of a journey made by the hero Hadding down to the underworld to obtain a magic sword, and this weapon was guarded by an old man whose name is Mimingus, and who is called a 'satyr of the woods'. Possibly this too may be Mimir, and he may have been the giant credited with the making of the wonderful sword Mimming, one of the marvellous weapons of early Germanic tradition. In the confused state of the evidence as it stands, however, the figure of this wise giant has become lost in obscurity.

As to Mimir's silent companion Hoenir, he also has slid back into the mists of oblivion. Naturally many attempts have been made to identify him with one of the better known gods, but without conspicuous success.[1] It may be assumed that he was more than the handsome, brainless fellow who appears in Snorri's tale of the truce between the Aesir and the Vanir, since he is named among the gods present at the creation of man, and indeed in *Vǫluspá* is said to have given them the gift of intelligence. He is also said to survive the downfall of the old gods and to reign in the new world. The poets knew him as the friend of Odin and Loki, and Snorri describes him as swift and long-legged. In a prose source (*Sǫgubrot*) he is said to be the most timid of the Aesir. A clue perhaps may be sought in the value put upon silence in Old Norse literature; it was thought to be a sign of wisdom, and conceivably some form of mantic wisdom was represented by the figure of Hoenir the silent. But there is little trace remaining of his relationship to the other inhabitants of Asgard, and Hoenir has become engulfed in the silence which was his strength.

1. Also with birds of various kinds, on the strength of the adjectives applied to him.

3. The Twin Gods

There is good reason to believe that at one time the heathen Germans worshipped twin deities, two brothers who were the sons of the god of the sky. Traces of these have been sought in the myths of northern Europe, but without much success.

Here again we are dealing with a pattern familiar in many mythologies. The most famous twins were Kastor and Polydeukes, the *Dioskouroi*, twin sons of Zeus, who were Castor and Pollux to the Romans. They were celebrated horsemen, rescuing men from peril on sea and land, and they were worshipped in particular by the Spartans. They were represented by a strange symbol called the *dokana*, two wooden beams joined by a crossbeam, which has been explained as a primitive apparatus for kindling fire.

In the third century A.D. the Twins were said by Greek geographers to be worshipped along the coast of the North Sea. Tacitus mentioned the Germanic tribe of the Naharvali, near Breslau, who worshipped twin gods similar to Castor and Pollux. He himself was struck by the resemblance, but came to the conclusion that the cult was not an imitation of the Roman one, but was native to the Germans. These gods were called the Alcis; they were worshipped by priests in a forest sanctuary, and the priests were 'decked out like women' (*muliebris ornatus*). The gods were young men and brothers, but no images (*simulacra*) of them were found among the Germans. It happens that an urn of the La Tène period has been found in the region where the Naharvali lived, and this shows men on horseback, each pair fastened to a cross-beam. This resembles the symbol of the *dokana*, and suggests that a similar cult reached the Germans during Roman times.

Of the later history of the Alcis however we know nothing definite. It has been noticed that a number of Germanic peoples had a pair of rulers, described as brothers, included among the ancestors of their royal house. The Vandals had two early kings called Raos and Raptos, the Langobards two heroes Ibor and Aio, and there are brother kings mentioned in the early history of the Swedes, such as Alrik and Eirek, and Alf and Yngvi. The

Anglo-Saxons had two heroes with the strange names Hengest and Horsa (meaning 'stallion' and 'horse') who were said to have played an important part in the foundation of the kingdom of Kent. The association with horses is characteristic of the *Dioskouroi*, so that these two are of special interest. The idea that one brother kills the other, as in the case of the Roman twins, Romulus and Remus, is found as part of some of these traditions, for instance that of the Swedish brothers mentioned above. There are also the brothers called the Haddingjar, vaguely remembered in Scandinavia. Places in Norway have been named after them, and the Old Norse word *haddr*, used of women's hair, recalls Tacitus's description of the priests of the twin gods, adorned in some way like women. The Haddingjar must presumably be connected with the Hasdingi, the royal dynasty of the Vandals, and with the Hartungen of German tradition.

All this however is scholarly speculation. A more practical question is whether we can find any trace of the heavenly brothers, the protective deities who gave help in time of need, in the northern myths. They have been sought among the Vanir, and it has been suggested that Njord and Freyr are their descendants, or Freyr and Ull. But only faint traces remain of these protective gods who supported their followers in battle or on the sea. It would seem that the initiative has passed over to the greater gods, Thor, Freyr, and Odin, or possibly to the goddesses. There is some evidence for a pair of female deities. Hakon, the Jarl of Halogaland, called in time of need upon his protectress Thorgerda, and according to one story in *Flateyjarbók* she appeared in the sky in answer to his prayers with her sister Irpa, and they shot arrows against the Jarl's enemies. This is behaviour reminiscent of the *Dioskouroi*. There is also a passage in Saxo which is hard to interpret. When the Swedes were at war with the Danes, each was threatened in turn by the god protecting the other side, and while they fought:

Two hairless old men, of appearance fouler than human, and displaying their horrid baldness in the twinkling starlight, divided their monstrous efforts with opposing ardour, one of them being zealous on the Danish side and the other as fervent for the Swedes.

Gesta Danorum, I, 29 (Elton's translation)

There is, however, nothing which precisely resembles the picture associated with the *Dioskouroi*, that of the two young men on horseback appearing together to help their worshippers. The Alcis appear to have been forgotten in the north by the time Snorri came to collect his myths.

4. *Forseti*

Snorri mentions Forseti, the son of Balder, among the gods of Asgard. In *Grímnismál*, in a list of the dwellings of the gods, mention is made of Glitnir, a hall of gold and silver, which belongs to Forseti. He is said to dwell there, and to 'still all strifes'. This may be a late addition to the poem, but Forseti is worth notice because there are two independent traditions about him. One is a story in the eighth-century life of St Willebrord which tells of a visit by the saint to an island between Frisia and Denmark. This island had a holy spring, from which men had to draw water in silence, because of the sanctity of the place. Willebrord baptized three men in the spring, and killed a cow there, defiling the holy spot. However, he escaped death at the hands of King Radbod, because three times lots were drawn, and each time he avoided the death sentence, although one of his party was killed. This island was said to be called Fositesland after the god worshipped there. The name Forsetlund is also found near Oslo fiord, so that it is possible that at one time the cult of this god spread northward to Norway from the Frisian coast.

The other story is a Frisian saga[1] telling how Frisian law came to be recorded. Charles the Great had demanded of twelve representatives from Frisia that they should tell him their laws, and when they could not obey, he offered them the gloomy alternatives of death, slavery, or being set adrift in a rudderless boat. They chose the last of these punishments, and called on God to help them. Their prayer was answered, for a thirteenth man appeared among their company with a golden axe on his shoulder. He steered the ship with his axe, and as they drew near land, he threw it ashore, and a spring gushed up in the place where it touched the earth. The

1. B. F. von Richthofen, *Rechtsquellen*, p. 439.

stranger taught them the laws which they needed to know, and disappeared.

This story has been given Christian colouring, and it is possible that it is not of heathen origin. It has been thought by some, however, to be a memory of the god Forseti, who according to *Grímnismál* was associated with silver and gold (hence the golden axe?) and with the peaceful settlement of disputes. The company of twelve men with a god as their leader need not necessarily have been suggested by Christ and the twelve apostles, as there is plenty of independent evidence for the council of twelve in the north. Odin headed such a council in the story of the sacrifice of King Vikar (page 52). Nor indeed does the axe seem a fitting symbol for Christ, while the use of it to cause a spring to gush out from the earth is in agreement with the sacred spring on Forseti's island in the other story. The names Axenshowe and Eswei are mentioned as place-names associated with this incident, and Eswei might be related to the name of the Aesir. There is no full agreement however as to the reliability of these traditions as evidence for a cult of Forseti in the north. As usual, attempts have been made to identify him with the greater gods, but without success.

5. *Heimdall*

When we turn to the figure of Heimdall, we are faced with a problem of a very different kind from that involved in the study of nebulous deities like Hoenir or Forseti. We have a good deal of material about this god, and the figure which emerges from Snorri's description of him and from references in the poems is that of a mysterious, impressive power, with a strong personality of his own. He does not however fit into any recognized category among the divinities. Scholars have been most industrious in their efforts to fit Heimdall neatly into the religious scheme of the north. He has been interpreted as a sun god, a moon god, a ram god, and a woodpecker god. He has been seen as the spirit of ritual silence, as a personification of the World Tree or of the rainbow. He has been compared with the Indian fire god Agni, with the Persian Mithras, with the Christian St Michael, even with Christ himself. Pering, who gives a masterly survey of the different theories about Heimdall, ends with the conclusion that his true place is as guardian spirit of the gods, a kind of brownie in Asgard.[1] De Vries, however, emphasizes his function of sentry.[2] Such a variety of theories gives some idea of the wide diversity of Heimdall's character. None of them however seems completely satisfying, since in every case certain aspects of this many-sided god have been emphasized and isolated at the expense and neglect of the rest.

Heimdall's most dramatic aspect is that of the Watcher. Snorri describes him sitting tirelessly at the end of heaven to guard the rainbow bridge. He needs no sleep, and can see by night as by day, his ear is perpetually alert for the tiniest sound and the faintest threat to Asgard's safety. He holds *Gjallarhorn*, the horn of warning. It is this patient watchfulness of the god with which Loki taunts him in *Lokasenna*, and in *Voluspá* his horn is used as the trump of doom, to arouse the gods when the forces of evil converge upon them.

It has been suggested that Heimdall's horn in this poem is an imitation of the trumpet of the archangel Gabriel, and cannot be an early feature of the god. On Gosforth Cross in Cumberland a figure is seen holding a horn; this comes among a series of scenes which must be related to the doom of the gods, and implies that the horn formed part of the tradition by the tenth century. The theory of a Christian origin does not, however, explain why the horn was connected with Heimdall in the beginning, and the picture of him as the unwearying sentinel can hardly be attributed solely to imitation of Gabriel. One explanation favoured by the Finnish scholar Pipping[3] was that Heimdall had some special connexion with the horned ram, since one form of his name found in the texts is Heimdali, 'ram'. We have no real solution to the problem raised by two strange kennings quoted by Snorri; he says that a poetic name for a sword is 'Heimdall's head', and that a poetic name for a head is 'sword of Heimdall'. If myths have given rise to these puzzling kennings, they are now lost, and most of the theories evolved to

1. B. Pering, *Heimdall*, Lund, 1941.
2. In *Études germaniques*, 1955, pp. 266 ff.
3. H. Pipping, 'Eddastudier', *Studier i Nordisk Filologi*, 16, 1925, pp. 23 ff.

account for them are too complicated to be satisfactory. Pipping sees the basic explanation in the figure of a ram with the horn on its head as a sword, and thinks that perhaps Heimdall represents the ram sacrifice hanging from the World Tree, so that to some extent he came to be identified with the tree itself. The tree was the guardian of the dwelling of the gods, and this would account for the unceasing watch kept by Heimdall.

Pipping also sees in the figure of Heimdall links with north-eastern Europe, and in particular with the Finno-Ugric tribes, many of whom are accustomed to represent their gods by standing pillars of wood. Heimdall is called the White God, great and holy, and there are Yakut legends of a White Youth, the father of the human race, who was nourished by the spirit of the World Tree and fed on milk. This conception must have come from the south, and must be connected in some way with the image of the life-giving, nourishing tree of the Near East. On the other hand there are certain characteristics of Heimdall which seem to point to w___n origin. In the preface to *Rígspula*, one of the *Edda* poems, Heimdall is identified with the hero of the poem, Rig. This Rig, whose name is not mentioned elsewhere, is repre-sented as the progenitor of mankind and the father of the human race. He goes up and down the earth, and in his wanderings he visits representatives of three classes of men: the thrall, the farmer, and the earl. He stays a night at three typical houses in turn, and lies down to sleep in each house between the husband and the wife. Nine months after his visit, a child is born to each couple; the first is the boy who becomes the rough, labouring thrall, the second, the boy who becomes the hard-working, free-born farmer, managing his own lands, and the third, the boy of noble ancestry, who is to grow into the earl, the leader of men.

There appears to be Celtic influence behind this poem. First, the name Rig is presumably to be derived from the Irish word *ríg*, 'king'. Secondly, this story of the travelling god, going from house to house among his subjects and begetting children, shows a striking resemblance to certain Irish traditions connected with Manannán mac Lir and his son Mongán.[1] Manannán is a Celtic god of the sea, associated with the Isle of Man, and called Son

1. N. K. Chadwick, 'Pictish and Celtic Marriage . . .', *Scottish Gaelic Studies*, 7, 1953, pp. 85 ff.

of the Sea. The same name might be given to Heimdall. In the lost *Heimdallargaldr*, a poem about him known to Snorri, he is said to be the son of nine mothers. These appear to be sea-giant-esses, or perhaps waves of the sea (see p. 130). It is assumed that Heimdall is the being described in the *Shorter Vǫluspá*:

> One was born in olden days,
> of strength surpassing, kin to the Powers.
> He, nail-resplendent, was born to nine
> giant maids, on the edge of earth.

We have already seen that the idea of maidens of mighty strength, dwelling beneath the sea, is familiar in both Scandinavian and Irish tradition, and that they are linked with the giantesses of the underworld who play an important part in Norse mythology. It is further said in the poem quoted above:

> To him was added the might of earth,
> of ice-cold sea, and sacred swine-blood.

The swine we know to have been sacred to Freyr and the Vanir, and they in turn have close links with the giantesses. The strange word used in the poem, 'nail-resplendent', is found also applied to a great giant of the underworld, the father of the maid *Men-glǫð*, 'necklace-glad', who is believed to be connected with Freyja. To the Vanir and the powers of the underworld, then, Heimdall seems in some way to belong.

It is true that this connexion with the Vanir is implied rather than clearly obvious, but it is implied at several different points. Heimdall seems to have special links with Freyja. One of her names, Mardǫll, is the counterpart of his, with *mar*, 'sea', re-placing *heim*, 'earth'. In *Þrymskviða* it is Heimdall who gives counsel how Freyja is to be saved from the giants, and there his name is linked with the Vanir, although unfortunately one can-not be sure from the context whether he is regarded as one of them or merely resembling them in his knowledge of hidden things. Freyja is also linked with the sea, and the power of the Vanir extended over water as well as land. Heimdall is said to have done battle with Loki, and their conflict is referred to in a tenth-century poem *Haustlǫng*. Once more we are unlucky in that the text of this is exceedingly obscure, and scholars have been unable to agree as to the exact meaning of the words. It seems that Heimdall was successful in the struggle, and was left in possession of the 'precious stone', which has been thought to be Freyja's necklace, *Brísingamen*, stolen from her by Loki.

Much more could be said about Heimdall, but it would mean heaping up complexities and conflicting theories. The lost poem known to Snorri, *Heimdallargaldr*, is sorely needed to throw more light on the perplexing figure of the watcher of the gods. *Vǫluspá* begins with an invocation to the 'sons of Heimdall' to keep silent, and seems to imply that the sons of Heimdall are men, and that he is therefore regarded, as in *Rígspula*, as the father of mankind. In what sense he was so regarded it is difficult to determine. There is no indication of any cult associated with him, and place-names do not help us here. Yet the widely differing references to the White God have a convincing ring, and their very variety and inconsistency are an argument against the theory that Heimdall is a composite figure pieced together by the poets and Snorri. The link with the Vanir seems the most helpful clue to our understanding of him, since these would account for the different aspects in which he appears, his association with the protection of Asgard, with the sea, with the World Tree and the underworld, and finally with the fathering of mankind.

6. *Loki*

The place which Loki occupies in the circle at Asgard is as puzzling as that of Heimdall, although he is an even more prominent figure, and plays an important part in most of the well-known myths. Indeed to a reader of Snorri Loki is perhaps the most outstanding character among the northern gods, the chief actor in the most amusing stories, and the motivating force in a large number of plots. It is he who brings comedy into the realm of the gods, and tragedy into the story of Balder. On the other hand, to a reader of the poems Loki is a vaguer, more powerful and sinister figure. He is evidently an ambivalent character, neither wholly good nor wholly bad, although in Snorri's tales the bad side predominates. By the late Viking age the wicked and dangerous side of his character seems to have been strengthened by comparison with the Christian Devil. Loki appears in Snorri to have been directly responsible for the death of Balder, but outside Snorri the evidence is slender, and many have thought that the picture of him as Balder's murderer is a late development due to the gradual blackening of his reputation.[1] This is perhaps the most difficult of the many problems connected with Loki.

A characteristic of Loki, shared by no other gods except Odin and Thor, is his sociability. He has adventures in company with nearly all the important inhabitants of Asgard, Freyr being the exception. He is the companion of Odin and Thor; he fights Heimdall and kills Balder; he plays a part in both the creation and destruction of the world; he helps in the building of Asgard; he is at home among the giants and the monsters as well as the gods. There is no doubt as to his importance in the mythology of the north. Unsuccessful attempts have been made to identify him with the mysterious god Lóðurr, who is said to have taken part in the creation of man, but of whom little is known. But it has not been found possible to establish Loki as a major deity who has come down in the world of the gods, for there is no evidence of his worship among men, as in the case of Freyr and Thor, and even Tyr.

Here it is proposed to examine the picture of Loki given in the poems and the myths to see how far it is a consistent one. As to the age and reliability of the various sources in which he is mentioned, more will be said later.

It may be noted that even the Loki of Snorri's tales is a mischievous rather than a wicked being. Sometimes his actions cause inconvenience and suffering to the gods, as when he helps a giant to steal the apples of immortality, or, in his desire to steal a salmon, kills an otter who has powerful relations to avenge him. Yet on other occasions it is Loki who rescues the gods from serious predicaments, as when he helps to regain Thor's hammer by dressing him up as bride. Sometimes Loki acts under compulsion, either because the giants get him into their power or the angry gods insist on his righting some wrong he has done them. There is no doubt however that many of his acts, like the cutting off of Sif's hair, are the doings of a naughty boy rather than crimes against the righteous gods. While he is

1. Dumézil's work on Loki (*Loki*, 1959, and *Les Dieux des Germains*, 1959), provides arguments against this.

both cunning and ingenious, it may be noted that his plans do not by any means always succeed.

Loki has certain magic powers, and the most outstanding is the ability to change his shape. When the giant was building the walls of Asgard, Loki turned himself into a mare and lured away the giant's horse which served him so faithfully. It was while he was in mare's form, according to Snorri, that Loki gave birth to Sleipnir, Odin's eight-legged steed. When he was concerned in the theft of the apples, Loki was in bird form. When he went to look for Thor's hammer, he was said to borrow the 'feather form' of Freyja, which meant flying in the shape of a bird. To prevent the clever dwarfs from winning their wager, he turned himself into a fly and stung the smith at a critical moment. He is said to have taken the form of a flea when he wanted to steal Freyja's necklace. One interpretation of a difficult verse in *Haustlǫng* implies that Heimdall and Loki fought in the form of seals, while at the end of *Lokasenna* he is said to have become a salmon in the river to escape the anger of the gods. According to Snorri, Loki took on the form of an old woman to prevent Balder coming back to Asgard. Finally, as well as giving birth to Sleipnir, he is said to be the father of monsters, and thus to have been responsible for the creation of the wolf Fenrir and the World Serpent, as well as the terrible goddess Hel, the guardian of the realm of death.

In this way, Loki is connected with the darker elements in the northern mythical world, and this tie is at least as early as the skaldic poets of the ninth century. It has been explained by some scholars as a derivation from medieval works on demonology like those of Isidore of Seville. We cannot however rule out the possibility that the kennings which link Loki with the monsters are founded on genuine heathen tradition, even though they have a vague general resemblance to learned speculation on the origin of monsters and devils. The binding of Loki may also be an early tradition, although here again it is difficult to be sure how far there has been influence from learned works. Old English accounts of the Genesis story certainly emphasize the binding of the Devil to a surprising extent, and it was a favourite subject for illustration in Anglo-Saxon manuscripts of the tenth century. This may have been because the idea of a bound giant was already familiar in heathen times. In northern England there are carved stones from the Viking age showing monstrous bound figures, which could be identified with either Satan or Loki. On the Gosforth Cross in particular we have what seems to be a faithful representation of the story of Loki's binding as told by Snorri. The bound figure is lying in a position where snakes can drop venom on him from above, while a female figure catches it in a bowl to keep it from his face (see page 37). At Gosforth we have a cross where heathen motifs concerned with the end of the world – Heimdall's horn, the killing of the serpent and so on – appear to have been deliberately chosen because they can be presented in accordance with Christian teaching also, and interpreted as the victory of Christ over the powers of hell, and the coming of the Last Judgement. The fact that the bound figure is found among these suggests that Loki here is equated with the bound Devil of apocalyptic tradition, and that he was therefore a figure familiar to the early converts. Olrik made a detailed study of folklore connected with the bound giant of the Caucasus region,[1] and while few now would follow his conclusions all the way, he has shown that the idea of a bound giant is a pre-Christian conception, and seems to have existed independently of ideas about the binding of Satan from Christian sources.

Jan de Vries[2] has made a full analysis of the sources in which Loki is mentioned. Many of these are late, and the stories of Loki's tricks contained in them are likely therefore to be late additions to his character, told for the sake of entertainment. He came to the conclusion that the chief characteristic of Loki likely to go back to earlier myths is his talent as a thief. Again and again he steals or hides the treasures of the gods: the apples of youth, the belt and gloves of Thor, the necklace of Freyja. This side of Loki's character was certainly familiar to the early poets, while Dumézil would go even further, and trace the conception of Loki as the master thief back to remote antiquity, among the fundamental mythological concepts of the Indo-European peoples.

1. A. Olrik, *Ragnarök: die Sagen vom Weltuntergang*, Berlin, 1922.
2. 'The Problem of Loki', *F.F. Communications*, Helsingfors, 110, 1933, pp. 19 ff.

Attempts have been made from time to time to see in Loki some link with a fire god, on the grounds of the resemblance between his name and *Logi*, 'fire'. There seems however to be little real evidence to support this. When, in Snorri's tale of Thor's journey to Utgard, Loki takes part in an eating contest with Logi (see pp. 33–4), this seems to mean no more than that the Norse storyteller was also aware of the superficial resemblance between the two names. Loki does not behave like a fire-spirit, and indeed he seems to be as much at home in the water as on the earth, so that some scholars have even tried to see him as a water-spirit. Other theories which try to establish Loki as an early god in the Germanic world have not been very successful. In the nineteenth century a charm was recorded by a clergyman from Lincolnshire, who claimed to remember hearing it spoken by an old countrywoman when he was a boy :[1]

> Thrice I smites with Holy Crock,
> With this mell [hammer] I thrice do knock,
> One for God, and one for Wod,
> And one for Lok.

It is tempting to see this as a folk survival of belief in three heathen gods, Thor of the hammer, Woden, and Loki, and some Danish and German scholars accepted it as such, and built up elaborate theories accordingly. But this isolated scrap of doggerel, which moreover was recorded in at least three different versions by the clergyman in question,[2] is an extremely fragile foundation on which to base assumptions concerning the beliefs of the Danes in Lincolnshire in the ninth century. A verse claimed to have been heard once in boyhood and not recorded until many years later needs corroborating evidence before it can be generally accepted.

Loki, the thief, the deceiver, and the sharp-tongued scandal-monger who outrages the gods and goddesses by his malicious revelations in *Lokasenna*, yet who nevertheless seems to be accepted as a dweller in Asgard and a companion of the greatest gods, is hard to comprehend. However, it was in view of these

1. *Viking Club Saga Book*, III (I), London, 1902, p. 53.

2. H. R. Ellis Davidson, 'Folklore and Man's Past' (paper given to the British Association for the Advancement of Science, Aberdeen, 1963), *Folklore*, 74, 1963, pp. 534–6.

queer contradictions in his character that resemblances were pointed out between Loki and the supernatural Trickster who plays a great part in the myth and folklore of a number of North American tribes.[1] The trickster is greedy, selfish, and treacherous; he takes on animal form; he appears in comic and often disgusting situations, and yet he may be regarded as a kind of culture hero, who provides mankind with benefits like sunlight and fire. At times he even appears as a creator. He can take on both male and female form, and can give birth to children. He is, in fact, a kind of semi-comic shaman, half way between god and hero, yet with a strong dash of the jester element, foreign to both, thrown in. The figure of the trickster was clearly a popular one among storytellers, and tended to attract to himself all sorts of folk-tales.

There is no doubt that this figure bears a resemblance to that of Loki at many points, and particularly at those points which are most difficult to fit in with any other interpretation of his character. Loki also seems to have become the hero of many folk-tales, told for entertainment purposes only, and many of them late in date; in these he usually plays a comic role. Sometimes the Indian legends about the trickster contain two creator figures, one good and impressive, and the other, the trickster, appearing as a kind of parody of him: a creator whose schemes frequently go awry. Loki as the ambivalent mischief-maker might similarly be seen as a kind of Odin-figure in reverse. It is certainly easier to understand some of the puzzling elements in him if we regard him as a parody of the great creator-gods rather than as consistently in opposition to them. Certain elements in the myths and poems suggest that at one time he was a chthonic figure, connected primarily with the world of the dead, and this would be comprehensible if we see him as a kind of shadow of Odin. Besides his links with Hel, the serpent, and the wolf, and with the horse that carries Odin to the realm of the dead, he appears alongside the giants at Ragnarok, steering the ship that brings them over the sea. In *Svipdagsmál* he is said to have made the magic weapon *Laevateinn*, 'beneath the doors of the dead'.

1. P. Radin, *The Trickster: a Study in American Indian Mythology*, 1956.

It is important to remember that there was also a Loki of the outer-regions, Utgard-Loki, who dwelt somewhere to the east of the land of the gods, and was visited on one famous occasion by Thor. This Loki is a giant of tremendous size and power, but his power is not really greater than that of Thor: it depends largely on his cunning and his capacity to perform sight-deceiving magic which makes things appear other than they are. The straightforward Thor is taken in and humiliated, whereas Odin, we feel, would have been perfectly at home in this bewildering world of sleight and fantasy. Comic fabrication though this story may be, it perhaps contains an element of truth in the way in which the Loki giant is set up against Thor. In a similar story in Saxo, but one presented very differently, travellers penetrate into the realm of a terrible giant, who is lying bound in the midst of darkness, like Loki. This giant lies in a land of cold, corruption, and tainted treasures, in fact, in the realm of death itself.

No estimate of Loki can be complete which does not take into account the grim and terrifying background of death to which Loki seems at times to belong. If he were originally a giant of the underworld, with skill in deceiving and disguise, it is conceivable that he would gradually develop in later literature into the figure of the agile trickster, stirring up mischief and parodying the more dignified gods, and so have won a place of this kind in Snorri's Asgard. Continually following Odin and Thor, yet mocking at them and the goddesses, he has turned into the hero of a series of diverting, sometimes unseemly stories. Only at Ragnarok is it clear where Loki's real allegiance lies, when he seems to relapse again into the figure of a bound and monstrous giant, breaking loose to destroy the world. Then the nimble-witted Thersites of the court of the gods is replaced by a remote and terrible power. Concerning his relations with Balder, there will be more to say.

7. *Balder*

The last of the enigmatic gods to be considered is Balder, whose fortunes, according to Snorri, were closely linked with those of Loki, so that they cannot be considered wholly apart. Here the problem is not so much one of diversity, as with Heimdall, nor of inconsistency, as with Loki, but is one caused by the fact that we have two widely different pictures of Balder's death, given by Snorri and Saxo. There is little evidence of any early cult of Balder, and the question appears to be largely one of literary sources and traditions linked with his name.

The earliest mention of Balder is in the Second Merseburg Charm, where he is mentioned along with Phol and Wodan:

> Phol and Wodan rode to the wood.
> Then Balder's foal sprained its foot.
> Then chanted Sinhtgunt and Sunna her sister,
> Then chanted Friia and Volla her sister,
> Then chanted Wodan, as he well knew how. ...

This however does not prove that he was known as a god in heathen Germany. Here we have mention of Wodan and his wife (Friia) and perhaps a fertility pair, Vol (Phol) and Volla. Sunna and Sinhtgunt have been taken as the Sun and Moon, but Balder, which (like Freyr) means 'lord', could be no more than a title, and the horse could have belonged to Vol, the fertility god, the only character in the rhyme who does not take part in the spell. Alternatively, Balder might be a hero, aided by the gods and goddesses. The name *Baldæg* is found in some of the early genealogies of the kings of Anglo-Saxon England. In this form it could mean literally 'bright day', and a theory was constructed to establish Balder as a deity of the sky on the grounds of this, and in accordance with Snorri's description of Balder as a god of radiance and beauty. All this however is mere surmise. There is no real evidence for myths about Balder as a god surviving in heathen England or among the continental Germans.

The early skaldic poets use Balder's name frequently as a kenning for warrior. In Saxo, it is as a warrior that he appears, although he is said to have 'sprung secretly from celestial seed'. Saxo's account, as a piece of literature, is far inferior to that of Snorri; it has received far less attention, and yet can scarcely be set aside, as has been done in a recent account of the religion of the Vikings,[1] as 'of no great interest'. In Snorri's tale (pp. 35–7), Balder was the fair young son of Odin, beloved of all in Asgard. Invulnerable to weapons, because all things had given

[1]. J. Brøndsted, *The Vikings*, Penguin Books, 1964, p. 277.

a promise to Frigg not to hurt him, he was finally slain by a shaft of mistletoe, a tiny plant which had gone unnoticed by the goddess. It was Loki who guided the hand of the blind god Hoder and prompted the shot, and Loki again who kept Balder in Hel's kingdom, since he, disguised as an old woman, refused to weep for the dead god, and accordingly Balder could not be freed from Hel.

In Saxo's tale,[1] the supernatural world is present, but the form is different. Balder the warrior was aided by a group of supernatural women, who appear to have been Valkyries, since they claimed to have the power to grant victory in battle. These women kept for Balder a special food which rendered him invincible, over which snakes had dropped poison. Balder had a human rival in the hero Hoder, since both wished to wed the maiden Nanna, and Hoder too met the women, who were willing to give him counsel, and even a special belt which could give him victory. Hoder learned that to slay Balder he would have to gain possession of a special weapon, a sword which was guarded by Mimingus, a satyr of the woods. To come by this, he had to go a long and perilous journey through cold and darkness to a mysterious land which seems to be the underworld. He took Mimingus by surprise, overcame him, and took away the sword.

Several battles were fought between Hoder and Balder, and in this part of the story Saxo has almost certainly repeated the same incident more than once. In one battle Balder, supported as he was by all the gods, was defeated, and his ships put to flight. On another occasion he won the victory, and uncovered a spring of clear water to quench the thirst of his soldiers. Saxo claimed that this spring still existed and was known as *Baldersbrynd*, 'Balder's spring'. In spite of this victory, Hoder married Nanna, and Balder began to pine away with grief and was carried round in a wagon. Finally Hoder met Balder after he had obtained the magic sword, and wounded him. Next day the final battle was fought, and the wounded Balder carried in a litter on to the field. Proserpine appeared in a dream and foretold his death, and after three days Balder indeed died from the wound which Hoder had given him. He was given a

1. Saxo Grammaticus, *Gesta Danorum*, III, 70–81.

royal funeral and buried in a great barrow. A certain Harald broke into his burial mound in the twelfth century, but he and his party were overtaken and nearly drowned by a stream which flooded out of the hill as they were digging, and after that the mound was left undisturbed. Odin was so determined to avenge the death of Balder his son that he wooed a princess called Rind, and, after some dubious adventures, had a son by her, called Boe; when Boe grew up, he killed Hoder in battle.

On the surface there are wide divergences between these two accounts of Balder's death. Apparently we have on the one hand the traditions preserved in Iceland and recorded by Snorri, opposed to those of Denmark, collected by Saxo; possibly one (or both) of the compilers has misunderstood or twisted the available sources. Much ingenuity has been expended in attempts to decide what these sources were, and whether they were in the form of poetry or prose saga. A saga of Hoder seems to have been known to Saxo, who tells the story of Balder throughout from Hoder's viewpoint. His account of the journey to the Other World, however, strongly suggests that it came from a poem, not known or ignored by Snorri, of the same type as *Svipdagsmál* and *Skírnismál*, two poems in the *Edda* which deal with supernatural journeys and magic weapons. Snorri on the other hand seems to have known poems not used by Saxo, including one describing the ride of Hermod across the bridge of the dead and down the road to Hel's abode. Other Norse poems which have survived give us comparatively little help. Only *Lokasenna* supports Snorri in inferring that Loki was responsible for Balder's death, since there Loki declares to Frigg that it is because of him that she will never again see Balder ride back to the hall. *Lokasenna* however is not thought to be an early poem. In *Vǫluspá* there is an allusion to Balder as the 'bleeding offering', struck down by the weapon of Hoder. In *Baldrs Draumar* Odin rides down to the land of the dead to consult a dead seeress as to why Balder has had ominous dreams, causing distress to all the gods. Her reply foretells Balder's entry into the realm of the dead:

> Here stands brewed the mead for Balder,
> shining cups, with shields for cover,
> but the Sons of the Gods must suffer anguish. . . .

She then goes on to predict the death of Balder by the hands of Hoder, and how Hoder in turn shall be slain by a son of Odin yet unborn, whose mother will be Rind. Again in *Eiríksmál*, a poem to commemorate the death of a tenth-century Norse king, and therefore one of our earliest sources, the noise of the dead kings coming to feast in Valhalla is said to sound 'as if Balder were returning to the hall'.

Apart from *Lokasenna*, there is nothing in the poems to conflict with Saxo's picture of Balder slain by Hoder, and of his death after a great battle. We may remember in this connexion that in Snorri's story the guardian of the bridge to the land of the dead told Hermod that the day before, when Balder had come that way, the bridge had resounded to the marching feet of many slain men, five troops of warriors passing down to Hel. This implies that Balder had not travelled alone, but had come with a host of men who had died on the battlefield.

When we compare the two stories, it is interesting to find that there is after all agreement between them and with the poems on a number of points, even though the presentation is so different that the initial impression is one of contradiction and confusion. It is worth noticing how far this agreement goes: Balder has a prophetic dream or dreams foretelling his death; Balder is warmly supported by Odin and the gods; supernatural powers both help and oppose him; he is slain by Hoder; the slaying is done by a special weapon, because in general Balder is invulnerable to weapons; Odin receives a terrible set-back from Balder's death; another of Odin's sons, born after Balder dies, is destined to avenge him; a journey to the land of the dead forms part of the tale. This last point is one of the most interesting features of the Balder story, since it implies that the struggle for Balder's survival took place partly on earth and partly in the Other World. There is not complete agreement as to when and why this journey was made. In the *Edda* poem, Odin rode down to the world of the dead to find out what threatened Balder; in Snorri, it was Hermod who rode down to Hel to fetch Balder back; in Saxo, it was Hoder who went down to the land of darkness and cold to obtain a special sword to kill Balder. Another interesting point is that in Saxo's tale three days elapsed between Balder's wounding and his death; it is possible that this was the period when the struggle for his spirit took place and the powers fought for Balder's life. In all sources also there is mention of Balder's magnificent funeral. Snorri describes how he was burned on his ship (and part of his account at least comes from an early poem). Saxo mentions the funeral and his burial in a mound; he also has a reference to ship-funeral, and to the corpses of those dying in battle being burned on ships, at another point in the story. Finally it is interesting to note that Snorri alludes to a folk-belief that all things weep for Balder when the dampness of a thaw sets in after frost, while Saxo, on the other hand, claims to know local traditions concerning Balder's battle with Hoder and his place of burial.

The special weapon with which Balder was killed was said by Snorri to have been mistletoe, and this has received great prominence in view of the importance of the 'golden bough' and the sacredness of mistletoe among the Druids, brought out by Frazer in his monumental work on early religion. Saxo however thought of this fatal weapon as a sword, and a famous sword Mistletoe was known in Norse heroic tradition, and is mentioned several times in the legendary sagas. It seems likely in any case that the motif in the Balder story was one which is found in other traditions of Odin, that of a seemingly harmless rod or stick becoming a real and deadly weapon through the magic of the god (see page 52). The plant mistletoe moreover is not native to Iceland, and some have thought that it is unlikely to have been an original feature of the myth.

On the whole it seems that both Saxo and Snorri, when they came to tell the tale of Balder's death, were dealing with obscure and puzzling sources, of the kind which cause us considerable bewilderment when we meet them in the *Edda* collection, poems full of esoteric allusions to magic and the Other World. Both writers have no doubt tried to clarify and to some extent rationalize their material, as we know them to have done else-where. Snorri was a great storyteller and Saxo was not, and consequently Snorri has come out by far the best in the contest. His version appears in all the popular mythologies, while little attention is paid to Saxo. But though Saxo's account may be muddled, full of repetition, and wretched from a literary point of view, it is nevertheless of value in preserving certain traditions about Balder which go back to an early period.

When Loki is blamed for Balder's death, this accusation may be based on the conception of some power of the underworld opposing Odin, and bringing about the death of his son. In Snorri the hostile old woman Thokk refuses to weep for him, and was believed, according to Snorri, to be Loki in disguise. In *Baldrs Draumar* it is the seeress whom Odin accuses of hostility towards Balder:

> You are no *vǫlva*, no wise woman,
> rather the mother of three giants!

he explains in sudden fury. The dead *vǫlva* makes the strange reply that none shall see her again until Loki bursts free from his bonds. The implication is that the mother of three giants is Loki himself, speaking through the lips of the dead, and that Angrboda, Boder of Grief, in Snorri's account is another name for Loki in female form. The giants are the three monsters, Serpent, Wolf and Hel, who are said to be his children and the threat that he will appear again at Ragnarok is consistent with the idea of Loki as a terrible bound giant of the underworld. It was perhaps in his character as this giant that Loki originally brought about Balder's death, rather than as in the tale told by Snorri, where he appears in the role of the nimble-witted mischief-maker of Asgard.

Balder is called the son of Odin, and Snorri and many others after him have assumed that this makes him a god. It has already been indicated (p. 109) that certain features in Snorri's account of his death seem to be influenced by the cult of the gods of the Vanir. On the other hand, Saxo thought of Balder as a warrior on earth, who was said to be Odin's son only in the sense that he was one of his followers, or that he was born to some human mother visited by the god. He received special favours from his celestial father as did many others of Odin's famous heroes. Allusions to Balder in the poems, as we have seen, do not appear to contradict this picture. In a study on Balder, de Vries[1] has given weighty reasons for accepting the

1. Jan de Vries, 'Deh Mythos von Balderstod', *Arkiv för Nordisk Filologi*, 70, 1955, pp. 41 ff.

story of his death as one belonging among the tales of Odin's heroes rather than among the myths of the slaying of a god. It could have originated as a story of rivalry between two brothers, both 'sons of Odin', who were led by some tragic accident to become slayer and slain. Such a story was known to the Anglo-Saxons, and is briefly referred to in *Beowulf*. The son of King Hrethel of the Geats, Herebeald, was accidentally shot by his brother Haethcyn with an arrow, and slain. A strange and moving passage follows the brief account of the happening, and the grief of the father over his dead boy – whom in the circumstances he is unable to avenge – is compared to that of a father whose son dies on the gallows. A youth hanged in this way must have died either as a criminal or – in heathen days – as a sacrifice to Wodan. The juxtaposition of the names Herebeald and Haethcyn is perhaps significant; it was pointed out long ago that they bear a resemblance to those of Balder and Hoder of the Norse story. Death upon the gallows is associated with the followers of Wodan, and these points led to the suggestion that here we have an early heroic version of the Balder story remembered in Anglo-Saxon England. As in Saxo, we have here two princely warriors, one of whom, perhaps through the power of a curse or hostile magic, unwittingly becomes the slayer of the other.

The story of Balder is perhaps the most tantalizing of all the puzzling myths which have survived in the north. I have been unable to deal with it in detail, because this would mean going far beyond the scope of this book. But it seems necessary to show that Snorri's story, for all its beauty and pathos, may have misled us in our estimate of Balder. Under his magic touch, Balder has taken on the lineaments of the dying god, derived from the cult of the Vanir. If however Balder in earlier tradition was a human hero struck down in spite of the favour of the gods, and against the will of Odin, he could then belong to the company of great northern heroes whose exploits belong partly to this and partly to the other world.

Chapter 8

The Beginning and the End

There is no doubt that before the universe was
created there was no place in which these created
gods could have subsisted or dwelt. And by 'universe'
I mean not merely heaven or earth which we see with
our eyes, but the whole extent of space which even the
heathens can grasp in their imagination.
 Letter of Bishop Daniel of Winchester
 to St Boniface, A. D. 723–4

When Snorri came to write his account of the gods, he assumed
that they dwelt in a community and had a definite place in
which to live, just as the deities of Ancient Greece were said to
dwell on Mount Olympus. The Aesir and the Vanir lived together in Asgard, and Asgard itself formed part of a larger
world-picture. The World Tree, Yggdrasill, formed the centre
of the universe, and beneath its roots lay three regions, those
of the gods, the giants, and the dead. This of course is an over-
simplification of the deeply-rooted beliefs of men in the Other
World and its powers. In the myths there is no exact boundary
to hedge in the giants, to confine the dead to a realm far from
their burial mounds and the hills of home, or to wall in the gods
in an upper region far above mankind. These different realms
however meant something significant to men, and recognition
of their existence went far deeper than the wealth of stories,
many frivolous or half-mocking, which were woven about them.
The World Tree formed the fixed centre of this series of worlds
which were believed to have had a definite beginning and to be
destined to eventual destruction.

1. *The World Tree*

The idea of a guardian tree standing beside a dwelling place
was once a familiar one in Germany and Scandinavia. We have
even a few examples left in the British Isles, some of which, as

at the Old Manor House at Knaresborough, are trees round which the house itself has been built.[1] Not only the family dwelling, but the house of the gods, the temple, had its own guardian tree in heathen times. The great heathen temple at Uppsala, where both Odin and Freyr were worshipped, is described in the eleventh century by Adam of Bremen in words which sound like an echo of the description of Yggdrasill in the poems:

Near to this temple is a very great tree, stretching its branches afar, and green both in winter and summer. No one knows what kind of tree it is.

Many scholars have thought that they knew, and elaborate theories have been built on the conviction that it was the sacred yew, the evergreen tree. This cannot however be proved from the literature, where more than one conception of the tree can be found. In poetry and prose, the word *askr*, 'ash', is used. We know however that in parts of north-western Europe the oak was especially sacred to the gods, and particularly to Thor, and that like Yggdrasill the sacred oak often had a sacred spring at its foot. There are hints too of a tree which provided food and drink for the gods, an idea which probably came from the Near East in the first place.[2]

Yggdrasill was certainly a guardian tree, and when the end of the world drew near, it was said to shake and tremble. Its doom, like those of the sacred trees cut down in Germany by Christian missionaries, was held to be inseparably linked with that of the gods whom it watched over and protected. But it was more than this: it was also the World Tree, the symbol of universality. It was said to spread its limbs over every land, and the fact that it formed a link between the gods, mankind, the giants, and the dead meant that it was visualized as a kind of ladder stretching up to heaven and downwards to the underworld. This conception of a road between the worlds is one which is familiar in the beliefs of the shamanistic religions. It is developed with rich abundance of detail in the mythologies of the peoples of north-eastern Europe, northern and central Asia, and even further

1. A. B. Cook, 'The European Sky-God', *Folklore*, 17, 1906, pp. 172 ff.
2. For early beliefs in the milk-yielding tree, see G. R. Levy, *The Gate of Horn*, London, 1948, pp. 120 ff.

afield, in the regions where shamans are trained to cultivate the mantic trance, and claim to have the power to send their spirits out of the body for long journeys to the other world. In these various mythologies, the tree which links the different regions plays an essential part.

The tree marked the centre of the universe, and united the cosmic regions. Some Finno-Ugric tribes believed that the gods feasted upon its fruits, and that souls were born among its branches. It was characteristic of this World Tree that its life was renewed continually: thus it became a symbol of the constant regeneration of the universe, and offered to men the means of attaining immortality. Sometimes it was symbolized in shamanistic ritual by a post with steps cut in it, a ladder, or a small birch tree, up which the shaman climbed to indicate his ascent to the heavens. When he entered into his state of ecstasy, he was believed to pass through a series of heavens, one above the other, until at last he penetrated in his flight into the highest realm of the gods. So in Norse mythology the beliefs about the nature of the world of the gods are inextricably linked with the powerful symbol of the World Tree. This marked resemblance to the beliefs of the Finno-Ugric and other eastern peoples is very significant for our understanding of the religious thought of the heathen peoples of the north.

At certain points in the *Edda* poems we find the inference that the realm of the gods was not at one level in space, but viewed as a series of worlds, one above the other. The seeress in *Vǫluspá* begins by remembering nine worlds, 'nine in the Tree'. On Odin's seat *Hliðskjálf* the god could sit out and look over 'all the worlds', suggesting that this seat may have been in the tree itself.[1] Clearly these worlds must not be thought to lie close together; only in the visionary gaze of Odin or of the inspired seeress could they thus be glimpsed as one. The plan of a small neat universe which might be suggested by Snorri's description is soon destroyed by the picture given many times of a long and

---

1. The suggested meaning, 'hill or rock with an opening' (Turville-Petre, *Myth and Religion of the North*, 1964, p. 64), suggests rather the Cosmic Mountain at the centre where the gods dwell (Eliade, *Images and Symbols*, 1961, pp. 42 ff.). This, of course, is closely linked with the World Tree.

perilous journey from one world to another over mountains and desolate wastes of cold and darkness, or of a tedious and fearsome road down to the abode of the dead. Long before astronomy revealed to men the terrifying extent of the great starry spaces, the idea of vastness and of distances to tantalize the mind was already present in heathen thought. In Norse mythology also, as in that of many other peoples further east, we find the image of a bridge that links the worlds. This may be fragile and steeply poised above the abyss, as thin as a needle or a sword-edge, so that only the man with tremendous mantic power may cross it. When Hermod rode to seek Balder, he rode over the *Gjallarbru*, the 'echoing bridge', and the hoofs of Sleipnir rang out loudly upon it. We hear also of the bridge *Bifrost*, a rainbow span of three colours, or sometimes called a bridge of flame, which linked earth and heaven. Over this the gods rode each day, and Snorri connects it with the Milky Way, the road of stars across the sky. This bridge was to be shattered by the enemy hosts at Ragnarok.

We hear also of a great gate, called by various names (*Helgrind*, *Nágrind*, *Valgrind*), which cut off the realm of the living from that of the dead, and over which Sleipnir leapt when he bore Hermod down to Hel. When the dead return to visit the earth, this gate is said to stand open for their passage. There is also mention of rushing waters to be crossed. But while we have thus the impression of boundaries and barriers and great distances, the idea of the World Tree as a fixed and eternal centre persists through the confusion, an image of tremendous power.

This image indeed appears to have once dominated the religious thought of much of Europe and Asia. The main lines can probably be traced to ancient Iranian and Mesopotamian religions, and the conception is one which has had wide and lasting effect on literature and art. Even the creatures which are said to inhabit Yggdrasill can be paralleled in the myths and legends of other regions. The eagle at the top and the serpent at the foot have been traced back to prehistoric monuments. In south Borneo, where the tree represents the cosmos in its entirety, the feminine principle is represented by the serpent, and this battles continually with the masculine principle, the eagle. Their strife is said ultimately to destroy the tree, but it always springs up anew. Hostility between the serpent and the bird is also found in pre-Homeric Greece. Thus when we learn from the *Edda* that the tree constantly suffers attack, both from the serpent at the foot and from the hart that gnaws its branches, we are dealing with a conception that is very old and widespread throughout Europe and Asia:

> The Ash Yggdrasill endures anguish,
> more than men know.
> A hart gnaws it on high, it rots at the side,
> while *Niðhǫggr* devours it below.

We are told in the same poem, *Grímnismál*, that a squirrel, called Ratatosk, runs up and down the tree, carrying messages – presumably hostile ones – between serpent and eagle. The battle between a serpent and an eagle is something which does indeed take place in nature; it was filmed with considerable effect by Walt Disney in *The Living Desert*. Its value as a symbol is obvious: the eagle, bird of heaven, and the serpent, creature of the earth, are fundamentally in opposition. The shaman, like the squirrel, can act as a link between them, for man, if he fully realizes the possibilities of his dual nature, can partake both of earth and heaven.

The meaning of the name Yggdrasill has not been finally determined. The usual interpretation is 'horse of Ygg', for Ygg is one of the names of Odin. One would expect to find the genitive form of the name, *Yggsdrasill*, in this case, but apart from this difficulty, it is an interpretation fruitful in meaning. The tree could be the horse of Odin in the sense that he hung upon it as a sacrifice (see p. 144). To *ride* on the gallows is found as a familiar expression in Old English and Old Norse, and in one of the King's sagas the dream of a great horse is taken as a portent of death by hanging. Besides Yggdrasill, the Tree has other names: *Læráðr*, 'shelterer', *Hoddmímir*, 'treasure of Mimir', *Mimameiðr*, 'pole of Mimir'. It seems clear that the World Tree is referred to in each case, and that it is visualized as affording both shelter and nourishment. The spring at its foot is connected with Mimir (see page 167) and also with Urd, the Norn of destiny. Snorri at one point speaks of three springs, one under each main root of the tree, but it seems more likely that there is one spring only, like that below the tree beside the temple at Uppsala, and that this spring, like the tree itself, had many names.

It is said that the ash is sprinkled with *aurr* from the spring; the meaning of this word is uncertain, but de Vries[1] takes it to mean clear, shining water. We are told that dew comes from the tree, and that when the hart feeds on its branches, her milk becomes shining mead which never gives out, and is used to provide drink for the warriors in Valhalla. It is said also that a man and woman are hidden in the tree during the terrible winter which devastates the earth when the end of all things draws near. They are nourished on morning dew, and Rydberg made the suggestion that another obscure name given to the tree, *Mjǫtviðr*, should really be *Mjǫðviðr*, 'mead tree', because of this conception of its life-giving liquid. Here again we have something in common with the milk-giving tree of the Finno-Ugric peoples, a symbol which must go back ultimately to Mesopotamia, and be of great antiquity.

Another aspect of the tree is that it is the source of new life. Not only do a man and a woman come forth from it to re-people the earth, but the Norns, who are said to dwell beneath it and water it from the spring, are connected with the birth of children. It is said in the poem *Svipdagsmál* that the tree has the power of healing, and that its fruits are burned in the fire and given to women in childbirth, 'that what is within may pass out'. This seems to agree with the widespread shamanistic idea that the tree is the source of unborn souls. Some of the Finno-Ugric peoples believe that the souls of the unborn congregate on its boughs, and that the destinies of men are written on its leaves, so that when a leaf falls, a man dies. This particular symbolism plays a very important part in the initiation dreams of shamans in many different regions of northern and central Asia.

Such close resemblances between the Scandinavian picture of the World Tree and the recorded beliefs of the Finno-Ugric people from more recent times are so striking that they can hardly be explained by a common European heritage of pre-

1. Jan de Vries, *Altgermanische Religionsgeschichte*, Berlin, 1957, II, p. 380.

Christian belief. Admittedly certain ideas connected with the tree seem to be very old, and we know too that the Germanic peoples had the idea of a World Pillar, associated with the cult of the supreme sky god. In a Saxon Chronicle of about 970 written by Widukind, there is a description of the setting up of a column in honour of Mars, to celebrate the victory of the Saxons against the Thuringians. He states that the name of Mars was Hermin. Another chronicle, written about thirty years after the event it describes, records how Charles the Great destroyed the temple and the sacred wood of Irminsul of the Saxons. Irminsul is mentioned again by a ninth-century writer, who states that it was the 'column of the universe, upholding all things'. It is thought that Irmin was another name for the sky god, Tîwaz, among the Saxons, and that the World Pillar, which upheld the sky, was associated with his worship.[1] However the clarity and detail of the picture of Yggdrasill is such as to suggest that new inspiration concerning the World Tree had come into Scandinavia from the east during the Viking age. The penetration of the Viking settlers down the rivers of Russia to the Black Sea opened the road to Byzantium and the East, and there must have been links between the Swedes and the Asiatic tribes, with their shamanistic lore.

The image of the tree that occupied the centre of the world did not wholly die out. It was replaced by the conception of the Christian cross, believed to stand at the mid point of the earth when it was raised at Calvary, at the spot once occupied by the fatal tree of Eden. No idea of this resemblance however seems to have occurred to Snorri when he wrote his description of the World Ash, taken from a number of *Edda* poems which still survive. An interesting question to consider is that of the kind of audience for which the strange collection of facts about the nature of the cosmos given in these poems was intended. It is one to which we must return later.

1. Jan de Vries, 'La Valeur religieuse du mot germanique *irmin*,' *Cahiers du Sud*, 314, 1952, pp. 18 ff.

2. *The Creation of the World*

The series of worlds whose centre was the tree was held to have had a definite beginning and to await a final destruction. Near the close of the heathen period, an unknown poet composed a poem of considerable power on this theme, and it is this poem, *Vǫluspá*, which was the chief source of Snorri's unforgettable account of the creation and destruction of the universe. We do not know how far this poet has himself pieced together isolated fragments of beliefs into a coherent whole, or whether he was dealing with a theme which already formed part of the recognized teaching about the gods. We are however able to conclude, from odd surviving references from other sources, that *Vǫluspá* did not exist in complete isolation.

We are told in this poem that at the beginning there was neither earth nor heaven, sand nor sea nor green grass, but only Ginnungagap, a great emptiness which was nevertheless pregnant with the potential power of creation. De Vries has interpreted the word *ginnunga* as associated with the idea of deceit through magic, with the altering of appearances to mislead the eyes, and this interpretation has been generally accepted.[1] There is a similar use of the term in Snorri's title for one section of the *Prose Edda*, *Gylfaginning*, 'the beguiling of Gylfi'. It is a more satisfactory explanation than to take the phrase to mean 'yawning gap', or to assume that Ginnung was a giant.

It appears that in the eleventh century Adam of Bremen was familiar with this name for the abyss, for he uses what must be the same term: *ghinmendegop*. Again in a fragment of an early poem from southern Germany, *Wessobrunner Gebet*, it is significant to find that the creation of the world is described in language very like that of the Norse poem:

There was neither earth nor high heaven, neither tree ... nor mountain.... No sun shone, no moon gave light. There was no glorious sea.

Although in this poem the creation is given a Christian interpretation, the close similarity suggests that a similar tradition

1. 'Ginnungagap', *Acta Philologica Scandinavica*, 5, 1930–4, pp. 41 ff.

to that in *Vǫluspá* existed among the continental Germans. The popularity of the creation as a subject of Old English poetry may be due to this. It was said to be the subject of the first inspired Christian poem of Caedmon. More surprisingly, it was the subject of the song sung by Hrothgar's minstrel in the new hall at Heorot, as related in the poem *Beowulf* (90-8):

He who knew how to tell of the creation of men in the far past related the tale of how the Almighty wrought the earth, the bright and radiant expanse encircled by the waters. Exulting in victory, he set up sun and moon, lights to give light to the earth-dwellers, and he adorned the surface of the ground with branches and foliage. Life also he created for every race of beings that move and live.

This was the song which tormented the monster Grendel, when he came prowling round the newly built hall, and heard sweet music within. The contrast between the order and beauty of creation and the dark formless world of the monsters is an effective artistic contrast; it is moreover something which may well come out of heathen tradition. The shaping of the earth out of formless chaos and the raising of the bright lights of heaven was an important part of pre-Christian teaching also, judging from the emphasis upon it in northern literature. The building of a bright hall in the wild country where the monsters ranged is like an echo of the creation of the fair world whose destruction was sought by the evil powers, an image likely to be familiar to those who could remember the old tales of the gods.

The original form of the creation myth in the north is not easy to determine. Snorri knew at least three different accounts. First there is a picture of layers of ice forming in the void, while sparks and embers rise from the warm region further south. Life was formed from the meeting of heat and cold, and the giant Ymir took shape in the ice as it melted. He was the ancestor of all the giants, and when he was slain, the earth was formed from his body. Secondly the sons of Bor were said to have been licked out of the salty ice-blocks by the cow *Auðhumla*. She emerged from the ice in the beginning, and Ymir was nourished on her milk. Thirdly there is a reference to the giant Bergelmir, who escaped in his boat from the flood caused by the blood of Ymir which overwhelmed the world, and who founded a new race. This last story sounds less convincing than the other two, and Snorri may have based it on a rather free interpretation of a verse about Bergelmir in *Vafþruðnismál*, grafted on to the Biblical story of the Flood. The name Bergelmir itself is suspicious, and seems to belong to a group of river names, like Hvergelmir and Vaðgelmir. The idea of a destroying flood is also in contradiction to that of the sacrifice of Ymir which created the world.

In the first two myths however we have two concepts of creation for which there are many parallels in different parts of the world. In the story of Ymir we have the slaying of the primeval being, in order that the earth may be formed, and there is good reason to believe that such a myth formed part of early Germanic tradition. Ymir's name has been related to Sanskrit *yama*, meaning 'hybrid' or 'hermaphrodite'. According to Tacitus, the Germans had a primeval ancestor Tuisto, whose son Mannus was the father of mankind. Attempts have been made to connect Tuisto with Tîwaz, but it seems more likely that his name is connected with Old Swedish *tvistra*, 'separate', and that, like Ymir, it means a two-fold being.[1] An explanation of such a name is given in *Vafþruðnismál*, where we are told that a man and woman were born from under the arm of Ymir, and a giant engendered from his two feet. Another example of a primeval being from which the first male and female spring is found in Indian mythology. Ymir indeed is a two-fold being in another sense, since from him both giants and men are born. Attempts have been made to account for the Ymir legend by borrowings from the Talmud and other sources which trace the creation of the world from the body of Adam. But expressions such as 'Ymir's skull' for heaven in the skaldic poets show that the idea of the slaughtered giant was widespread, and can hardly be due to a late borrowing from Christian or Jewish sources. Moreover, the wide distribution of the creation myth in this form provides us with plenty of parallels from non-Christian thought.

The idea of part of the giant's body being flung up into heaven to become a star seems to have been remembered in various myths. Thiazi's eyes were said to be thrown up to heaven by Odin, making two stars (see p. 40), and again the frozen

1. J. de Vries, *Altnordisches Etymologisches Wörterbuch*, Leiden, 1961, *tvistra*.

toe of Aurvandil was said to have been thrown up by Thor (p. 41). These myths are evidently connected with names of constellations, but the strange reference to a frozen toe suggests that there is some connexion with the creation legend of the giant who emerged from the ice.

There are parallels also for the other primeval figure, that of the cow. She was the symbol of the fruitful earth in Egypt and the Near East from the time of the earliest religious records. However *auðhumla* is a native word for a rich, hornless cow. The streams of milk from her udders which became rivers echo the idea of the World Tree as a source of nourishment, although there is some confusion as to whether it is the cow, the goat, or the hart from which the life-giving streams come. The cow, like Ymir, emerged from the melting ice, and licked the salty ice-blocks. It has been suggested that there is some link between the creation legend and the holy place of the Germans, mentioned by Tacitus (p. 55), by the salt springs of the River Saale near Strassfurt, for which a great battle was fought. At this spot it was believed that 'men's prayers received ready access',[1] and it was thought to be close to heaven. The Germans obtained salt there

... by pouring river water on heaps of burning wood, and there uniting the two opposed elements, fire and water.

Thus we have the same conjunction of water, salt, and fire as in the creation myth, associated with a definite holy place in Germany. Another possible origin for the impressive picture of life forming from the union of intense heat and intense cold might however be sought in the volcanic conditions in Iceland. Eruptions of boiling lava, flames, and steam have recurred there at fairly frequent intervals throughout historic times, and must have been known in the Viking age. Iceland is unique among volcanic regions in the meeting of cold and heat which takes place when the ice-covered volcanoes erupt, and the snow and ice melt in the burning flood of lava to send down disastrous floods to the plains below. This is a point to be discussed again in the section on the destruction of the world described in *Vǫluspá*.

There seems to be no trace in Scandinavian sources of the other widespread form of the creation legend, deriving the world

1. Tacitus, *Annals*, xiii, 57.

from a primeval egg, whose upper shell forms the heavens and lower shell the earth. This myth is found in Egyptian, Greek Orphic, and Mithraic tradition, and it has been preserved in Finland, in the story of Väinämöinen creating the world from an egg which a duck laid on his knee in the midst of the watery wastes.[1] It appears that the traditional ideas about the creation which have inspired *Vǫluspá* and other Eddic poems are distinct from those which reached Finland.

The slayers of Ymir are said to be three brothers, Odin, Vili, and Ve. There is a parallel to this in Manichean sources, where a demon was slain by three brother gods in order to form the world. Again however a late borrowing seems unlikely, as there are traces of Odin's brothers elsewhere in Scandinavian tradition. In *Lokasenna*, Frigg is accused of taking Vili and Ve as lovers, and again in *Ynglinga Saga* there is an allusion to the long absence of Odin during which he left his brothers to rule and they took over his wife as well as the kingdom. The names of the brothers are known to the skaldic poets, and Vili's name has two genitive forms, Vilja and Vilis, so that it must have been known for a considerable time in the north. The names could be interpreted as 'will' and 'holiness', but can hardly be mere abstractions in imitation of the Christian Trinity, for reasons given above. We do not know the origin of the strange setting which Snorri gives to the *Prose Edda*, when Gylfi meets three mysterious powers, called High One, Just-as-High, and Third, who sat on high-seats, one above the other, and replied to his questions with wit and irony. This may be based on memories of the brothers of Odin.

A trio of gods appears once more in the story of the creation of man. Here Odin's companions are Hoenir, the silent god, and Lodur, of whom we know almost nothing. According to *Vǫluspá*, they found two trees on the seashore, Askr and Embla, and breathed into them the gift of life. Odin gave them spirit, Hoenir understanding, and Lodur senses and outward form (although the exact meaning of the terms used is debatable). The name *Askr* links up with the World Ash, and also with an Anglo-Saxon tradition that Aesc was the founder ancestor of

1. M. Haavio, 'Väinämöinen, Eternal Sage', *F.F. Communications* (Helsinki), 144, 1952, pp. 145 ff.

the tribe of the Aescingas. Embla may be the same as *elmla*, 'the elm', but if so the reason for choosing this tree is not clear. We have also the other myth of two human beings emerging from a tree to people the world, found in the *Edda* poems. Their names are given as Líf and Lífþrasir, and they are said to shelter in the World Tree and to be nourished by dew from its branches while the rest of the world suffered the great winter. Snorri however interprets this to mean that the two remained in the tree throughout the destruction of the worlds, and repeopled the earth after the time of terror was over. If indeed we are to view the whole series of events as a recurring cycle, as seems to be the case, then there must be a new creation after every destruction of the world. It is in accordance with the teaching concerning the World Tree that it should be from here that life once more emerges after the catastrophe.

3. *The End of the World*

The most memorable stanzas of *Vǫluspá* are those which describe the doom of the gods, and Snorri has paraphrased them into noble prose in his account of Ragnarok. This doom is to be first foreshadowed by the great winter (*fimbulvetr*), which is to last three years on end, and by suffering, wickedness, and bitter warfare among men. Then there are to be mighty earthquakes, darkening of the sun, and the breaking loose of the monsters from their bonds. The serpent will leave the sea, and cause the waters to rise and overwhelm the earth. The giants will arrive in their ship, made from the uncut nails of the dead, and another band under the leadership of Surt will come by land and ride over the rainbow bridge to storm Asgard. The armies of the gods and the giants will meet on a great plain for the final battle.

In this conflict all the great gods must be destroyed, and the monsters with them. Only the sons of the gods survive, and Surt too is left to destroy earth and heaven with fire. Then at the close of *Vǫluspá* comes the calm and lovely picture of the renewal of life, when earth rises green and fertile from the sea, and the sons of the gods remember the past only as men recall an evil dream.

In this account only small additions here and there seem to be due to Snorri; the account of the time of destruction and the renewal that follows must be credited to *Vǫluspá*. Although the language of the poem is in many places obscure, and the clues to some of the allusions lost – for instance we can only guess at the identity of Gullveig who was three times burned by the Aesir – its imaginative strength is still potent for a modern reader. The conclusion of the poem has been taken by some to describe the triumph of Christianity over the old religion, but if this were the deliberate intention of the poet, surely he would have been more explicit. To read it in this way is to narrow down its significance. We have here a vision of death and rebirth which is the essence of all great religions, the eternal re-enactment of which Eliade writes.[1] A whole-hearted Christian poet would scarcely have left us so objective a picture of the old faith, without rejection or condemnation, for such calm detachment would be a rare quality to find in the early days of Christianity. Snorri, it is true, possessed the double vision to a marked degree, but he took care to tell us clearly at the beginning of his book where his real allegiance lay. On the other hand, a heathen poet may well have sensed that the days of his gods were numbered, and there is something of this tragic sense of loss and of the passing of old truths in the moving lines of *Vǫluspá*.

We can be fairly confident at least that this poem is not a wild improvisation, bringing separate concepts together for the first time. There is sufficient scattered evidence to show that the conceptions of the end of the world here used were known elsewhere during the heathen period. In his justly famous study on Ragnarok,[2] the Danish scholar Olrik turned to folklore to throw light on this poem. He found widespread folk-beliefs in Denmark and further afield to provide a fascinating commentary on it. The belief in a ship made of dead men's nails, the devouring of the sun by a monster, the legend that the earth will finally sink into the sea, and the picture of a bound giant one day to break loose and destroy the world – all these can be found in folklore in Denmark and elsewhere. On a different level, parallels to *Vǫluspá* can be found in other mythologies. In Iranian tradition there is the myth of a terrible winter to come upon

1. *The Myth of the Eternal Return*, trans. Trask, 1955.
2. *Ragnarök: die Sagen vom Weltuntergang*, Berlin, 1922.

men, and certain men and beasts given shelter from it in the fold of Yima.[1] Another Iranian belief was that finger-nails should be consecrated to the bird Askozushta, lest they should be used by the forces of evil. In Celtic literary tradition there is a myth of a battle between gods and giants on a vast plain, in which most of the gods will fall. There is no detailed resemblance here to suggest imitation or borrowing between Celtic and Norse peoples, but the fundamental concept behind the two accounts appears to be the same. We know that the Celtic peoples in the ancient world feared lest the earth would be destroyed. Strabo[2] recorded that their Druids taught that 'the soul and the world are indestructible, but one day fire and water will prevail'.

Much has been made of such points of resemblance, and also of parallels with Christian accounts of the burning of the world at doomsday, the darkening of the sun, and the falling of the stars. It is obvious that if one contemplates the destruction of the world, whether in a religious context or not, certain possibilities are bound to occur to the mind. Destruction by intense heat and cold and inundation by water are likely to be among them. As we shall see later, this was particularly so for the people of Iceland. It must be admitted too that the falling of the stars and the darkening of the sun could well come into a poet's mind, even if he had not studied apocryphal literature or the writings of the early church. Robert Burns could swear to love his girl

> Till a' the seas gang dry, my dear,
> And the rocks melt wi' the sun ...

and cosmic imagery of this kind is part of the common literary and imaginative heritage of others beside theological scholars. Therefore I would discount much of what has been written deriving the material of *Vǫluspá* from Christian sources. It is true that the morbid insistence on the terrors cf Judgement Day in the writings and sermons of churchmen may well have had an effect on those outside the pale of the Christian church. But it would be insufficient in itself to account for the idea of the ending of the world among the heathen Scandinavians.

1. R. C. Zaehner, *The Dawn and Twilight of Zoroastrianism*, 1961, p. 135.
2. *Geography*, IV, 4.

It is worth noting that both in the *Edda* and in the work of the early skaldic poets we find traces of a conception of the universal destruction of the world. There is a reference to the falling of the stars in a ninth-century poem of Kormak, and one to the overwhelming of the earth by the sea in the *Shorter Vǫluspá*. A passage in Saxo describing the battle in which Harald of Denmark fell reads as if it were based on some poetic account of the world's ending:

The sky seemed to fall suddenly on the earth, fields and woods to sink to the ground; all things were confounded, and old Chaos come again; heaven and earth mingling in one tempestuous turmoil, and the world rushing to universal ruin.   *Gesta Danorum*, VIII, 262

Of particular interest is an inscription carved in runes on a Swedish memorial stone from Skarpaker, read by von Friesen as: *iarp s[k]al rifna uk ubhimin*, which he interprets: Earth shall be torn asunder, and high heaven.[1] If this reading is correct, this brief inscription implies that the idea of the destruction of the world was familiar in Sweden, and that it was taken as a fitting subject for a memorial stone to the dead. A scholar's theory from a foreign source is not likely to find its way on to a gravestone. This stone is not a conventional Christian one, for a kind of cross is shown with its base in a boat, which it has been suggested might represent the ship of the dead. It seems likely that the inscription is a quotation from a poem.

Besides the destruction of earth and heaven, we have a second theme in *Vǫluspá*, the breaking loose of the monsters. In the tenth-century court poem *Eiríksmál*, composed on the death of a king of Norway, Odin is asked why he has caused the king to be slain. His reply is: The grey wolf is watching the dwellings of the gods. The implication here is that Eric was needed to join the warrior host of Odin in readiness for the last great battle, and the oblique style of the reference presupposes that Ragnarok was a theme familiar to the poet's audience. Whether it was usual to visualize the other gods dying along with Odin when he was devoured by the wolf is not certain. Valid reasons why they should perish can be found in the myths: Thor's special adversary was known to be the World Serpent; Tyr bound the monster, and therefore might expect vengeance if it broke loose;

1. Brate and Wessen, *Södermanlands Runinskrifter*, p. 117.

Freyr, the bright god who gave away his sword when he wooed Gerd, is matched against Surt, the fire-bringer, whose weapon shone like the sun; Loki was an old enemy of Heimdall, and Snorri brings them together once more. The deaths of Odin, Thor, and Freyr are already given in Vǫluspá, and the others may have been added by Snorri on his own initiative.

There seems little doubt that the destruction of the worlds and the breaking loose of the monsters were ideas familiar to heathen thought. It would be remarkable if a poem of tenth- or eleventh-century date, as this is judged to be, should be completely devoid of Christian influence, and when a resemblance is seen between the horn of Heimdall and Gabriel's trumpet, or reference to the sins of men or to the return of Balder suggests Christian teaching, this could be due either to vague influences from the new faith, or to a deliberate sense of parallels in the poet's mind. But this is a different matter from assuming that the whole concept of Ragnarok in the poem is an imitation and refashioning of Christian ideas about the Last Judgement. One cannot but feel that scholars who have made such a suggestion have been driven on by the pursuit of isolated details and their own theories, and have neglected to sit down and read the poem through again with an open mind.

As with the World Tree, we are very conscious of associations with thought and imagery outside northern Europe in this picture of the world's ending. A tenth-century Bavarian poem about the world's destruction uses the word *Muspilli* in a Christian context, apparently referring to the fire which is to burn the earth. The same word occurs in a ninth-century Old Saxon Christian poem, *Heliand*; this has a reference to the power of *Mudspell* over mankind, and a statement also that *Mutspelli* comes like a thief in the night. Some scholars have thought that this must be the name of some ancient power hostile to the gods, remembered and used in a Christian setting. In that case the sons of Muspell mentioned in *Vǫluspá* may have been an early conception once familiar in Germany. Others have tried to prove that the idea of a world of fire in the south, from which the sons of Muspell come, was of Iranian origin. It has already been noticed that several points in the account of the ending of the world can be paralleled from Iranian sources.

Reitzenstein[1] and others have claimed that there must be Manichean influence behind the Norse conception of the destruction of gods and men. The points which they make are of interest, but they are concerned with minor resemblances only, and no direct proof of influence for the whole conception has been found. Nor is it easy to see how Manichean ideas could have reached the north so as to be embodied in a tenth-century poem. However, in view of other resemblances noted by Olrik and mentioned earlier, in particular the idea of the sheltering of men and beasts from the great winter, the possibility of new influences coming into Scandinavia during the Viking age must be borne in mind.

In considering Ragnarok, we must take into account a series of carvings on stone which were executed about the tenth century in northern England at a time when the Viking settlers were well established there, some of which have already been mentioned (pp. 173 and 179). There seems little doubt that the scenes on the cross at Gosforth in Cumberland have been based on an account of Ragnarok closely resembling that given in *Vǫluspá* and Snorri. Here monsters struggle in bonds; a woman holds a bowl beside a bound figure, suggesting Sigyn and Loki; a figure battles with a monster, holding open its jaws with hand and foot, precisely as Vidar was said to do when he slew the wolf that had swallowed Odin. In addition we have a figure with a horn, and a warrior riding into battle. So many separate points of resemblance seem to establish the fact that the artist was working on a series of scenes deliberately grouped together. All these scenes were capable of a Christian as well as a heathen interpretation, and as there is a Crucifixion scene on the other side of the cross, there is no doubt that it was erected as a Christian monument.[2] In the same church where this famous cross was erected, we have a stone, probably part of another cross, which appears to show Thor fishing for the World Serpent. There are also two much-worn hog-back tombstones, which are covered with elaborate carvings. One shows figures struggling with serpents, and the other, two armies approaching

1. R. Reitzenstein, *Die nordischen, persischen und christlichen verstellungen vom Weltuntergang*, 1926.

2. See K. Berg, 'The Gosforth Cross', *Journal of the Warburg and Courtauld Institutes*, 21, 1958, pp. 27 ff., where excellent illustrations are given.

with spears and shields as though for a great battle. Other carved stones which have been thought to show incidents from the final battle of the gods have been pointed out in the Isle of Man.

The existence of these stones implies that there was a body of material available in the tenth century dealing with the end of the world and with the destruction of gods and men, which has been used in *Vǫluspá*. It was of sufficient importance to be used as a symbol of the overthrowing of the forces of evil by Christ, since this seems to be the message of the Gosforth Cross as a whole. When we remember the number of stones from Gosforth, it seems probable that there was some artist or patron in this district with a particular interest in the theme of the gods and the monsters. The existence of the Swedish rune-stone at Skarpaler also suggests that Ragnarok was a traditional subject to be shown on memorial stones for the dead. The destruction of the world, and even of the gods themselves, by the monsters was a fitting symbol of the sombre power of death, like the devouring dragon. Certainly these carvings give us the right to assume what the literary evidence implies, namely that Ragnarok was a widespread popular image in the heathen north, and need not be accounted for by imitations of scholars, or borrowings by bookish men from the written literature of the East.

We do not find anything to suggest the figure of Surt on the carvings. Bertha Phillpotts[1] believed that he was a volcano demon, and that the scene where he set fire to heaven and earth so that steam and flames rose to the stars might have been inspired by one of the Icelandic volcanic eruptions. Surt's name is found in Icelandic place-names, and in particular the gloomy and impressive caverns of the volcanic region in the centre, Surtshellir, are called after him; he may have been one of the northern giants believed to inhabit the underworld.

Certainly when one reads accounts of some of the outstanding eruptions in Iceland in fairly recent times, in particular that of Skaptar Yökul in 1783, the suggestion made by Bertha Phillpotts appears worthy of consideration. The sequence of events was the same as in *Vǫluspá*: first earthquake tremors shook the mountains, then the sun was darkened by clouds of smoke and ashes, then came blazing flames, with smoke and steam, while the

1. 'Surt', *Arkiv für Nordisk Filologi*, 21, 1905, pp. 14 ff.

melting ice caused serious flooding by water as well as by burning lava; if we add a tidal wave from the sea to this series of catastrophes, the situation is very close to that in the poem. As life was said to begin from the meeting of intense cold and heat, so too it ended with the union of water and fire, when the flames mounted to heaven and the sea covered the earth. This vivid picture of creation and destruction was surely most likely to emerge in Iceland itself, where the result of the interaction of cold and heat was constantly before the eyes, and where Hekla erupts on an average every thirty-five years. The poet of *Vǫluspá* could well have been inspired by such a terrible scene as that which took place in 1783, and at many other periods of Iceland's history.

In any case, the burning in *Vǫluspá* is linked with two natural catastrophes which men must have feared constantly in the northern settlements: destruction of life by intense cold, and the flooding of rivers and sea over inhabited land. Both these conceptions are widespread through the world, but they are such as would occur with special force to the minds of the men of the north-west, a region of long, dark winters and stormy seas, as well as occasional volcanic eruptions. The emphasis on the carved stones, on the other hand, was on the overthrowing of the gods by the monsters breaking loose from their bonds. It may have been the genius of the poet of *Vǫluspá* which brought these two ideas together. Certainly the clarity and conviction which one feels in Snorri's account of the destruction is such as to make it hard to believe that here we have merely a hotch-potch of assorted ideas about the world's ending, pieced together from outside sources. If the account in *Vǫluspá*, from which most of his material is taken, was based on an actual experience such as a major volcanic eruption, this would explain how old heathen ideas about the last battle and the overthrow of the gods have been linked up with teaching concerning the end of the world, and all given a new freshness and significance.

There seems no doubt that a vigorous tradition about the end of the world and its subsequent rebirth out of the sea existed in pre-Christian times in the north. This was strong enough to survive until late in the heathen period, when new ideas coming in from outside may have helped to give it new life. The sinking of earth into the sea, the triumph of cold, fire, and darkness, the breaking loose of monsters long held in check – such images lie deep in men's minds, and we can understand their long survival. The picture of Ragnarok might indeed be viewed as a great and terrifying image of a mental breakdown, or as the complete disintegration of the mind in death. It is this which gives the picture which Snorri took from *Vǫluspá* such unmistakable power. He rightly saw it as a fitting climax to his account of the northern gods.

Conclusion

The Passing of the Old Gods

Kjartan said: 'As for me, I mean to accept the Christian faith in Norway, on one condition, and that is that I shall still put a little reliance on Thor next winter, when I get to Iceland.' The king said, with a smile: 'You can see from Kjartan's manner that he feels he can put more trust in his strength and his weapons than in Thor and Odin.'

Laxdoela Saga

This brief survey of heathen religion in the north has shown us that certain of the gods who appear in the myths were once of considerable importance in the lives of men. In the Viking age there were four powerful deities. First Odin, god of inspiration, whether in the form of battle-frenzy, intoxication, or secret wisdom from the land of the dead. Secondly Thor, god of the sky and the thunderbolt, preserver of the community where men pitted their strength and wits against the hardship of the weather and the attacks of their enemies. Thirdly Freyr, who with his sister Freyja brought peace and prosperity to men, the blessings of fertility in the home and the field, healthy children and rich harvests. This group of deities can be traced back to the days when the Germans were a heathen people and worshipped Wodan, god of inspiration and the dead, Tíwaz, god of the sky and of battle, and a god of fertility, along with the goddess of many names whom the Danes called Nerthus. The symbols associated with these gods, the starry heavens and the mighty tree, the unloosing of fetters, the hammer that shattered rocks and slew giants, the ship and the wagon that brought the deity to men, the horse that galloped through the air, the spear that determined victory, the women bearing gifts – all these symbols of power appear to have been known to the Germans in the early period; and to have retained something of their potency into the late Viking age, so that they have left their mark on the myths that remain to us. The background of these deities, the cosmic region surrounding the World Tree, also seems to be of great antiquity. Above was the home of the gods, below the great depths, with middle earth, the home of mankind, poised between them. The doors between the worlds were not hard to open, given the necessary knowledge and the courage to choose so perilous a path.

Many of the myths are concerned with the conception of a journey to the Other World, through the cold and darkness that acted as a barrier. The rich symbolism of roads and bridges, dark holes and caves leading to the underworld, the open burial mound, the journey through the air in bird form, all this emphasizes the belief in a passage between the worlds both for men and other beings. The creatures of the depths are strongly and vigorously portrayed in the myths. The giants, sometimes monstrous and sometimes fair to see, the wolf held in bonds, the ancient dragon in his den, the serpent encircling the world, are never long forgotten. They are continually contrasted with the realm of the gods, the shining heavens with their bright dwellings. The underworld, either below the earth or the waves, is the abode of darkness and death, threatening always to destroy the ordered world of light and overrun the inhabited earth. Yet at the same time it is the place from which new life comes, and to which the gods may look for their brides. We are reminded from time to time in the myths that the seemingly dead earth sends up shoots in spring, that wisdom may come from the sea depths, and that the characteristics of dead men appear again in their children's children.

Finally in this picture of gods and monsters, we find the idea of the continual re-enactment, *l'éternel retour*, as Mircea Eliade calls it. The gods themselves were doomed to fall before the powers of darkness, and heaven and earth to pass away. But rebirth must follow destruction, and a newly cleansed earth and heaven emerge from the sea and the flames. The sons of the gods and the survivors of mankind would again people earth and heaven, new dwellings arise in Asgard, and green fields once more yield their harvest on middle earth.

Such is the picture which we discern at the heart of the old religion, behind the succession of rich, entertaining, and often moving myths which have survived from the northern world. It was claimed at the beginning that myths are a comment on human existence and a model of social behaviour, an attempt to define the inner realities. Although some of the surviving myths are clearly shaped by the hands of poets, scholars, and entertainers, there is much which appears to be basic material from heathen times. There is moreover a certain amount of information collected in the *Edda* poems, particularly that which has to do with the World Tree, the divisions between the worlds, and the dwellings of the gods, which has certainly not been put together for its value as entertainment. It has the appearance of a body of knowledge about the gods and their world brought together for purposes of memory or teaching. This enables us to correct the more frivolous impression given by some of the racier myths, products of an age when the gods offered a tempting target for northern wit.

We can see the myths as a vigorous, heroic comment on life, life as men found it in hard and inhospitable lands. The gods never cease their struggle against the creatures of cold and darkness. Thor, perhaps the best-loved deity of the north, is characteristic of the Vikings in his resolute pertinacity. The values for which he stood – law and order in the free community, the keeping of faith between men – were those by which the Vikings set great store, even though they themselves often appeared to the outside world as the forces of destruction unleashed. Odin represented the other side of life, the inspiration granted to the warrior and the poet, and the secret wisdom won by communication with the dead. In his cult and in the religion of the Vanir we see most clearly the shamanistic tendencies of northern religion, the emphasis on man's powers to reach out beyond this harsh and limited world. Above all, the northern myths are clear-sighted in their recognition of the reality of the forces of destruction. The fight in a narrow place against odds, which has been called the ideal of heroic literature in the north, is given cosmic stature in the conception of Ragnarok, the doom of the gods, when Odin and his peers go down fighting against the monsters and the unleashed fury of the elements. The depths and dark mysteries of the subconscious are given full recognition in the myths. The greatest terror to be faced, that of the disintegration of the mind in madness or death, is not pushed to one side. At Ragnarok a rich and wonderful world was shattered and the monsters had their fill of destruction. After that facing of reality, it was possible to see beyond the catastrophe and to imagine a new world built upon the ruins of the old.

This does not mean that all who accepted the old heathen faith had a deep philosophy and acceptance of life. For the ordinary man, the myths might be very limited in their significance, and his religious ideas fragmentary and perfunctory. Like Kjartan, he might prefer to trust in his own strength and weapons rather than spend much time considering the gods, although he enjoyed hearing stories about them and paid them lip-service at the popular festivals. He might find more satisfaction in the popular beliefs which formed a large part of the heathen heritage for many people. Many must have paid more attention to the land-spirits, for instance, than to the high gods, to the spirits said to follow men who were lucky at hunting and fishing, who dwelt in hills and stones round the farms, and sometimes appeared in animal form or sometimes like little men with wives and children of their own. They could either help or hinder, and men and women would instinctively turn to them – as to a favourite saint – in the little troubles and hopes of everyday life in the fields or on the sea. Similarly they thought a good deal of the dead in their mounds, and remembered with awe and terror tales of local hauntings by characters who had been fearsome influences in their lifetimes and would not rest quiet in their graves. They respected the giants said to dwell in local caves or wander over the mountains behind their settlements, who could give help to men or prove terrible enemies if their hostility was aroused. Nearer even than these were the protective spirits attached to certain families, whose friendship would pass from father to son, who might be seen in dreams walking over the hills or the sea, and would give warning of approaching death. There were many popular beliefs such as these, peopling the waste places and giving a sense of significance to life, linking man with the powers which he could not control, even while they might also fill the long dark winter nights with terror.

Such popular beliefs were part of the common heritage of men, and flourished in the lonely, isolated communities among the mountains. There must always have been men however who were fanatical devotees to the cults of Odin, Thor, the Vanir, or one of the lesser gods, to whom the local shrine of the deity they chose for special worship was the centre of the world. Between the two extremes there was every variety of attitude towards the gods, inconsistencies, doubts and fears, cynical appraisal of the old tales and scorn of the ancient rites, sentimental faithfulness to the old ways and the well-known customs. There was no central organization to formulate a body of beliefs, and so ideas about the gods must have varied from one district to another, as we have seen that the names of the deities varied also. But men shared the body of myths which grew out of their beliefs about the gods, even though to some they were no more than a source of entertainment. Thus it is that certain assumptions which we find there are enlightening for our understanding of the northern peoples.

We realize anew the value which they set on individualism. Greek and Latin writers, commenting on the methods of warfare among the Germanic peoples, noted that while they were intensely loyal to leaders and kinsmen, they could not be relied on to cooperate in large numbers, or to obey a general's commands without question:

If it comes about that their friends fall, they expose themselves to danger to avenge them. They charge swiftly with much spirit, both foot-soldiers and horsemen, as if they were of a single mind, and quite without the slightest fear. They do not obey their leaders well. Headstrong, despising strategy, precaution, or foresight, they show contempt for every tactical command.

Such was the shrewd description of the sixth-century Germans recorded in *Strategicon*. The same characteristics can be recognized in the Vikings later on, and help to explain why, brilliant campaigners as they were, they made no lasting conquests, and their gains soon melted away. The myths are very much stories of individuals, and their reactions to one another; they show lonely gods going their wilful ways, with certain responsibilities to the community or the family to which they belong, but little more to hold them.

While there is constant recognition of the fact of death and its seriousness, it is faced without undue fear. The emphasis in the myths is the same as that in the heroic poetry, on the importance not of holding on to life at any cost, but of acting in a way which will be long remembered when life is over. There are many noble expressions of this desire for renown, and they have often been quoted, but it is nevertheless worth while recalling two of them again. First a passage from the poem *Beowulf*, the consolation offered to a king when one of his best-loved followers has been killed:

> O wise man, do not grieve. Better for every man to avenge his friend rather than lament for him overmuch. Each of us must endure the ending of life in this world. Let those who can therefore achieve glory before the coming of death. That is the finest lot for the warrior when life is over. *Beowulf*, 1384-9

And secondly, lines from the Norse *Hávamál*, presented as the wisdom of Odin:

> Cattle die, kinsfolk die,
> oneself dies the same.
> I know one thing only which never dies –
> the renown of the noble dead.

After a life of courage and achievement and a glorious death, a man will be remembered for many generations. His burial mound will be a lasting memorial and a reminder to his descendants of their splendid heritage. Such ideas are enshrined in the myths. They are in accordance with the worship of Odin, the god who sought out young heroes and inspired them with unflinching courage, and with the religion of Thor and the Vanir, where the emphasis is on the continuity of the family and the community rather than any personal immortality in the Other World. A man's heroic deeds will win renown, and his fine qualities will be passed on to his descendants. Such is the noblest form of immortality, and the great gods themselves achieved no more.

But to accomplish great things, a man must avoid excesses. 'He knows everything who knows moderation', it is said in one of the Icelandic sagas, and this is characteristic of the spirit of the heroes at their wisest and best. One of the most telling qualities of Snorri is the quick irony with which he deflates the pretentious: the wolf Fenrir gapes so hugely with his jaws that they stretch from earth to heaven – and he would gape even more widely, were there more room to do so; the gods laughed when the wolf was bound – all except Tyr: he lost his hand. Man must not take himself or even his gods too seriously, and this is an attitude which goes deeper than the wit of Snorri, it is part of the spirit of the myths themselves. The exuberant exaggerations of the Irish sagas are not for the northern gods; Freyja, Thor, Loki have the robust common sense which the Vikings themselves admired hugely, and although they take part in the comedies of the regaining of the hammer or the visit to the land of the giants, they survive virtually unscathed. The man who could make a joke when wounded to death or gasp out a witty remark when men were removing an arrow from his throat after battle is honoured in the sagas, because even in pain and weakness he could still keep his sense of proportion, and it is this sense which is perhaps the great quality of these northern stories.

This sense of proportion is gained by viewing men and gods objectively, by standing back, as it were, to see them clearly and without prejudice. It is this ability which helps to preserve in the myths a keen realization of the strength of fate. This is the main lesson in the story of Balder, against whose destined fate Odin and the gods struggled in vain. Fate runs like a scarlet thread through the tales both of the gods and the great heroes. *Wyrd*, the Old English word for Fate, was still much used in Christian literature, being equated with Providence and the will of Almighty God. There is little doubt that men were conscious of its sombre power before Christianity came to Anglo-Saxon England. The men of the north knew that they walked along a precipice edge, their precarious security threatened constantly by the sword, the storm, the attack of an enemy. Disaster might reach them at any time, whether heralded by gloomy omens or falling from a blue sky. The crops might fail, the fish disappear from the coastal waters, or an invader come upon them from the sea. Many a minor Ragnarok was enacted in the halls of Anglo-Saxon England, Norway, and Iceland, when the roof crashed down in flames, and a noble, courageous band of men perished at the hands of a stronger or more cunning enemy. A blunted sword-blade, a chance encounter, or a snow-storm in the hills might result in the loss of all that made life worth living, and even the most far-seeing could not guard against such accidents. It has been remarked that the favourite tales of the Germanic peoples and the Scandinavians, the most moving themes of their poetry, were concerned with the deaths of young heroes and with defeats in battle. The myths emphasize the remorseless power of fate: the curse of Andvari's ring dogged Sigurd the Volsung and brought him to an early death; Balder fell in spite of all the wisdom of Odin and the protection of Frigg; the grey wolf watches the abode of the gods, for he knows that his destined time will come and the bonds will snap, long though the waiting must be. When an Anglo-Saxon poet[1] composed the line: 'Fate is stronger, and God mightier, than any man can imagine', he was thinking as a Christian, but he was also expressing an idea implicit in heathen thought. Behind the great achievements of the heroes and the mighty power of the gods, there was something yet more powerful, the law of implacable fate, leading to Ragnarok and beyond.

In spite of this awareness of fate, indeed perhaps because of it, the picture of man's qualities which emerges from the myths is a noble one. The gods are heroic figures, men writ large, who led dangerous, individualistic lives, yet at the same time were part of a closely-knit small group, with a firm sense of values and certain intense loyalties. They would give up their lives rather than surrender these values, but they would fight on as long as they could, since life was well worth while. Men knew that the gods whom they served could not give them freedom from danger and calamity, and they did not demand that they should. We find in the myths no sense of bitterness at the harshness and unfairness of life, but rather a spirit of heroic resignation: humanity is born to trouble, but courage, adventure, and the wonders of life are matters for thankfulness, to be enjoyed while life is still granted to us. The great gifts of the gods were readiness to face the world as it was, the luck that sustains men in tight places, and the opportunity to win that glory which alone can outlive death.

This attitude is an adult one, far removed from that of a spoilt child. It explains why the myths have still a strong attraction for us, bred in so different a world from that of our fore-

1. The unknown composer of the poem known as *The Seafarer*.

fathers, cut off from them by barriers of new learning and knowledge. The dangers of this view of the world lay in a tendency towards lack of compassion for the weak, an over-emphasis on material success, and arrogant self-confidence: indeed the heroic literature contains frank warning against such errors. It is easy to see how such a conception of life fitted in with the worship of the northern gods. To live fully and richly, a man needed boldness and wisdom, and these Odin could grant him. He must be a loyal member of his family and community, and in this Thor would give him support. He needed to win the struggle with the earth and make it fertile, and to beget male children, so that his family might continue after him, and for this he depended on the blessing of the Vanir. It is sometimes assumed that this heathen religion was essentially a man's one, but we have seen that women had their place in it also. Indeed in view of the part which women play in the heroic legends and the sagas, we can scarcely doubt it. The early priestesses of the north, the women who were prepared to die by sacrificial rites, and the seeresses who helped to link men with the gods, all contributed something of great importance to the heathen faith. There was a place for woman's gifts of divination and wise counsel, as well as that other side emphasized in the rites of the fertility cult.

The weaknesses of the heathen religion when it came into contact with Christianity were largely practical ones. There was no real central authority, no recognized body of doctrine to which to appeal, few deep certainties for which men were prepared to die. The worship of the old gods was a very individual affair, suiting the independent people who practised it. A man usually chose one of the deities for his special friend and protector, with whom he entered into a kind of partnership, and this did not prevent him from acknowledging the existence of the rest, or from taking part in communal ceremonies in which they were worshipped. The images of several gods stood side by side in the little local temples and in the great temple at Uppsala, even though there might from time to time be rivalry between the cults of the battle and fertility deities. When in the seventh century King Redwald of East Anglia provided one altar in his church to sacrifice to Christ, and another small one to offer

victims to devils,[1] he was not behaving childishly, or cunningly
hoping to get the best of both worlds, but merely acting according to normal heathen custom, since acceptance of one god did
not mean that one wholly rejected one's neighbour's deity. This
indeed must have been one of the most difficult lessons for the
new converts to Christianity to learn, and while they gained in
single-mindedness, it is to be feared that they lost much of their
old spirit of tolerance.

The upkeep of a temple was in general the business either of
the ruler or of a family, and in the latter case the man who built
the shrine and his descendants would act as its priests. Something of the nature of communities or colleges of priests must
presumably have existed in the early days of heathenism, but
we hear little of them in the sources which remain to us. In any
case, the power of priesthood in the last resort depended largely
on the approval of the king. Once he was converted to Christianity, the main prop of the old faith disappeared, and in the
Anglo-Saxon kingdoms, according to Bede's detailed records of
conversion, there appears to have been very little genuine opposition to the new faith.

. The believer in the old religion would find a great deal in
Christianity which would seem to him familiar and right. The
idea of a dying god was already known to him from the fertility
cults, and the lament for Christ's death on Good Friday followed by rejoicing in the Resurrection on Easter Day would
follow a familiar pattern of death and renewal. The cycle of the
Christian year was something to which he was already accustomed. Even the idea of God himself hanging upon a tree as a
sacrifice was foreshadowed in the image of Odin upon Yggdrasill. Welcome also must have been the teaching that his
new god would speak to him 'as a man speaks with his friend',
for he had grown up with the idea that it was natural to seek
counsel from Thor or Freyr, to visit the seeress who spoke out of
a trance, uttering words of wisdom from the great powers to
guide his steps in life. The idea of direct guidance in the early
Church, often by men who act as 'angels' of God, is very
marked in the pages of Bede. The Christian teaching concerning
creation and doomsday moreover echoed ideas to which men

1. Bede's *Ecclesiastical History*, II, 15.

had grown accustomed in their days of heathenism, and which were firmly established in their poetic tradition. The new faith was presented to them as a fighting one, and this they saw as natural and desirable. The picture of Christ as a warrior, combating the forces of evil, was a development and a reflection of their vague ideas about their Sky God. We can assume from the choice of carvings on the Gosforth Cross, where the fight with the monsters is placed alongside the Crucifixion, that this parallel was recognized by their teachers in the Christian faith. We see it too in the fine imaginative poem *The Dream of the Rood*, where Christ appears as a young warrior, stripping himself voluntarily for the conflict, and mounting the Cross as a hero turns to meet death in battle. The old heroic conception of life was found to be still in harmony with the new teaching. 'Do not pray me out of God's battle', were the words of Gizur, one of the early Christian bishops of Iceland, dying in great pain, in response to those who stood round his bed praying that God would give him a merciful release from his sufferings.

At the same time the new faith was strong just where the old one had been weak. When in 625 King Edwin of Northumbria asked his nobles to tell him their reactions to the proposal that they should accept the Christian faith for their kingdom, one of them, according to Bede's account,[1] spoke of the brevity and uncertainty of life on earth, comparing it with the flight of a sparrow through the king's hall on a winter afternoon :

For a short time he is safe from the wintry storm, but after a little space he vanishes from your sight, back into the dark winter from which he came.

Such, he said, was man's life here on earth, a short space in the warmth and light between the darkness that preceded his birth and the unknown into which he passed at death :

Of what went before and of what is to follow, we are utterly ignorant. If therefore this new faith can give us some greater certainty, it justly deserves that we should follow it.

Whether these words were in truth spoken in Edwin's hall in Northumbria does not greatly matter. Here Bede has caught the authentic voice of the heathen Northumbrian, faced with a cold

1. Bede, *Ecclesiastical History*, 11, 13.

and hostile world, and has put into memorable words his urgent questionings. In the seventh century in northern England, it must indeed have seemed that light and joy were momentary things, and that men were under the constant threat of violence and a return to chaos. Not long after the meeting in the hall, the hopeful kingdom of King Edwin, won with such determination and courage from his enemies after years of exile, was to be shattered by invasion from heathen Mercia. There was a deep longing among thinking people for a clearer message and for a greater authority than the old religion could give them, for an answer to the question 'Why are we here?', for something which would endure in spite of threats of disintegration and loss of all the material goods for which they struggled so hard and, it often seemed, so unavailingly.

The power of the Christian religion lay also in the welding together of the different aspects of the heathen faith into one united whole, with a God who was the father of all men, not the fickle All-Father of Asgard, and with Christ as their heroic leader. The new heroism of the cloister and the wilderness and the missionary journey – with martyrdom, perhaps, at the end – was open to those who could find no full satisfaction in the life of a warrior. There had been a striving in the old religion to find a link between heaven and earth, through the shaman who could travel between the worlds, but now men were given a new link in the incarnation of Christ, something for which the ancient faith had no parallel. All this must have been profoundly exciting and satisfying for the thinking convert. As for the unthinking, of whom there were many, it was largely a matter of new ceremonies replacing the old. 'They have taken away the ancient rites and customs, and how the new ones are to be attended to, nobody knows,' was the lament of the country people against the monks, recorded in Bede's *Life of St Cuthbert*. One has immense sympathy for them, and for the men in Norway who shrank from breaking their pledges to Thor and Freyr, who, as they said courageously in the face of the angry young missionary king Olaf, had given them help and counsel as long as they could remember. But the old faith could no longer offer men what they needed; it was incapable of further development to satisfy the new needs and questionings when fresh know-

ledge and a different way of living came into the north. To realize the tremendous impact of Christian teaching, it is only
necessary to read of the life of St Aidan or St Cuthbert in newly
converted Northumbria. Men flocked to these inspired leaders
for help which the old faith could not offer them, and the saints
did not fail the suppliants, but wore themselves out with generous and unceasing response.

In many ways the old religion had pointed forward to the
new, but while much of the pattern was the same, the Christian
conception of the relationship between God and man was im-
measurably richer and deeper. When we lament the passing of
the old faith, it is largely a lamentation for a simpler way of life,
and for the heroic ideas which belonged to that life, doomed to
be lost when a more complex and organized society replaced the
old one. As the way of living changed, and new vistas opened
before the eyes of the young, the old deities could no longer
satisfy, and men had reached the point of no return. The story
of their struggles and problems in striving after a different goal
and taking Christ as their leader is indeed an absorbing one, but
falls outside the scope of this book.

Works of Reference

References to special books and articles are given in footnotes. For those who wish to follow up any branch of the subject in detail, there are three works which contain extensive bibliographies. The fullest and most valuable book of reference on both Germanic and Scandinavian religion is:

Jan de Vries, *Altgermanische Religionsgeschichte*, 2 vols., 2nd edition, Walter de Gruyter, Berlin, 1956.

Additional information about recent work on Scandinavian mythology will be found in:

E. O. G. Turville-Petre, *Myth and Religion of the North*, Weidenfeld & Nicolson, 1964.

An earlier book in English which may be useful is:

J. A. MacCulloch, *Mythology of All Races*, Vol. 11 (Eddic), 1930.

Where reliable English translations are available of the works referred to, they are given in the list of names and sources.

Names and Sources

In accordance with the usual English custom, I have throughout this book simplified Old Norse and other unfamiliar names when this seemed desirable, in particular omitting accents and final *r*, and replacing the letter ð by *d* and Þ by *th*. In the following list of names and sources which may be unfamiliar to the reader, the Old Icelandic or Old English form has been given in brackets where a change has been made.

The following may serve as a rough guide to pronunciation of Old Icelandic names:

ð – voiced sound of *th*, as in English *then*
Þ – voiceless sound of *th*, as in English *thin*
á – as *oa* in English *broad*
ǫ – as *o* in English *not*
ø – as *eu* in French *peur*
æ – as *ai* in English *air*
au – as *ou* in English *loud*

The final *r* is not pronounced as a separate syllable, therefore *Garmr* and similar words are not pronounced as two syllables.

The accent normally falls on the first syllable.

ADAM OF BREMEN: Author of the History of the Archbishops of Hamburg-Bremen, *Gesta Hammaburgensis ecclesiae pontificum* (translated by F. J. Tschan, Columbia University Press (New York) 1959), who lived in the eleventh century.

AEGIR (ÆGIR): God of the sea.

AESIR (ÆSIR): Race of the gods to which Odin and Thor belong

ALFHEIM: Home of the light elves

AGNI: Early king of Sweden, married to Skialf, who caused his death

ALAISIAGAE: Female supernatural beings, connected with the war god, called 'goddesses' on an altar of the Roman period on Hadrian's Wall

ALCIS: Twin gods, said by Tacitus to be worshipped by the Germans

ANDVARI: Dwarf who possessed a golden treasure, taken from him by Loki to pay the ransom for Otter

ANGLO-SAXON CHRONICLE: Set of annals in Anglo-Saxon, giving a year by year record of events, begun in Wessex in the mid ninth century and continued, in a number of local versions, until the Norman Conquest

ANGRBODA: 'Boder of Grief', giantess on whom Loki begot monsters

ASGARD (ASGARÐR): Home of the gods

ASKR: 'Ash tree'. Name of the first man created by the gods from a tree on the sea-shore

AUÐHUMLA: 'Rich hornless cow'. The primeval cow which nourished the first being, Ymir, and licked the ancestor of the gods out of the melting ice

Names and Sources

AURVANDIL (AURVANDILL): The husband of a seeress who tried to charm the whetstone out of Thor's head, whose toe Thor threw up to become a star

BALDER (BALDR): Son of Odin, called the Beautiful, slain by Hoder

BALDRS DRAUMAR: 'Balder's Dreams', poem in the *Edda* telling how Odin sought to discover the fate of Balder. Also known as *Vegtamskviða*

BATTLE OF THE GOTHS AND HUNS: Name given to poem in *Hervarar Saga*, a survival of earlier heroic poetry (translated by N. Kershaw, *Anglo-Saxon and Norse Poems*, Cambridge University Press, 1922)

BAUGI: Brother of Suttung, the giant who held the mead of inspiration

BEDE (BEDA): Known as the Venerable. Scholar and historian in the Northumbrian monastery of Jarrow in the eighth century, who wrote many Latin works, including *A History of the English Church and People* (translated by Leo Sherley-Price, Penguin Classics, 1955)

BEOW: Or Beaw. Name occurring in genealogies of Anglo-Saxon kings, thought by some to be a heathen deity of fertility

BEOWULF: Anglo-Saxon epic poem, surviving in one MS. of about A.D. 1000, known by the name of its hero, Beowulf of the Geats (translated by David Wright, Penguin Classics, 1957)

BERGELMIR: Giant who survived the flood caused by the blood of the slaughtered Ymir

BERSERKS (BERSERKIR): Warriors possessed by battle fury, usually impervious to wounds

BEYLA: 'Bee' (?). Companion of Byggvir, a minor inhabitant of Asgard, mentioned in *Lokasenna*

BIARKI (BOÐVAR-BIARKI): 'Little Bear'. Famous Danish warrior who could fight in bear form, follower of King Hrolf

BIFROST (BIFRǫST): Rainbow bridge linking earth and heaven

BOBD: Female spirit of battle in Irish sagas, who often appeared in bird form

BOE (BOUS): Son of Odin and Rinda in Saxo, who avenges Balder's death

BOR (BORR): Son of Buri and father of Odin

BRAGI: God of poetry, married to Idun. Also the name of the ninth-century Icelandic poet, Bragi Boddason

BRIAN BORU (BORUMH): Christian High-king of Ireland, who fell at Clontarf in 1014 fighting against the Vikings of Dublin and their allies

BRISINGAMEN (BRÍSINGAMEN): 'Necklace of the Brisings' (?). The great treasure of Freyja, thought to be a necklace, obtained from the dwarfs

BROSINGAMENE: A great treasure, thought to be a necklace or collar, said in *Beowulf* to be taken from Eormanric Hama

BRYNHILD (BRYNHILDR): Valkyrie and princess, loved by Sigurd the Volsung but married to King Gunnar. Burned herself to death when Sigurd was killed

BURI (BÚRI): First being created from the primeval ice, father of Bor

BYGGVIR: From *bygg*, barley (?). One of the minor companions of the gods, mentioned in *Lokasenna*

CAEDMON (CÆDMON): Anglo-Saxon poet of the seventh century who was famous for his Christian poems on Biblical subjects. His story is told by Bede

CODEX REGIUS: Icelandic MS. of the thirteenth century (now in Copenhagen) containing a number of poems about the gods and heroes, known as the *Edda*

COIFI (CEFI): High priest of the heathen gods in Northumbria in the seventh century, according to Bede's account

DARRAÐARLJÓÐ: 'Lay of the Spear'. Poem preserved in *Njál's Saga*, a chant of supernatural women before battle (translated by N. Kershaw, *Anglo-Saxon and Norse Poems*, Cambridge University Press, 1922)

DÍSIR: Female supernatural beings

DONAR: Thunder god worshipped by the heathen Germans

DRAUGR: Inhabitant of a grave mound who is restless after death

DRAUPNIR: Gold ring of Odin, from which other rings are produced

DREAM OF THE ROOD: Name given to Old English Christian poem about Christ's Cross, preserved in the Vercelli Book of the tenth century, and also written in runes on a carved cross of about the seventh century at Ruthwell (translated by R. K. Gordon, *Anglo-Saxon Poetry*, Everyman Library, 1927)

EDDA: Name given to collection of poems preserved in the *Codex Regius*, known as the *Elder Edda* to distinguish them from the *Prose Edda* written by Snorri Sturluson (translated by L. M. Hollander, Texas University Press, 1929, 1962)

EDWIN: King of Northumbria who was converted to Christianity in the seventh century

EGILS SAGA: Story of Egill Skallagrímsson, the famous poet and adventurer who lived in Iceland in the tenth century. One of the longest and best known of the Icelandic family sagas (translated by E. R. Eddison, Cambridge University Press, 1930)

EGILS SAGA OK ÁSMUNDAR: One of the legendary sagas in the *Fornaldar Sǫgur* collection, telling of the adventures of two foster-brothers

ERIC BLOODAXE (EIRÍKR BLOÐØX): Norwegian king of the tenth century who was driven out of Norway and reigned in Northumbria, where he finally died in battle

EIRÍKS SAGA RAUÐA: Saga of Eric the Red, an Icelander who discovered Greenland and settled there in the tenth century. One of the Icelandic family sagas. Also known as *Þorfinns Saga Karlsefnis* (translated by G. Jones, World's Classics, 1961)

ERIC THE VICTORIOUS (EIRÍKR INN SIGRSÆLI): Famous Swedish king of the tenth century

EIRÍKSMÁL: Tenth-century poem composed at the death of Eric Bloodaxe (translated by N. Kershaw, *Anglo-Saxon and Norse Poems*, Cambridge University Press, 1922)

ELENE: Old English poem about St Helena, attributed to the poet Cynewulf (translated by R. K. Gordon, *Anglo-Saxon Poetry*, Everyman, 1927)

ELLI: 'Old Age'. The old woman who outdid Thor in a wrestling match in the hall of Utgard-Loki

Names and Sources

EYRBYGGJA SAGA: One of the longer Icelandic family sagas, the history of the people living at Snæfellsness in western Iceland (translated by Paul Schach, University of Nebraska Press, 1959)

EXODUS: Old English poem about the departure of the Israelites from Egypt (translated by R. K. Gordon, *Anglo-Saxon Poetry*, Everyman, 1927)

EYVIND KELDA (EYVINDR KELDA): Descendant of Harald Fairhair who worked magic and was drowned by Olaf Tryggvason

FAFNIR (FÁFNIR): Dragon who guarded a golden treasure and was slain by Sigurd the Volsung

FENRIR: The wolf, said to be son of Loki, who was bound by Tyr, and will break free at Ragnarok

FIMBULVETR: The 'mighty winter', to last for three years on end, which is to precede Ragnarok

FJǪRGYNN: Mother of Thor, thought to be a fertility goddess. Also found in the masculine form Fjǫrgyn

FLATEYJARBÓK: MS. book containing a version of the sagas of the Norwegian kings, with short episodes interpolated, written in the Flatey monastery, Iceland

FLÓAMANNA SAGA: One of the Icelandic family sagas, telling of an expedition to Greenland from Flói, Iceland

FOMOIRI: Company of supernatural beings in Irish mythology, hostile to the Tuatha Dé Donann

FORNALDAR SǪGUR: 'Sagas of Old Time', a series of legendary and heroic sagas, written late, with some romance material but also preserving some early traditions and verses (edited Jónsson, Reykjavik, 1950)

FORSETI: Son of Balder, named as a law-giver among the gods, worshipped in Frisia

FREYFAXI: 'Mane of Freyr'. Horse of hero of *Hrafnskels Saga*, dedicated to the god Freyr. Also name of horse in *Vatnsdœla Saga*

FREYJA: Sister of Freyr, daughter of Njord, a powerful goddess of fertility among the Vanir

FREYR: Son of Njord and one of the Vanir, the chief god of fertility in Norway and Sweden

FRIDLEIF (FRIÐLEIFR): Frideuus in Saxo. An early king of Denmark, the son of Frodi III

FRIÐÞJÓFS SAGA: Story of the hero Fridiof the Bold, one of the sagas in the *Fornaldar Sǫgur* (translated by R. B. Anderson, in *Viking Tales of the North*, Scott (Chicago), 1889)

FRIGG: Wife of Odin and Queen of Asgard, associated with fertility

FRIJA: Wife of Wodan, worshipped by the heathen Germans

FRODI (FROÐI): Frotho in Saxo. Name borne by several legendary kings of Denmark, thought to have been the Danish equivalent of Freyr

GARM (GARMR): Hound of the Underworld, who will break loose at Ragnarok and kill Tyr

GAUTREKS SAGA: One of the legendary sagas in the *Fornaldar Sǫgur* collection, the story of King Gautrek

GEFION (GEFJUN): Goddess worshipped at Leire, who ploughed round Zealand and made it into an island

GEIRROD (GEIRRØÐR): Giant hostile to the gods, slain by Thor

GERD (GERÐR): Fair maiden of the Underworld, wooed by Freyr

GERMANIA: Account of the way of life, customs, and religions of the German tribes, written by the Roman historian Tacitus in A.D. 98

GILLING (GILLINGR): Giant killed by the dwarfs who made the mead of inspiration

GINNUNGAGAP: Space preceding creation, in which the worlds were made

GÍSLA SAGA: One of the Icelandic family sagas, the story of the outlaw Gisli (translated by George Johnston, University of Toronto Press, 1963)

GJALLARBRÚ: 'Resounding bridge', the bridge crossed by Hermod on his way to the realm of Hel to seek Balder

GJALLARHORN: 'Echoing horn', horn of Heimdall, to give warning of danger to Asgard

GOÐI: Priest of a heathen temple in Iceland, who presided over the local assembly and had his own followers

GOLDMANE (GULLIFAXI): Horse of the giant Hrungnir, which he raced against Sleipnir

GREGORY OF TOURS: Bishop of Tours in the sixth century, author of History of the Franks (translated by O. M. Dalton, Oxford University Press, 1927)

GRENDEL: Monster who attacked the Danish king's hall, and was slain by Beowulf, as recounted in the Anglo-Saxon poem

GRÍMNISMÁL: Poem in the Edda, the utterance of Grímnir, who is Odin in disguise

GULLINBURSTI: 'Golden-bristled'. Golden boar made by the dwarfs, owned by Freyr

GUNGNIR: Spear of Odin

GUNNAR HELMING (GUNNARR HELMINGR): Hero of short humorous story inserted into Flateyjarbók, a Norwegian who impersonated the god Freyr in Sweden

GYLFI: Early king of Sweden who let Gefion take Zealand. Appears in the Prose Edda as the questioner of the gods in the section called Gylfaginning (the beguiling of Gylfi)

GYMIR: Father of Gerd, and said to be the same as Aegir

HADDING (HADDINGR): Famous hero in Denmark. Hadingus in Saxo

HADDINGJAR: The Haddings. Pair of brothers sometimes named among early kings of Norway or Sweden, thought to have been twin deities

HAETHCYN (HÆÐCYN): Second son of Hrethel, king of the Geats in Beowulf, and slayer of his brother

HAGBARD (HARBARÐR): Lover of Signy, put to death by her father. Hagbarthus in Saxo

HAKI: Early king of Norway, sent to sea in a burning ship as he was dying

HÁKONARMÁL: Tenth-century poem by Eyvindr Finnsson on the death of the Norwegian king Hakon the Good (translated by N. Kershaw, Anglo-Saxon and Norse Poems, Cambridge University Press, 1922)

Names and Sources

HAKON THE GOOD (HÁKON GÓÐI): Christian king of Norway in the tenth century

HALFDAN THE BLACK (HÁLFDAN SVARTI): Early king of Vestfold, Norway in the ninth century

HARALD FAIRHAIR (HARALDR INN HÁRFAGRI): 'Harald with the fine hair', the king of Norway who united most of the country under his rule in the ninth century

HARALD WARTOOTH (HARALDR HILDITǪNN): King of Denmark who worshipped Odin

HARÐAR SAGA: One of the Icelandic family sagas, the story of Hord the outlaw

HÁVAMÁL: 'Utterance of the High One'. Poem in the *Edda*, purporting to be spoken by Odin (translated by D. E. Martin Clarke, Cambridge University Press, 1923)

HAUKSBÓK: One version of *Landnámabók*, giving an account of the settlement of Iceland

HAUSTLǪNG: Ninth-century poem about the gods, by Þjóðólfr ór Hvini

HEIDRUN (HEIDRÚN): Goat which provided mead for Valhalla, fed on the World Tree

HEIMDALLARGALDR: Lost poem about Heimdall, quoted by Snorri

HEIMDALL (HEIMDALLR): God called the White, who kept watch over Asgard

HEIMSKRINGLA: 'Round world'. History of kings of Norway, compiled from old sagas and poems by Snorri Sturluson (translated by E. Monsen and A. H. Smith, Heffer, 1931)

HEL: Daughter of Loki, given the rule of the kingdom of death, name also used for the kingdom itself

HELGAKVIÐA: Lay of Helgi. A number of Helgi lays in the *Edda* have different titles in various editions. They are concerned with Helgi Hjǫrvarðsson and Helgi Hundingsbani, and, as the latter was linked with the Volsung family, lays about him are sometimes called *Vǫlsungakviða* and *Vǫlsungakviða hin forna* (this last contains the episode of Helgi and Sigrun)

HELGI THE LEAN: Early settler in Iceland, of mixed faith, who came out from the Hebrides

HELGRIND: 'Death gate', between the worlds of the living and the dead

HELIAND: Old Saxon poem of the ninth century about Judgement Day

HEOROT: Hall built by the Danish king Hrothgar, as recounted in *Beowulf*

HEREBEALD: Son of King Hrethel of the Geats, killed accidentally by his brother, according to *Beowulf*

HERMOD (HERMÓÐR): Son of Odin, who rode to Hel to seek Balder

HERVARAR SAGA OK HEIÐREKS: One of the legendary sagas in the *Fornaldar Sǫgur* collection, the story of King Heiðrekr and his descendants (translated by N. Kershaw, *Stories and Ballads of the Far Past*, Cambridge University Press, 1921)

HILDISVÍN: 'Battle Pig'. Boar owned by Freyja, and also name of helmet possessed by Swedish kings

HLIÐSKJÁLF: Seat of Odin from which he can look out to all worlds

HODER (HǪÐR): Hotherus in Saxo's account. A god, said to be blind, who slew Balder, but a hero in Saxo

HOENIR (HŒNIR): A god, renowned for his silence

HÓLMGANGA: 'To go to the island'. Term used for the official duel, fought at an accepted duelling place, which at Thingvellir in Iceland was an island beside the place of assembly

HORD (HǪRÐR): Famous outlaw, hero of *Harðar Saga*

HRAFNKELL: Hero of *Hrafnskels Saga Freysgoða*, one of the Icelandic family sagas, where he is represented as a worshipper of Freyr (translated by G. Jones, *Four Icelandic Sagas*, Princeton, 1935)

HRAFNSMÁL: Poem by Þorbjǫrn Hornklofi, composed in the ninth century, about the followers of Harald Fairhair. Also known as *Haraldsmál* and *Haraldskvæði* (translated by N. Kershaw, *Anglo-Saxon and Norse Poems*, Cambridge University Press, 1922)

HRETHEL (HREÐEL): King of the Geats in *Beowulf* and grandfather of the hero of the poem

HROLF KRAKI (HRÓLFR KRAKI): Famous warrior-king of Denmark, whose story is told in one of the legendary sagas, *Hrólfs Saga Kraka* (translated by G. Jones, in *Eric the Red and other Icelandic sagas*, World's Classics, 1961)

HROTHGAR (HROÐGAR): King of the Danes who built the hall Heorot and was visited by Beowulf

HRUNGNIR: Giant who was killed in a duel with Thor

HUGI: 'Thought'. Youth who competed with Thialfi in a race in the hall of Utgard-Loki

HUGINN: From *hugi*, thought. One of Odin's ravens

HÚSDRAPA: Tenth-century poem by Ulfr Uggarson describing various mythological scenes

HYMIR: Sea giant with whom Thor went fishing on his expedition to catch the World Serpent, as told in the poem *Hymiskviða* in the *Edda*

HYNDLULJÓÐ: Lay of Hyndla, a giantess who appears as the rival of Freyja and is persuaded to reveal the ancestry of Ottar. A poem in the *Edda*

IBN FADLAN: Arab traveller and diplomat who visited Swedish settlers on the Volga in the tenth century and left an account of them

IDUN (IÐUNN): Wife of Bragi and goddess who guarded the golden apples of youth for the gods

ING: God or hero of Anglo-Saxon tradition, connected with Denmark, and the founder of the royal dynasty of Bernicia

INGIMUND: Icelandic settler, the story of whose family is told in *Vatns-dœla Saga*, one of the Icelandic family sagas

IRMINSUL: Pillar which supports the world in Germanic tradition

JOMSBORG: Viking stronghold, said to be built by Harald Gormsson of Denmark, somewhere on the coast of Wendland, in the late tenth century. Held by garrison known as Jomsvikings

JORDANES: Historian of the sixth century who wrote a history of the Goths, *De origine actibusque Getarum* (translated Mierow, Princeton, 1915)

Names and Sources

JOTUNHEIM (JQTUNHEIMR): Realm of the Jǫtnar, or giants

KALEVALA: National epic of the Finns, put together from old lays by Elias Lönnrot (translated by W. F. Kirby, 1907)

KETILS SAGA HŒNGS: One of the legendary sagas telling the story of the Norwegian hero Ketill, in the *Fornaldar Sǫgur* series

KJALNESINGA SAGA: One of the Icelandic family sagas, containing legendary material similar to that in the *Fornaldar Sǫgur*

KORMÁKS SAGA: One of the Icelandic family sagas, the story of Kormak, a poet and adventurer of the ninth century (translated by L. M. Hollander, New York, 1949)

KVASIR: Called the wisest of the gods, a being made from the saliva of the Aesir and Vanir, from whose blood was made the mead of inspiration

LANDNÁMABÓK: Book of the settlement of Iceland, originally written by Ari the Wise in the eleventh century, but added to by others

LEMMINKAINEN: Hero of some of the lays in the *Kalevala*, who was killed and brought to life again by his mother

LODUR (LÓÐURR): One of the gods said to take part in the creation of man

LIF (LÍF): 'Life'. Said in *Vafþruðnismál* to be preserved through Ragnarok in order to found a new race of men

LIFTHRASIR (LÍFÞRASIR): 'Eager for life' (?). Companion of Lif

LOGI: 'Flame'. Competitor who outdid Loki in an eating contest in the hall of Utgard-Loki

LOKASENNA: 'Loki's Mocking'. Poem in the *Edda* which describes Loki mocking and abusing all the gods and goddesses in turn

LOKI: Inhabitant of Asgard who frequently causes mischief, and who was bound under the earth for his part in the slaying of Balder, to break loose at Ragnarok

LYTIR (LÝTIR): God who according to a story in *Flateyjarbók* was worshipped by the Swedes

MAGNI: Son of Thor and the giantess Járnsaxa, who survives Ragnarok and has part possession of Thor's hammer

MANANNÁN MAC LIR: Celtic god of the sea

MENGLAD (MENGLǪÐ): 'Necklace-glad'. Maid of supernatural realm, wooed by Svipdagr in the *Edda* poem *Svipdagsmál*

MERSEBURG CHARMS: Two pagan spells found in 1841 in a ninth-century MS. in the Merseburg Cathedral Library.

MIDGARD (MIDGARÐR): The world of men, midway between the gods and the giants

MIDGARD SERPENT (MIÐGARÐSORMR): The World Serpent, curled round the earth, beneath the sea, which is to break loose at Ragnarok

MIMIR (MÍMIR): Also found as Mímr and Mími. A wise being associated with the World Tree and the Spring of Urd. Put to death by the Vanir, after which his head was kept by Odin and consulted in time of perplexity

MIMINGUS: Old man from whom Hotherus (Hoder) obtained a magic sword with which to kill Balder, in Saxo's account

MIST-CALF (MǪKKURKALFI): Clay man made by the giants to support Hrungnir in his duel with Thor

MISTLETOE (MISTILLTEINN): Name of a wonderful sword possessed by Hromund Greipsson and others

MJOLLNIR (MJǪLLNIR): Hammer of Thor, made by the dwarfs, to protect the gods from their enemies

MODGUD (MOÐGUÐR): Maiden who kept the bridge on the road to Hel

MOTHERS: Group of female deities connected with plenty who were worshipped by the Germans and Celts in Roman times

MUSPELL (MÚSPELL): Realm of fire, the heat from which helped in the creation of the world. The sons of Muspell ride out against the gods at Ragnarok

MUSPILLI: Name given to a German poem about the end of the world, where this word is used. The poem is in a tenth-century MS.

MUNINN: From *muna*, to remember. One of Odin's ravens

NAGLFAR: Ship of dead men's nails, which is to bring Loki and the giants against the gods at Ragnarok

NANNA: Wife of Balder, who died at his funeral and was burned with him

NEHALENNIA: Goddess of plenty worshipped on the Island of Walcheren in Roman times

NERTHUS: Fertility goddess worshipped in Denmark in the first century A.D., as described by Tacitus

NIÐHǪGGR: Serpent at the foot of the World Tree, also described as a flying dragon, who feeds on corpses

NIFLHEIM: The abode of darkness, beneath the roots of the World Tree

NJÁLS SAGA: Also called *Brennu-Njáls Saga*. Longest and most famous of the Icelandic family sagas, the story of the burning of the Icelander Niall and his family (translated by Bayerschmidt and Hollander, Allen & Unwin, 1956)

NJORD (NJǪRÐR): God associated with ships and the sea. The father of Freyr and Freyja, and one of the Vanir

NORNA-GEST (NORNA-GESTR): 'Stranger of the Norns'. Hero of a tale inserted into Olaf Tryggvason's saga in *Flateyjarbók* (translated by N. Kershaw, *Stories and Ballads of the Far Past*, Cambridge University Press, 1921)

OD (ÓÐR): Husband of Freyja, who deserted her

ODIN (ÓÐINN): Leader of the Aesir, god of battle, inspiration, and death

OLAF ELF OF GEIRSTAD: Oláfr *Geirstaðaálfr*. Early king in Vestfold, Norway, to whose burial mound men sacrificed after his death

OLAF THE HOLY: St Olaf, great Christian king of Norway, 1016–30

OLAF TRYGGVASON: King of Norway 995–1000, who set out to convert the country to Christianity

OROSIUS: Paulus Orosius, author of *Historiae adversum Paganos*, a history of the world, in the fifth century A.D.

ǪRVAR-ODDS SAGA: One of the legendary sagas in the *Fornaldar Sǫgur* collection, the story of the hero Odd and his travels abroad

OTTER (OTR): Son of Hreidmar, killed by Loki

Names and Sources

OTTAR THE SIMPLE (OTTARR HEIMSKI): A worshipper of Freyja, helped by her to discover his ancestry, as told in the *Edda* poem *Hyndluljóð*

PAUL THE DEACON: Paulus Diaconus, author of a history of the Lombards, *Historia Langobardorum*, in the eighth century (translated by Foulke, New York, 1907)

PHOL: Vol (?). Mentioned with Volla in the 2nd Merseburg Charm, and thought to be a fertility deity

PROCOPIUS: Greek historian of sixth century B.C. who wrote a history of the Gothic Wars

PROSE EDDA: Book about poetic imagery and diction by Snorri Sturluson, containing many myths and quotations (translated by Brodeur, Oxford University Press, 1916, and partially by J. I. Young, Bowes & Bowes, 1954)

RAGNAR LODBROK (RAGNARR LOÐBRÓK): 'Leather-breeks'. Famous hero who slew a dragon, and whose sons conquered England, in *Ragnars Saga Loðbrókar*, one of the *Fornaldar Sǫgur* (translated by O. Schlauch, 1949)

RAGNAROK (RAGNARØKR): 'Destruction of the powers'. Term used to describe the end of the world, when the monsters slay the gods, and Midgard and Asgard are destroyed

RAGNVALD OF ORKNEY (RǪGNVALDR): Famous Earl of the Orkneys, 1135–58, poet and adventurer

RAGNVALD RETTILBEINI (RǪGNVALDR): Son of Harald Fairhair of Norway, who practised witchcraft and was finally put to death by his father

RAN: Wife of the sea god Aegir, who catches drowned seamen in her net, and gives them hospitality in her halls

RAGNARSDRÁPA: Ninth-century poem by Bragi Boddason about the gods

RATATOSK (RATATOSKR): Squirrel who runs up and down the World Tree

RAUD (RAUÐR): Worshipper of the heathen gods, especially Thor, in Northern Norway, put to death by Olaf Tryggvason

REDWALD (RÆDWALD): King of East Anglia in the seventh century, who was partially converted to Christianity

REGIN (REGINN): Famous smith, son of Hreidmar, who slew his father and helped Sigurd the Volsung to slay his brother Fafnir, the dragon

RÍGSÞULA: Poem in the *Edda*, telling how Rig (thought to be Heimdall) fathered the different classes of men

RING (HRINGR): Nickname of Sigurd, King of Sweden, who defeated Harald Wartooth of Denmark in Saxo's account

ROSKVA (RǪSKVA): Farmer's daughter who went with Thor to the hall of Utgard-Loki

SAXNOT: (Seaxneat to the Anglo-Saxons.) 'Sword-companion'(?). God worshipped by the Old Saxons, and remembered as ancestor of the kings of Essex

SAXO GRAMMATICUS: Danish antiquarian of twelfth century who wrote a history of the Danes (*Gesta Danorum*), the first nine books of which contain much mythological material (translated by Lord Elton, Folklore Society, 1894)

SCEAF: Child who came over the sea to rule in Denmark, according to William of Malmesbury

SCYLD SCEFING: First king of the Danes according to *Beowulf*, who came over the sea and was set adrift in a ship after death

SEIÐR: Form of magic and divination, said to be originated by Freyja

SIDONIUS: Sidonius Apollinaris, Bishop of Clermont, who left a number of Latin poems and letters, written in the fifth century (translated by W. B. Anderson, Heinemann, 1936)

SIF: Wife of Thor, with wonderful golden hair

SIGNY: Daughter of Sigar, king of Denmark, who loved Hagbard, the slayer of her brothers, and killed herself when he was put to death by her father, according to Saxo's account

SIGMUND (SIGMUNDR): (Sigemund in Anglo-Saxon tradition.) Famous hero, father of Sigurd the Vǫlsung

SIGRDRÍFUMÁL: Poem in the *Edda*, containing magic lore spoken by Sigrdrifa, a Valkyrie

SIGRUN (SIGRÚN): Valkyrie, lover of Helgi Hundingsbani, who is said to be an earlier Valkyrie, Svafa, reborn

SIGURD THE VOLSUNG (SIGURÐR): Also called Fáfnisbani, slayer of Fafnir the dragon. Famous hero of the Volsung family

SIGVAT (SIGVATR ÞORDARSON): Icelandic poet of early eleventh century

SIGYN: Wife of Loki who tended him when he was bound under the earth

SKADI (SKAÐI): Daughter of Thiazi the giant, who married Njord, but left him to go back to the mountains

SKÁLDSKAPARMÁL: 'Poetic diction'. Second section of Snorri's *Prose Edda*, containing many of the myths used by poets

SKEGGI (JÁRNSKEGGI): Worshipper of Thor in Trondheim, Norway, killed by Olaf Tryggvason

SKIALF (SKIÁLF): Wife of Agni of Sweden, who caused his death

SKÍÐBLAÐNIR: Magic ship of Freyr

SKIOLD (SKJǪLDR): Son of Odin, who ruled over Denmark and married Gefion. Ancestor of Danish kings

SKÍRNIR (SKÍRNIR): Servant of Freyr, went to woo Gerd for him, according to *Edda* poem *Skírnismál*

SKJǪLDUNGA SAGA: Lost saga about early legendary kings of Denmark, surviving in sixteenth-century Latin version

SLEIPNIR: The eight-legged horse of Odin

SNORRI STURLUSON: Icelandic writer, who lived *c.* 1179–1241, author of the *Prose Edda* and *Heimskringla*

SǪGUBROT: Fragmentary history of the Danish kings, in Icelandic MS. of about 1300

SOLOMON AND SATURN: Anglo-Saxon poem in dialogue form

SONATORREK: 'Loss of the sons'. Ninth-century poem by Egill Skallagrímsson (translated by N. Kershaw, *Anglo-Saxon and Norse Poems*, Cambridge University Press, 1922)

STARKAD (STARKAÐR): Famous hero who comes into the legendary sagas and Saxo's history

STRATEGICON: Sixth-century Greek treatise on warfare

STRABO: Greek geographer, who described a number of the German tribes in the first century

Names and Sources

SURT (SURTR): A fire giant from Muspell who burns earth and heaven

SUTTUNG (SUTTUNGR): Son of the giant Gilling, who took back the mead of inspiration from the dwarfs who killed his father

SVAÐILFARI: Sagacious horse of the giant who built the wall round Asgard; the sire of Sleipnir

SVEIN: King of Denmark, father of Canute, who conquered England 1014

SVIPSDAGSMÁL: Poem in the *Edda* about the supernatural journey of Svipdagr to woo Menglad. Also known as *Grógaldr* and *Fjǫlsvinnsmál*

TACITUS: Roman historian, who lived A.D. 55–118. The *Histories*, *Annals*, and *Germania*, are three of his major works

THIALFI (ÞJÁLFI): Farmer's son who went with Thor to Utgard

THIAZI (ÞJÁZI): Giant who stole Idun and her apples of youth, and was slain by the gods when he chased Loki back into Asgard

THING (ÞING): Public meeting for the passing of laws and hearing of law cases, held regularly at places of assembly

THIÐRIKS SAGA: Þiðriks Saga of Bern, written in Norway in the thirteenth century, containing German material

THOKK (ÞǪKK): Giantess who refused to weep for Balder, said to be Loki

THOR (ÞÓRR): God of thunder, specially venerated in Norway and Sweden

THORBIORN BRUNARSON (ÞORBJǪRN BRÚNARSON): Eleventh-century Icelandic poet, of whom a few verses have survived

THORGERDA (ÞORGERÐR HǪLGARBRÚÐR): 'Bride of Helgi'. Goddess worshipped by the Jarls of Halogaland, and connected with Freyja

THORGRIM (ÞORGRÍMR ÞORSTEINSSON): Brother-in-law of hero of *Gísla Saga*, whom Gisli killed; called the priest of Freyr

THORHALL (ÞORHALLR VEIÐIMAÐR): 'The hunter'. Worshipper of Thor who took part in expedition to Vineland

THOROLF (ÞORÓLFR MOSTRARSKEGG): 'Beard of Most'. One of early settlers in Iceland, great worshipper of Thor, who came from island of Most in Norway

THORD FREYSGOÐI (ÞÓRÐR): Thord priest of Freyr. A name found in several Icelandic genealogies, though little is known of him

THRYM (ÞRYMR): Giant who stole Thor's hammer. The story of its recovery is told in the *Edda* poem *Þrymskviða*

THUNOR (ÞUNOR): Thunder god worshipped by the Anglo-Saxons

TÎWAZ: God of battle worshipped by the Germans

TIW: Or Tig. Name under which Tîwaz was worshipped by Anglo-Saxons

TYR (TYR): One of the gods of Asgard, thought to be an early war god

TÚATHA DÉ DONANN: Originally 'peoples of the goddess Donu', a spirit folk. The gods of pagan Ireland

ULL (ULLR): One of the gods of Asgard. Famous archer and skier

URD (URÐR): One of the Norns who guarded the spring by the World Tree

UTGARD-LOKI (UTGARÐAR-LOKI): The giant ruler of Utgard, a realm outside Asgard

VAFÞRÚÐNISMÁL: Dialogue poem in the *Edda* between Odin and Vafþruðnir the giant

VAÏNÄMÖINEN: Great magician of Finnish epic *Kalevala*

VALASKJÁLF: The seat of Odin, from which he could see all worlds

VALHALLA (VALHǪLL): 'Hall of the slain'. The dwelling of Odin where he welcomes those slain in battle, and where they spend their time fighting and feasting

VALKYRIE (VALKYRJA): 'Chooser of the slain'. Female spirit attending the god of war, who helps to decide the course of battle and conducts the slain to Valhalla

VALI (VÁLI): Son of Odin and Rind, who avenges Balder by killing Hoder, and who survives Ragnarok

VANIR: The race of gods to which Njord, Freyr, and Freyja belong, connected with fertility

VATNSDŒLA SAGA: One of the Icelandic family sagas, telling of the men of Vatnsdale (translated by G. Jones, Princeton, 1944)

VE (VÉ): Son of Bor and brother of Odin

VIDAR (VÍDAR): Son of Odin, who avenged him by slaying Fenrir

VIGA-GLÚMS SAGA: One of the Icelandic family sagas containing much early material. The story of Glum, a famous Icelandic fighter and poet (translated by Sir E. Head, London, 1866)

VIGRID (VÍGRÍÐR): Plain on which the last great battle is fought

VIKAR (VIKARR): Norwegian king who was sacrificed to Odin

VILI: Son of Bor and brother of Odin

VINELAND (VINLAND): Settlement of the east coast of America established by Icelanders from Greenland

VITAZGJAFI: 'Certain giver'. Name of a field beside the temple of Freyr in *Viga-Glúms Saga*

VOLSUNG (VǪLSUNGR): Founder of the Volsung family, father of hero Sigmund

VǪLSUNGA SAGA: One of the best-known of the *Fornaldar Sǫgur*, telling of the history of the Volsung family, and especially of the famous hero Sigurd (translated by O. Schlauch, New York, 1949)

VǪLUSPÁ: 'Sooth-saying of the vǫlva'. Poem in the *Edda* telling of the beginning and ending of the worlds. The *Shorter Vǫluspá* is another poem about the origin and doom of the gods

VǪLVA: Woman with powers of divination, a seeress

WACHILT: Giantess mother of Wade in Germanic tradition, said to live under the sea

WADE: Giant remembered in Anglo-Saxon and Danish tradition. Connected with great stones and with the sea, father of Weland the Smith

WÆLCYRGE: 'Chooser of the slain'. Term used to translate the names of the Furies in Old English word lists of eighth and ninth centuries

WELAND: Supernatural smith of the early Anglo-Saxon tradition. Vǫlundr in Old Norse poetry

WIDIA: Son of Weland. Wittich in German tradition

WILLEBRORD: Bishop of Utrecht. Missionary in the Netherlands in the eighth century. Life written by Alcuin of York (translated by C. H. Talbot, *The Anglo-Saxon Missionaries in Germany*, London, 1954)

WILLIAM OF MALMESBURY: Writer of twelfth-century Latin history of the kings of England, *Gesta Regum Anglorum* (translated by Sharpe in the G. Bell Bohn Library, 1847, 1876)

Names and Sources

WODAN: Or Wotan. God of battle and death worshipped by the heathen Germanic peoples

WODEN: God of battle and death worshipped by the Anglo-Saxons in England

WULFSTAN: Lupus. Anglo-Saxon Archbishop of York, 1002–23. His homilies have survived, and the most famous is *Sermo Lupi*, a sermon about the sins of the nation (ed. Whitelock, Methuen, 1939)

YGGDRASILL: Probably 'Horse of Yggr (Odin)'. The World Tree, forming the centre of the worlds of gods, men, and giants

YMIR: Primeval giant, from whose body the world was formed

YNGLINGA SAGA: First section of Snorri's *Heimskringla*, which gives an account of the early kings of Sweden, the Ynglings, from whom the Norwegian kings were descended

YNGLINGS (YNGLINGAR): Royal dynasty of Sweden

YNGLINGATÁL: Ninth-century poem by Þjóðólfr ór Hvíni, giving a list of the early kings, how they died and where they were buried, from which Snorri took much of his information for *Ynglinga Saga*

Index

Index

Index

246

Index

Index

About the Author

Hilda Roderick Ellis Davidson was born at Bebington, Cheshire, in 1914. She was educated at the Park High School for Girls, Birkenhead, and Newnham College, Cambridge, where she took Firsts in English and Archaeology. She received her Ph.D. in 1940 after three years of research under Professor and Mrs Chadwick into the pagan beliefs of Scandinavia.
She was Assistant Lecturer in English at the Royal Holloway College from 1939 to 1944, after which she worked as a part-time lecturer in English at Birkbeck College. Since 1955 she has been engaged in writing and research. She is a Fellow of the Society of Antiquaries and a member of the Council of the Folklore Society. Married with two children, she lives just outside Cambridge.

H. R. Ellis Davidson's other publications include *The Road to Hel* (1943), *The Golden Age of Northumbria* (1958), *The Sword in Anglo-Saxon England* (1962), many articles in literary and archaeological periodicals, and the article on *Hero* in the *Encyclopaedia Britannica*. She is a lecturer, and also holds a Calouste Gulbenkian Research Fellowship at the Lucy Cavendish College, Cambridge, and is working on eastern influences on the pre-Christian religion in Northern Europe.

h   1/2012 P

(Due to patron taped, can't fix well)